FOURTH UPDATED EDITION

HOW TO

By Royce Diener

Merritt Publishing
A Division Of The Merritt Company
Santa Monica, California

How to Finance a Growing Business

Merritt Publishing
1661 Ninth Street
P.O. Box 955
Santa Monica, California 90406

For a list of other publications or for more information, please call
(800) 638-7597. In Alaska and Hawaii, please call (310) 450-7234.

Library of Congress Catalog Card Number: Pending

Diener, Royce
How to Finance a Growing Business
Includes index.
Pages: 327

ISBN 1-56343-100-9
Printed in the United States of America.

PREFACE
TO THE FOURTH EDITION

When I wrote the first edition of this book more than a decade ago, I intended that it be understandable to anyone interested in learning finance, and I was gratified when the hardcover edition appeared in most American libraries. It was used as a course guide and as a text, and it was listed as recommended reading by a number of financial groups and at least one executive "book of the month" club. Oddly enough, that did not represent the readership I had intended primarily to reach.

Therefore I welcomed the offer of Merritt Publishing to bring out this fourth edition. This book was not written in the format of a text to confer an academic understanding of the subject (although I can't deny its usefulness in that sector). Rather, I desired primarily to set forth in simple terms every practical means of structuring and accomplishing the entire spectrum of business finance. I wanted not only to describe the various types of finance that might be tapped, but also *how* to go about obtaining this funding.

Ten years ago the initial chapter of the book included the following two statements:

> *Every business needs money in order to grow.*

> *The availability of capital keeps pace with greater and more varied business growth needs.*

Looking at the scene today, I see no reason to change the above two statements. Corporate growth continues to be the most important measurement of business success. Capital requirements for individual business — and for the world economy — are today greater than ever.

Table Of Contents

CHAPTER 1
THE PARADOX
OF BUSINESS FINANCE

This book is based on a simple fact: that every business needs money in order to grow.

Businessmen and women can no longer limit their activities to being solely manufacturers, retailers, or providers of services. They must also become seekers of capital.

Paradoxically, although there are numerous capital sources, the means of tapping them are not generally known. This is because, to many individuals, the field of finance is an area of mystery — and it is easy to understand why.

Banks and other financial institutions have not in the past provided clear explanations of the basis on which they make capital available. To those seeking funds, the operations conducted in these temples of finance seem esoteric. The picture is clouded by ivory-tower doubletalk and insider jargon.

Meanwhile, the need for proper financing for growing businesses has become increasingly acute. As costs have risen, sales dollar volume figures increased, markets have broadened, and more working capital to sustain these higher levels has become necessary. Taxes take a much greater portion of earnings, decreasing the availability of funds arising from company profits which could otherwise be used in financing growth. Capital planning has therefore inevitably become — far more than it used to be — a factor which requires almost continuous attention during the development of any business.

Fortunately, the availability of capital has kept pace with today's greater and more varied needs. In this book I hope to bridge the gap between the need and the availability. I will explain simply the details of most financeable business situations, identify the appropriate financial solution, and describe *specifically* the actual procedures which should be followed in order to obtain such financing. Here are some of the subjects covered:

- How to calculate your working capital and your need for same;
- When to seek a secured loan — and when an unsecured loan;
- How to mix long-term, short-term and revolving loans;
- How to make sure that your lending officer sees the incentives in sponsoring your loan;
- How to make sure that your accountant's statement reflects your business in the best possible light;
- How to analyze your enterprise's financial statement from the financier's point of view, and how to enhance the picture;
- How to determine cash flow and use it to best advantage in obtaining certain types of financing;
- How to obtain financing far in excess of the net worth of your company;
- How to arrange purchase and sale leasebacks and chattel loan financing;
- How to arrange export and import financing, including foreign letters of credit;
- How to turn the legal structure of your business — proprietorship, partnership, corporation, or "sub-S" — to best advantage in obtaining financing;
- How to finance LBOs (leveraged buyouts);
- How to finance employee ownership of business through ESOPs;
- How to use investor loans, debentures, or new classes of stock to obtain capital without giving away a proportionate share of profit;
- How to tap into the market for private placements from institutions, the Small Business Administration, investment companies, venture capitalists, subordinated private lenders and REITs;
- How to leverage your own capital by creating a captive finance company;

- How to arrange time sales financing for your customers as a means of increasing volume and profits;

- How to evaluate and finance acquisitions;

- When and how to go public through an investment banker;

- How to reduce loan interest cost by issuing commercial paper; and

- How to take advantage of the Eurodollar and world-wide financial marketplace.

Parts of this book may appear elementary to some readers, but the book's basic approach makes sure to cover all the ground for those less experienced in financial management. The early parts of the book establish important terms and definitions which the reader needs in order to understand the more advanced financing techniques discussed later on.

Chapter 2
The Different Types of Capital

A dynamic economy brings changes to the field of business finance every year. Indeed, change is so rapid and so continuous that it creates sources of business finance today that didn't exist a decade ago, not to mention a quarter century ago. And markets don't just grow. They change. In the last quarter century — in the last *decade* — the economy hasn't just grown bigger. It has become fundamentally different.

The field of business finance has also changed.

Financial institutions compete to devise new funding mechanisms to put more of their money to work and, not coincidentally, to meet the changing needs of their clients. One result of this competition has been the creation of a broad spectrum of business finance whose analysis is a must for every seeker of capital.

The Source and Function of Capital

Financial experts usually categorize capital by referring to its *source* and its *function.* In simple terms, this analysis asks two questions: Where does the money come from? And where does it go?

Here, then, with these questions before us, is our starting point — and we begin by differentiating among the three generic *sources* of capital: public, institutional, and private financing.

Public financing involves the issuance of securities to more than a very small group of investors and, with the exception of intrastate issues, requires registration with the Securities and Exchange Commission. Public financing almost always involves the services of stock brokerage firms, which refer to this end of their business as investment banking. It usually applies to established businesses which have already travelled the other routes of financing, so we defer our discussion of public issues to the latter part of this book.

Institutional financing multiplies your options — so it comes as no surprise that businesses make heavy use of institutional financing. In doing so they tap into:

- Commercial banks;
- Insurers;
- Commercial finance companies;
- Pension funds;
- The Small Business Administration;
- Factors;
- Venture capitalists;
- Industrial loan banks and real estate investment trusts; and
- Investment bankers who can arrange private placements.

The length of this list gives you an idea of the wide variety of sources for institutional investing.

In one respect, however, all of these institutions stay on one side of a very definite line. They stop short of what we might call "100 percent financing." They may advance as much as 90 percent of the capital required to get an enterprise up and running, but entrepreneurs err in believing that they may occasionally lend *all* the necessary money. Instead, they want to see some of the owner's capital at risk, too.

Private financing stands as the remaining source from which the other increment of capital may come. This group ranges from relatives and friends, or a small group of hopeful investors, to substantial backers of new ideas and operations known as venture capitalists. Professionals in the larger cities — attorneys, accountants, and particularly financial consultants — are often helpful in providing access to private investors.

Venture capitalists don't operate under strict rules governing security and return. They invest their money with a frank view of the risks and with meager or no security, in a gamble for substantial return. Unlike institutions, which primarily seek interest income, venture capitalists seek an ownership interest. They invest for the long haul. They want to cash in on the increase in the value of the business operation once it establishes itself in its market.

In short, they want capital gains, not interest income. This makes for subtle differences in the way they approach a business venture — and for subtle differences in the way you approach them with your idea. We go into the details later in this book, but suffice it to say for now that what you keep in mind, in presenting your idea to a venture capitalist, is the fact that the venture capitalist is primarily interested in substantial capital gains in the future. Institutions, on the other hand, accept a lower return in exchange for lower risk.

Basic Equity

This brings us to the notion of *basic equity*, or a distinction based on the *function* of capital.

Equity is the foundation stone in the financial structure of the business enterprise. It commonly represents the original investment in the business plus retained earnings. Technically, on the balance sheet equity reflects *ownership* of the enterprise as held by principals and other investors. It also represents the total value of the business, since all other financing (except for stock) amounts to some form of borrowing which the business must repay.

Thus a lending officer who asks you, "What do you have in the business?" wants to know about your equity. And as we demonstrate later in this book in our analysis of financial statements, we mean equity when we discuss the book value or net worth of the business. Keep in mind, however, that the meaning of equity changes somewhat in connection with certain sophisticated financial instruments. For example, subordinated debentures or notes are usually considered equity by lending institutions even though they are a form of borrowing. We show later on how these shadings of meaning can help you to pyramid the borrowing power of a business.

For now, let us list the three functional types of funding:

- Equity capital;
- Working capital; and
- Growth capital.

The differences among them are not academic, and an understanding of them is crucial for the very practical reason that, in order to obtain adequate financing for a growing business, you must know the nature of what you seek.

Some lending officers won't make these distinctions for you. They may consider only exactly what you apply for — and reject your application because your company does not qualify for the type of financing you specify. Yet you might qualify for a different form of financing. During my years as chief financial executive of companies whose capital structure I sought to build, I would occasionally encounter a lending officer who would not make a meaningful counter-suggestion if he thought my company did not qualify for the particular type of funding I proposed. Later, when I became a lending officer myself, I tried to fill this void. If I could not approve, for example, the long-term fixed asset loan my client requested, I might still satisfy the client by arranging a revolving line of secured credit on receivables or inventory that, although short-term, would remain available for the time the client needed the money.

Working Capital

Let's return for a moment to the three types of capital. You will find that institutions do not generally provide equity capital, as we describe it — at least, not in the early stages of a venture. But working and growth capital, on the other hand, come from a variety of sources. Both become necessary when the enterprise has used equity capital to the limit of its availability. They extend the effectiveness of equity by providing the *leverage on investment* present in the financial picture of every successful enterprise.

The need for working capital arises from the ongoing activities of business. As sales increase, so do accounts receivable — that is, money owed to the business by its customers but not yet received. The enterprise needs money to "carry" accounts receivable for the very good reason that no business can precisely match income and outgo. Your enterprise also needs money to satisfy the costs of increasing inventory to meet rising demand.

Fortunately, you can usually obtain working capital on a steady, revolving basis. Note that although your needs for working capital fluctuate over time, the need itself continues. Accounts receivable and inventory buildup tend to run in cycles, usually based on seasonal demand. It is to satisfy those needs that working capital is required. Although borrowed funds may be used for working capital for fairly long periods of time, the amount *fluctuates*, depending on the cyclical aspects of a particular business.

It is precisely here — in the varying use of greater or lesser sums of money over a single year — that we hit upon the essence of *working capital.*

Makers of personal computers know these cycles very well. So do makers of gifts and toys, to an even greater extent. The personal computer industry took off when manufacturers targeted the consumer, as opposed to the office market. Computer makers wanted one in every household — and to get them there, the makers geared their advertising dollars to the Christmas shopping season. Thus, like gift and toy makers, they built up inventory during the summer and fall in order to meet the demands of pre-Christmas shipping to retailers.

Their own need for working capital followed the pattern of any industry whose peak sales coincide with the Christmas shopping season. The manufacturer needs money to produce, market, and ship well before Christmas, and then more money to carry accounts receivable until retailers pay for their shipments. The need for working capital in these industries peaks in November and December and dips in the middle of January, when checks from retailers flow in and create a high liquidity. At that time the loans are reduced as the need for working capital decreases.

In contrast, in an ordinary year the home building industry posts its greatest demand for working capital in the early summer, when construction crews begin the big push of warm-weather work. The industry shows its greatest liquidity in midwinter, when bad weather cuts into construction.

Whatever the timing and whatever the industry, working capital plays the same role. It provides the business enterprise with funds to carry it through its period of greatest cash need. It provides a ready source of outside money when the business most needs it.

Growth Capital and the Future

Growth capital differs from working capital because the need for it does not spring from the cyclical nature of the enterprise. Some financiers lump the two together, but in fact, the need for growth capital springs from the desire to expand the business, improve production facilities, develop and market new products, or even cut costs. You justify the financing when you can project greater profits to result from your program. In making growth capital available, institutions don't look toward seasonal liquidity but rather to increased profits from which the business may repay the loan in orderly fashion over time.

Every business needs all three types of capital as time goes on — equity capital for permanent needs, working capital for seasonal needs, and growth capital for expansion. No enterprise can look to any single financing program, maintained for a short period, to meet every future need.

Why? Let's assume that you did $12 million in sales last year and earned an after-tax profit of $840,000, or 7 percent. You see a bigger demand for your product and arrange for some growth capital to expand your production facilities. As a result, your sales this year double to $2 million a month and your annual profit hits $1.7 million.

Does the extra profit eliminate your need for working capital? Not at all. When you did $1 million in sales per month, you carried accounts receivable of, say, $1.5 million. As your sales double, so do your accounts receivable. You need money — working capital — to carry these accounts receivable to the tune of *another* $1.5 million, or $3 million in all.

But your profit *last year* came to only $840,000 — or $660,000 less than you need *this year* to carry the additional accounts receivable. Moreover, you need to use that profit for other purposes — perhaps to expand inventory, perhaps to amortize a loan that allowed you to buy the equipment that yielded the increase in your sales in the first place. Although you are doing well, your need for working capital continues to mount — a fact which a financier will immediately recognize.

It should come as no surprise that, under these circumstances, you will get the additional financing without much trouble, as we describe later on in this book.

The Analysis of Function

Let's go back to the three types of capital and analyze them according to their function:

- Working capital provides for *fluctuating* needs.
- Growth capital provides for *amortizing* needs.
- Equity capital provides for *permanent* needs.

Your loan officer makes these distinctions automatically. If you ask for a *working capital* loan, your loan officer wants to know whether you can reduce or eliminate the loan during your annual period of greatest liquidity. If you ask for *growth capital,* your loan officer wants you to demonstrate how the money will buy fixed assets or perhaps additional marketing to yield a profit substantial enough to repay the loan over time.

If you don't make it clear that you need either working or growth capital, your banker may explain that the loans he or she makes are temporary and that the bank can't lock its money into a business. "We would like to accommodate you," your banker may say, "but we can't invest in a business. We only make loans."

Indeed, lending institutions *don't* invest in businesses. Stockholders do — by investing their money in the hope of capital gains in the future and, in the meantime, perhaps a flow of dividends. Lending institutions advance money to businesses on which they earn interest.

Still, the modern financial marketplace allows you to line up "working capital" to serve "equity capital" purposes, if you know how to do it. But we get ahead of our story. A substantial part of this book seeks to explore your options in obtaining working and growth capital, the principal means of financing a growing business.

Equity capital comes first, of course, as it is the financial base upon which the entire capital structure of the enterprise rests. Accordingly, in the next chapter we cover equity capital in detail.

CHAPTER 3
EQUITY CAPITAL

Before any business starts up, the entrepreneur must decide what equity capital structure to use. At the root of this process are three questions:

- How much capital does the business need?
- What should the promoter of the business give in return for that capital?
- What form should the capital take?

In discussing the methods of business finance, this book concerns itself mostly with going businesses, not startups, but many of the equity problems encountered during later growth are the same as those which arise even before a new business begins. Whether you are starting from scratch, with nothing but an idea in mind, or whether you are looking for a means to capitalize a going business which is ready to take its first giant step forward, you must make basic decisions about the capital structure of your venture.

Planning

Equity planning requires an objective approach. When you seek to implement your financing plan, it must appeal to potential investors' interests as well as to your own. The plan must include two basic considerations:

- Potential investors must have enthusiasm for your plans and confidence in the management of the enterprise.
- They must find the offer of an equity interest, whether as stockholders or partners, attractive when compared to other investment possibilities.

In satisfying these requirements, you pave the way to obtaining equity capital from partners or backers. It should come as no surprise at this point that your most important tool is an effective and accurate presentation.

I have seen some amazing results produced by good presentations. In one case, a man with a background in jewelry sales came into my office with an idea to distribute a tastefully designed line of costume jewelry which, though modestly priced, used new metal alloys to reproduce effects previously seen only in much more expensive pieces. His pieces were original, and he had a clever promotional campaign, too. The line targeted teenagers and young women, and my client had obtained an endorsement from a leading designer of junior dresses, who agreed to use the costume jewelry in all of his fashion shows and in fashion magazine ads.

My client showed me a series of display cards illustrating some of the items in the line, the packaging, several merchandising schemes, and a few rough layouts for trade ads. He showed me an actual sample, demonstrating the workmanship and finish.

Together we worked out his need for capital at $150,000, and we discussed what he would give up to his investors in return (of which more anon).

I arranged for the embryonic jewelry manufacturer to meet several private investors in my office several days later. In less than two hours the investors committed to provide the equity capital he needed — mainly because he gave them such a fine presentation.

Key Elements

Over the years I have seen many startup business proposals ranging from this simple one involving jewelry to proposals in such high tech fields as telecommunications, computer software, biotechnology and medical diagnostics. Obviously, such projects require special technical expertise on the part of the promoter — and on the part of the investor. In each case, however, success depended on a carefully prepared presentation and business plan which included the following elements:

- A description of the product or service. Remember, a picture is worth a thousand words. A sample is probably worth two thousand.
- An estimate of the size of the market, along with projections for sales volumes over several years.
- Cost breakdowns, pricing policies, a break-even analysis, and profit projections.
- Past sales volume and earnings (in the case of an existing business).

- The nature of the competition.
- Information about the management of the enterprise, including general background and details of experience bearing directly on the venture.
- References, including trade, banking and personal.
- Sources of supply.
- The specific financing necessary to get the venture going.

Your accountant can help you in gathering some of this information, but a professional financial consultant is probably the specialist most familiar with all aspects of the presentation, particularly the actual financing arrangements.

Note that the last item on the list is the most important. In discussing the financing needed to get your venture going, you must give investors the details as to how much money you need and what you're willing to give up in return for it.

How to Determine Your Equity Need

You can determine how much money to seek only after you analyse the question in detail. And you must come up with a specific figure; ballpark numbers don't work. Investors want to know exactly how you arrive at the numbers you show them.

Indeed, they worry just as much about your asking for too little as for too much — because in either case, it shows that you haven't thought things through. Too little capital can be as bad as none at all. All of the funding may disappear if you ask your investors for a capital sum insufficient to accomplish your purpose. On the other hand, to a sensible investor, no one presents quite such a ridiculous figure as the promoter who asks for a ridiculously high sum. It is surprising how many seekers of capital think that they add luster to their presentation when they ask for big, rounded-off numbers. The investor knows that such people have little idea of their specific needs.

When approached with requests for many more times capital than a proposition would normally seem to require, I usually find that the seeker has made little effort to delineate the real need. I have received, for example, requests for "half a million" — a nice round figure, indeed — from misguided business people who, when pressed for analysis, could detail actual requirements for only $70,000 or $80,000. To the serious investor, such unrealistic thinking immediately proclaims a lack of experience with substantial sums of money and raises serious doubt as to the ability of the applicant to handle such sums. In the face of such requests, investor confidence melts like the spring snow.

A Common Mistake

Another mistake is to throw in a lot of extra cash as a standby or reserve, far in excess of any reasonable amount for this purpose. This type of thinking appears frequently in otherwise well prepared presentations. I remember one proposal from a former vice president of a big aircraft maker. He detailed a need for about $300,000 — but asked for $450,000. "You see," he explained, "I think the company should always keep about $150,000 in the bank, over and above its actual needs. I don't want to have to scurry around for more money if suddenly we should need it."

This well seasoned executive had spent years working in a government-subsidized industry — an experience which had insulated him from the realism of the sophisticated investor. As every student of economics knows, there is an "opportunity" cost of money consisting of its *not* earning the return it would yield if invested elsewhere. Every investor knows, for example, how much his or her capital would yield in government bonds, listed securities, or real estate if not invested in your enterprise. To the investor, money sitting idly in a bank account is unproductive and costly.

Whatever sum you decide on, it must be just right — neither too little nor too much. In a later chapter we present a cash-need flow analysis, but at the moment, we don't need such a detailed approach. Instead, our analysis of the need must cover the following:

1. *The cost of physical plant assets.* This includes the cost of equipment and plant improvements such as electric power, gas lines, compressed air lines. Equipment includes any tooling — dies, jigs, molds, etc. — necessary to manufacture product, whether you intend to make the item onsite or contract it out.

2. *The cost of ancillary physical equipment.* Distributors, contract manufacturers, retailers and even sales organizations may need materials handling equipment,

storage or display units, delivery trucks, and packing and shipping equipment.

3. *The cost of office equipment.* This includes furniture, computers, communications equipment, photocopying machines, mailing equipment, etc.

4. *Supplies.* This includes production supplies, office, shipping and mailing supplies, stationary and forms, etc.

5. *Deposits.* You may carry these as assets on your balance sheets, but they require cash up front. In this category go rent deposits, deposits for power and telephone, premiums for property and casualty insurance and workers' compensation coverage, and tax deposits. You must also provide for business license fees and sometimes consulting costs — for example, for environmental impact studies. And depending on the form of organization your enterprise takes — especially in the case of corporations and complicated partnerships — you must pay for organization costs: the fees of the attorneys who draw up the papers forming the enterprise, plus state and federal fees connected with same.

6. *The capital needed to carry you to break-even.* This category takes the most thought. You arrive at a figure for beginning capital (by which we mean capital for a new venture or for a new direction for an established business) by plotting two trends — expense versus income — against each other until they reach equilibrium. In this way you also calculate your break-even point.

Obviously, income comes from sales; it can also come from lease or royalty payments, licensing, or service fees. In order to make a meaningful projection, you predict the growth of income on a monthly basis, usually over one or two years.

Even if you are fortunate enough to possess purchase orders for your service or product before startup, these sales do not create income until you complete each order — that is, until you provide the service or make the product, ship it to your customer, and transfer title (which occurs, incidentally, even in over-the-counter sales). It usually takes several months after inception before a business can deliver goods or services. Thereafter, sales gradually approach a plateau through a series of monthly increases. Only the individual entrepreneur can project this trend, based on his or her own estimate of pricing and volume.

To illustrate, let us imagine that you wish to begin a business called the Potbellied Stove Corp. You project income thus:

Table A

Month	Sales
1st	
2nd	$ 3,000
3nd	5,000
4rd	10,000
5th	16,000
6th	20,000
7th	23,000
8th	25,000
9th	25,000
10th	25,000
11th	25,000
12th	25,000

Your business begins to create income at the end of the second month. Thereafter income climbs at a fairly steady rate until it stabilizes in the eighth month. Most businesses arrive at such plateaus, which give their managers time to assure efficiency and prepare to move forward by expanding product lines, sales efforts and marketing territories.

You plot your monthly cash outflow against this income trend. Monthly cash outflow consists of expenses which, in an operation of the size of Potbellied Stove Corp., would run more or less as follows:

Table B — Fixed Monthly Expenses

Salaries	$ 3,000
Payroll Taxes	150
Workers' comp and insurance	190
Rent	400
Maintenance	60
Telephone and fax	100
Utilities	40
Auto	65
Advertising	200
Legal and audit	100
Travel	200
Postage	25
Supplies	70
Total	$ 4,600 per month

You must add other expenses to this list once the business gets under way, among them depreciation, bad-debt reserves, commissions for your sales people, cash discounts for prompt payments by your customers, delivery expenses, and cost of goods sold. Depreciation and bad-debt reserves aren't cash expenses and so don't enter into your projection. More important are the variable costs, such as commissions, cash discounts for prompt payments, delivery expenses, and cost of goods sold. These are incurred as percentages of sales, not as fixed monthly expenses.

The *cost of goods sold* is what you pay for the products or services you sell. Later in this book, when we look at advanced cash need projections, we look more closely at the cost of goods sold. For the moment, however, we need only to compute the cost of the items you purchase either for resale or for conversion into a product you make and sell. Salaries and overhead items already appear in our list of monthly expenses in Table B, so you must concern yourself only with the actual cost of the outside purchases of raw materials, parts, subassemblies, or complete products or commodities. You express the relationship between such costs to the selling price of your product as a percentage.

If you intend to sell an item for $100, for example, and must spend $55 to purchase the parts and raw materials and pay for the direct labor needed to produce it, your cost of goods sold is 55 percent. Note that this is the complement of your *gross profit margin* (or operating margin), which in our example would be 45 percent. In some businesses — for example, retail and wholesale distributorships — these patterns are fixed. You purchase items for resale at a fixed discount off of established list prices, and this discount becomes your gross profit margin. So in such businesses you obtain your cost of goods sold by deducting your purchasing discount from 100 percent. If you enter an industry with established margins, you figure your cost of goods sold as the complementary percentage of that margin. In basic commodity distributorships such as lumber, for example, the gross profit margin may be as low as 15 percent — making the cost of goods sold 85 percent. Normal retailing margins average 40 percent (making the cost of goods sold 60 percent). Manufacturing operations can run from 25 percent to more than 50 percent. Service industries may show much higher gross profit margins since they receive income for services rendered, not for goods purchased and resold.

Let's return now to the income projection in Table A. Assume that the cost of goods sold for Potbellied Stove Corp. comes to 60 percent, a common figure for manufacturing firms. In the fifth month, according to the table, sales income reaches $16,000. Thus the cost of goods sold in the same month becomes $9,600. Now, to complete the example, assume cash discounts of 2 percent to customers who pay promptly, sales commissions of 10 percent, and delivery expenses of 1 percent. We combine these with the fixed monthly expenses of $4,600 as shown in Table B to arrive at the following picture for the fifth month of operation:

Table C — Analysis of Monthly Income vs. Expense

Sales income for fifth month (Table A)	$16,000
Cost of goods sold (60 percent)	9,600
Sales commissions	1,600
Customer cash discounts	320
Delivery expense	160
Fixed monthly expenses (Table B)	4,600
Total monthly cash costs	$16,280
under (need) for month	$ (280)

As this analysis shows, Potbellied Stove Corp. reaches *break-even* in the fifth month — and its break-even sales volume is therefore slightly more than $16,000 per month.

Now we apply the schedule of costs and percentages in Table C to the income projections in Table A and arrive at the following figures for net monthly cash need:

Month	Projected Income	Cash under (need)
1st	——	($ 4,600)
2nd	$ 3,000	(3,700)
3rd	5,000	(3,200)
4th	10,000	(1,900)
5th	16,000	(280)
Total Cash Under		($13,680)

Thus we arrive at a beginning cash requirement of $13,680 — the money that Potbellied Stove Corp. must spend merely on operations to reach the break-even point.

Now we add two more items to our list of expenses — money to carry inventory and money to carry accounts receivable. You can calculate these only after you compute your beginning capital requirement.

7. *Money to carry inventory.* This calculation depends on turnover, which in most cases runs to 60 days. This means that you must have an inventory on hand equal to about two months' sales at break-even level. (If turnover in your industry is slower or faster, adjust your figures accordingly.) We already know that the cost of goods sold in the fifth month — when Potbellied Stove Corp. reaches break-even — is $9,600. Thus you must buy at least twice this amount, or $19,200, to obtain a two-month inventory. But you don't have to pay out all of this money immediately if you obtain 60-day terms from your suppliers. Therefore you must plan on an inventory cost of half the total purchased for the two months, or $9,600.[1]

8. *Money required to carry accounts receivable.* You may sell on 10 or 30-day terms, but not all of your customers will pay on the due date. Hence the need for money to carry accounts receivable. Allow for a 45-day average for accounts receivable. In our example, once the company reaches break-even at $16,000 sales per month, you should allow for at least one and one half months' sales, or accounts receivable of $24,000.

What happens, you may ask, when your sales continue to climb? How do you carry the increasingly larger inventories and accounts receivable?

The answer is that when this happens, you have reached the point at which you need working capital. Your equity capital has carried you to break-even, and you now need working capital.

The Bottom Line

Now let's recapitulate. We project that Potbellied Stove Corp. will reach break-even after five months of operation. To calculate our total equity capital requirement, we take the costs detailed heretofore and — assuming that the company needs a physical plant and equipment — we list our needs for capital thus:

---

[1]Incidentally, this introduces a point which becomes increasingly important as a business grows — namely that *accounts payable constitute a part of the working capital of every company.*

1. Cost of plant physical assets	$25,000
2. Cost of ancillary physical equipment	6,000
3. Cost of office physical equipment	3,500
4. Cost of supplies (original equipment plus replenishment cost in Table B)	800
5. Pre-opening deposits	1,600
6. Beginning capital to break-even	13,680
7. Cash to carry inventory	9,600
8. Cash to carry accounts receivable	24,000
9. Contingencies (10 percent)	8,500
Total Equity Capital Requirement	$92,680

Thus we see that Potbellied Stove Corp. needs nearly $100,000 in capital. But if we project our cost versus income analysis through the eighth month, we see a business doing $25,000 in sales monthly and generating a monthly cash surplus of $2,150.

This, in turn, means that the company will produce a net positive cash flow at an annual rate exceeding $25,000 before the end of the first year — a projection with enough appeal to induce an investor to consider the proposition attractive compared to other investment opportunities he or she might have.

What to Give Up for Equity Capital

Once you know how much equity capital you need, the other side of the coin turns up: You must decide how much to give up to your investors in return for their capital.

There are no precise answers to this question, but precedent establishes some ground rules.

It is important that you consider one distinction as you address this question. When you seek equity investment, you don't sell out your position. You ask investors to *join* with you in an effort to achieve a goal of mutual benefit. When you sell out, you try to obtain the highest price for the asset. But when you take in partners, or investors, you do so with the attitude that all parties fare equitably, each receiving an equitable share in return for his or her contribution. Neither the promoter nor the investor seeks to profit at the expense of the other; rather, both look to profit mutually from the future progress of the business.

In the previous paragraph I refer to the *promoter.* This is a frequently misunderstood term, and — since I use it throughout this book — I would like to define it in the context of our subject. As I use it, I mean the founder and organizer of the enterprise — the individual with vision and ideas who innovates, plans, and inspires. The financial community means nothing derogatory when it calls someone the promoter of a worthwhile enterprise. The impetus of the promoter transforms lines on a drawing board and inchoate aspirations into tangible products and services. As the fountainhead of business activity, the promoter deserves the fullest respect.

The Simplest Arrangement

Returning to the question of what to give up in return for your investors' capital, we begin with the simplest — and the most frequently used — arrangement, the joining of a promoter with inactive partners or investors. In many such cases the promoter comes with little or no capital to contribute personally to the venture; instead, the promoter's contribution consists of the basic idea for the venture — that is, the idea for the product or service to be sold by the enterprise — along with the promoter's knowledge of the field of endeavor and his or her willingness to operate the business day to day. As a rule of thumb, in such an arrangement the promoter takes half of the equity in the venture and gives up half to the investors. Should the promoter also have personal capital to contribute, he or she would receive equity in the same proportion as the investors. Note that *additional cash* is implied in the previous sentence, since money spent prior to the presentation of the deal is usually included in the promoter's basic contribution. Also, the promoter commonly takes a deferred position on his or her own equity as a demonstration of good faith to the backers.

To illustrate, let's recall the manufacturer of costume jewelry mentioned earlier. He sought capital totalling $150,000 and agreed to contribute to the enterprise 1) the marketing tie-in with the designer of fashions for young people, 2) the product designs, 3) his experience as a salesman of jewelry, 4) his willingness to work full time as chief executive of the enterprise, and 5) $15,000 in cash, or 10 percent of the capital he sought.

Let's assume that he agrees to give up 50 percent equity to his investors in return for $150,000 in capital. On that basis, 100 percent of the company is imputed to be worth $300,000. Of the $150,000 in capital needed to begin operations, the promoter invests his own $15,000. He contributes this cash toward the total capital requirement, and in exchange he gets equity in the same proportion as his investors do — that is, 5 percent of total capital.

When we add this equity to the 50 percent represented by his other contributions, we see that the promoter holds 55 percent of the value of the enterprise. To show good faith, he puts his cash investment in a subordinate position to the capital of his investors, giving them voting rights for all stock he holds over 50 percent.

Evaluating the Contribution

As this simple example shows, you must specifically evaluate the contribution of the promoter — and in arranging equity so as to make the enterprise attractive to investors. Where the enterprise involves an existing business, the considerations vary considerably from those applicable to entirely new ventures.

Even in new ventures the usual 50-50 split between promoter and investor remains common only up to a point — namely, when the venture involves more than a nominal amount of capital. In today's financing market, the 50-50 arrangement may hold when outside investment ranges between $25,000 and $250,000. It may hold even when outside investment ranges to $1 million if the promoter brings extremely valuable experience, contacts or know-how to the venture. Beyond this level, if the promoter comes with little or no cash, he or she cannot ordinarily obtain 50 percent of the deal in the absence of something else of great value such as a patent, an advantageous option, an exclusive contract, or rights in a high tech product.

Occasionally promoters and investors disagree on the equity worth of some of these intangible contributions — for example, a promising but unmarketed patent. To resolve such a dispute, the promoter might retain the patent but contribute the right to use it in return for equity in the enterprise. In exchange, the venture could agree to pay a royalty to the promoter, based on profits or gross income. In this manner, if the patent proves as valuable as the promoter thinks, he or she receives benefits in the form of royalties over and above the equity accepted in return for the right to use the patent. If necessary, the promoter might sweeten the pot for the investors by giving the venture the right to purchase the patent in the future, at a higher price — at a value reflecting the success of the patent in the marketplace, in other words.

The Earnings Multiple

When the deal involves a going business, the promoter may include normal business assets in evaluating an equity. If the promoter presents only an opportunity for an investor to participate in the ordinary growth of the business, the promoter gets credit for the higher of the book value of the company or, in the alternative, for what financiers call *an earnings multiple*. But the promoter can't get credit for both book value and earnings multiple. With a little luck, the evaluation of a small company comes in at five times earnings (always computed after taxes) when a promoter seeks private equity capital. Larger private companies with long records of success may obtain multiples of six or eight times earnings, and the multiples may go higher for companies with publicly traded stock, as we see later on in this book. Whatever the multiple, after-tax earnings must be calculated on a *pro forma* basis — that is, using the tax and capital structure present after the new equity comes in.

Take, for example, a company having a $50,000 net worth and earning $18,000 after taxes. Using an earnings multiple of five, the value of the company comes to $90,000, to be credited to the promoter-principal. But assuming a higher net worth — say, $110,000 — and the same earnings, you would take the net worth as the value of the contribution.

If a promoter seeks equity capital to finance additional activity in an existing business — a new program which will greatly enhance the business's profit potential — he or she should receive credit for the value attributable to the contemplated new program. This is particularly true if the business provides unique opportunities for growth and/or cost savings to the new program.

For example, an importer of housewares might attract an offer for a promising distributorship of German cutlery on condition that it stock a large inventory. The importer needs equity capital to finance the inventory and can show investors that, in addition to contributing the new German franchise, he can utilize the unique advantages of an established distributorship in the field and a clientele. These factors position the importer to profit from a ready market, perhaps far more quickly than an importer starting from scratch. Circumstances such as these should entitle the importer to a 50 percent position in the new venture, plus the value of his present business.

Let's assume that the importer shows a net worth of $50,000, posts normal profits, and needs $25,000 in outside equity for the new venture in German cutlery. Assume also that the importer and his investors agree to value the importer's contribution to the new franchise at 50 percent *of the new equity,* or $25,000. The total valuation of the enterprise appears like this:

Net worth of existing distributorship	$ 50,000
Value of promoter's contribution to new franchise	25,000
Cash equity capital from investors	25,000
Total value of resultant entity	$100,000

Thus the promoter owns 75 percent of the resultant entity, which, considering that he contributes the new franchise *plus* his existing business, is reasonable.

Balancing the Scales

Sometimes investors feel that a promoter wants them to provide more money for a new venture than they should contribute for the percentage of equity the promoter wants to give up — even though the capital the promoter wants may indeed be the amount required to make the new venture fly. To break such a stalemate, the investors might offer part of their capital in the form of equity and part in the form of a loan. They limit their equity position to that percentage agreeable to the promoter. To balance the scales, part of the investors' contribution comes as a loan holding superior position to the equity. The promoter must pay interest on the loan, and the loan has a prior claim on the assets of the enterprise—which is to say that the loan must be repaid before equity holders can take any profits out of the business.

The point here is that you can find a format to satisfy almost any type of equity requirement. An investor may decline a greater share in the future profits of a venture in favor of a prior, safe position as a creditor. Another investor — or the promoter — may allow his or her funds to occupy a riskier position in return for a higher percentage of the equity. Given a willingness to negotiate, promoters and investors can find their way to positions toward one end or the other of this spectrum so as to satisfy everyone involved.

Forms of Equity Structure

The simplest form of business venture — the irreducible element — is *the individual proprietorship.* You establish a proprietorship the day you go into business for yourself. If you require no outside capital to start off and can hire any assistance you need, you do well to go it alone, for you give yourself the freedom to make your own decisions with no one looking over your shoulder and without worrying what effect your decisions may have on the investments of others. The sole proprietor also enjoys certain early tax advantages and a freedom from government regulation.

These advantages don't last, and in any case, the sole proprietorship also comes with certain drawbacks, among them the fact that all of the proprietor's personal assets become subject to business liabilities (assuming, of course, no corporate entity). More significant for our purposes is the fact that the sole proprietor faces enormous difficulty in obtaining equity capital. Indeed, the sole proprietor has few sources for equity capital outside of friends and family, and the great danger in bringing such people into your business is that you do so without firm arrangements — and then lose friends and family to misunderstanding.

Indeed, as a rule, friends and family stand willing only to *lend* money — and borrowed money is not equity capital even when the proprietor agrees to allow the friend or relative to share in future profits. Such money comes to the proprietor as a personal loan, with troublesome possibilities not usually found in formal business arrangements. To be sure, many grand business enterprises begin as proprietorships — a basic unit of our economic history — and along the line many such enterprises qualify for many types of financing. But the inability of the proprietorship to attract equity is a major shortcoming.

The next step up is the *partnership.* In many ways, partnerships and corporations rest on similar considerations and offer similar financing possibilities. Tax law treats partnerships and corporations differently, but other than that, some partnerships show the characteristics of corporations, and some corporations show the characteristics of partnerships. The closely held corporation in particular may be nothing more than a partnership superficially cast into the mold of a corporation. How many of us have heard two business people, each holding 50 percent of a corporation, refer to each other as "my partner"?

Few businesses actually qualify as true partnerships. In a partnership two or more individuals join in a business activity on an absolutely equal basis. The partners contribute the same amount of capital to the enterprise, and all devote the same amount of time to its activities. They take the same draw on the partnership[2] for their efforts, and they share equally in the accumulation of the net worth (the "partnership account"). They also stand equally liable for 100 percent of the partnership's liabilities.

Equity Capital In Partnerships

True partnerships, however, are the exception to the rule. Most partnerships, like corporations, arise from the need for equity capital. To the individual proprietor who seeks equity capital, there is sometimes little difference between taking some partners into the business and finding investors for same.

Equity capital may come from one or more partners on any basis mutually acceptable to promoter and investor. Some variations:

- Fifty-fifty partnerships in which the promoter takes an active role in managing the enterprise and the investor remains inactive (the *silent partner*). Usually the active partner takes a reasonable draw for work performed and all partners split the remainder of profits equally.

- Partnerships in which the partners own the assets equally and the operating partner receives no draw but does receive a greater share of the profits than the inactive partners.

- Partnerships in which the investor's contribution comes as a loan with interest and principal payments taking first claim on profits.

The partners, as we see, may arrange to share profits in any way agreeable to all, covering the priority of claims on

---

[2]Technically, there are no salaries in a partnership.

assets by promoter and investor as all see fit. They make their agreement formal by having a partnership agreement drawn up by an attorney.

Other Possibilities

Partners don't necessarily share profits in proportion to their investments. For example, the active partner may put up $10,000 for a new venture and the inactive partners $40,000. They may agree that the first $20,000 in profit each year go to repay the inactive partners and that any remainder be split equally between promoter and investors. Once the inactive partners recoup all but $10,000 of their investment — that is, once their equity in the partnership equals that of the promoter — the profits might split 50 percent to the promoter and 50 percent among the inactive investors, with no requirement that the venture reduce the inactive investors' contributions further.

Such an arrangement illustrates several points. It gives the inactive partners priority for their larger investment and — to balance the scales — ultimately puts the promoter in position to receive an equal share of the profits despite his or her smaller investment. The priority position of the investors reduces their risk, while the promoter takes a riskier position in return for a greater share of the profits than his or her investment would otherwise justify.

The *limited and general partnership* allows for more varied positions of risk versus profit sharing. In simple partnerships the acts of any partner bind all partners, and every partner stands liable for the acts of other partners to the full extent of the partner's personal fortune. In limited and general partnerships, on the other hand, only the general partner stands fully liable, while limited partners limit their liability to the extent of their investment in the partnership. Limited partners are almost always the investors in the partnership and usually hold a priority position on assets and profits. General partners are usually the promoters and contribute active management.

Land promotion companies provide a good example of this mixed kind of partnership. Typically, the promoters are experienced land developers who put up little money of their own. They begin a deal by obtaining an option on a large parcel of land with the intention of dividing it into salable lots. The promoters take in a number of partners who invest almost all the money required for the project.

The partnership agreement lists the promoters as general partners and the investors as limited partners. The general partners manage the operation, but the agreement typically calls for the limited partners to recoup their investments in full before the profits split. Thereafter the general partners may receive an amount equal to the sum repaid to the investors, after which general and limited partners share equally in the profits.

In one such venture for which I arranged financing, the limited partners invested $1.5 million in a project which ultimately achieved $7 million in sales of lots. As the profits developed, they went first to repay the $1.5 million investment of the limited partners. Next the general partners received $1.5 million, and then the remaining profits split 50-50 between limited and general partners. Expenses totalled $1 million, so — after the payments of $1.5 million to both limited and general partners — there remained $3 million to split. Thus the limited partners recovered their initial $1.5 million plus a profit of 100 percent, or $3 million in all. The promoters received an equal amount on an investment of zero. That's a handsome gain, to be sure, but they had to wait until the limited partners had been repaid in full before they collected a penny. Had the project fallen short of their expectations, the general partners might have received nothing, and the ownership of the remaining assets would have gone to the investors.

The Corporate Format

Partnerships enjoy certain advantages — a relatively simple form, freedom from government regulation, and favorable tax treatment, especially during the early stages of a venture. But if you need complete flexibility in financing, the most useful form of company structure is unquestionably the corporation. You don't need the corporate form to start a business, but almost inevitably, successful proprietorships and partnerships ultimately incorporate.

Why? Only corporations may take advantage of certain types of financing — for example, public stock offerings. And the many types of corporate securities present the greatest number of variations capable of satisfying equity funding requirements. With a corporation, you can issue various classes of common stock, preferred stock, debentures, notes, and so on. There is a corporate security to fill every need.

Classes of Securities

In order to choose among the types of securities, one should examine the major classes of such securities in the order of the priority of their claims on the assets of the corporation.

- *Capital notes.* These are obligations of the corporation, and they must be repaid. But financiers call them *capital* notes because they do not represent ordinary borrowing, as do loans from a bank, and because they are subordinate to ordinary borrowing. Capital notes are often part of the permanent capital of a business since, for tax or equity purposes, they may represent money invested by the principals. Sometimes capital notes represent long-term private placements from institutions, but only if they are subordinated to borrowings from banks and other financial institutions.

- *Debentures.* These are also corporate obligations like capital notes, but they stand more in the mold of a classic security. Debentures have definite terms of repayment and call for a fixed rate of interest payable semiannually or quarterly. They are evidenced by printed bonds bearing some indenture provisions and descriptions of the other types of securities authorized by the corporation. There is usually another document called the *indenture* containing protective provisions relating to missed payments, maintenance of certain stated levels of earnings, net worth, liquidity, and debt limits.

- *Preferred stock.* As the name implies, preferred stock has a claim prior to that of any other form of stock but subordinate to other types of securities such as capital notes and debentures. Preferred stock has no stated term of repayment because it is a true stock, not an obligation of the corporation. But the corporation may *call* the stock — that is, pay it off at face value — at any time the retained earnings of the corporation permit. Preferred stock usually earns *dividends,* not interest, payable semiannually or quarterly out of earnings. Normally, the holder of preferred stock has no voting rights, but if the corporation misses two dividends because of insufficient profits, the holder of preferred stock may take over voting rights from the holder of common stock. In the event of a corporate liquidation, preferred stock has a prior claim over common stock on the corporate assets.

- *Common stock.* This is the basic stock of every corporation and usually carries the only voting rights. Thus the control of the company vests in the common shareholders (except in case of certain defaults as described above). All increases in net worth accrue to the benefit of common stockholders, who thus hold the corporation's true "growth stock." But the corporation may pay no dividends to common stockholders until it has paid interest on notes and debentures plus dividends on preferred stock, since these have a higher priority, or claim.

Variations on the Theme

As we show later in this book, the forms of corporate securities permit many variations. Debentures may be convertible into common stock, for example. Preferred stock can be convertible, cumulative or noncumulative as to dividends; preferred stock can even have voting rights. The corporation may issue two classes of common stock (class A and class B). The chapter on public issues covers these matters in greater detail.

For the moment, the important distinction arises out of the priority of a security, and as we have seen, the higher the priority, the lower the risk. Conversely, the lower the priority, the greater the potential return. In the present economy, senior notes and debentures may earn interest ranging between 5 and 9 percent annually. Preferred stocks may yield dividends of 7 to 9 percent. Common stocks promise no set yield, but they may earn the highest return if the corporation does well.

The simplest corporate form issues only one class of common stock, and the individual investors generally hold stock in proportion to their equity in the enterprise. In a typical 50-50 deal, the dollar value of the investments shows up in the "capital" section of the balance sheet in the form of stock issued to the investors, and the offsetting entry shows up under "current assets" when the money is initially invested. The stock given to the promoter for his or her services also shows up under the listing for capital, with an offsetting entry in the "other assets" section of the balance sheet for "promotional stock" or "good will." Of course, the balance sheet treats cash invested by the promoter just as it treats cash invested by the investors.

The use of promotional stock provides a simple solution to the requirement that the promoter be compensated for his or her services, but the other investors don't always find this practice acceptable. They frequently object that the arrangement immediately gives the promoter an ownership interest in a sizable part of the cash investment even before the new venture begins operation. This happens when the stock allocated to the promoter gives him or her the same rights of ownership over the corporation's assets as enjoyed by the other investors, including an ownership interest in the cash invested by the others.

Diluted Interest

For example, if the investors pay $100,000 for their stock, and the promoter receives 50 percent of the common stock in exchange for his or her services — but makes no cash investment — the arrangement immediately dilutes the interest of the investors by 50 percent. Indeed, the cash asset value of their investment drops by $50,000 before operations begin. The investors may not object to sharing future profits with the promoter, but many balk at giving away half of their investment the moment they subscribe to the stock of the corporation.

Fortunately, the flexibility inherent in the corporation allows for several ways to fix this problem. The investors may give their money to the corporation in exchange for a capital note or debenture representing, say, 80 percent of the cash investment, with the balance represented by common stock. Thus with a $100,000 cash investment, the investors could receive corporate notes for $80,000 plus common stock for another $20,000 divided 50-50 with the promoter. In this manner they dilute only 10 percent of their cash investment (50 percent of 20 percent) and would receive repayment of 80 percent of their investment before the promoter begins to share in the profits.

In the alternative, the investors might receive *preferred voting* stock in exchange for the greater part of their investment, plus *common stock* for the balance. This arrangement enables the investors to share control and gives them a prior claim on the corporate assets, including the cash they have paid in. The corporation, meanwhile, has the option to call the preferred stock — that is, to redeem it out of earnings. Voting control shifts to the promoter once this happens. The investors, their cash recovered, retain an interest in the enterprise in the form of their common stock, which becomes worth many times what they originally paid for it as the enterprise grows.

The Unitized Combination

Still another arrangement — the *unitized combination* — avoids the problem of dilution entirely. This arrangement packages two types of securities, usually debentures and common stock, in such a way as to give the promoter no claim on most of the funds invested in the enterprise. For example, the corporation raises $100,000 by issuing $90,000 in debentures and $10,000 in common stock. It sells the $90,000 in debentures packaged with $5,000 of the common stock — a ratio of 18 to 1 — to the investors, and the other $5,000 in common stock to the promoter. It prices the debentures at $100 and the common stock at $1, and each unitized package consists of 18 bonds (at a cost of $1,800) and 100 shares of common stock (at a cost of $100) for a total unit cost of $1,900. The investors buy 50 unitized packages, each costing $1,900, to raise a total of $95,000. The promoter alone has the right to buy common stock without the debentures, and he or she invests $5,000 for 5,000 shares. In this way investors and promoter pay the same price for the common stock and own half of the outstanding shares respectively. But the *priority* of the debentures puts the investors first in line to receive repayment of their $90,000; it also strips the promoter of any claim whatever on the great majority of the money invested in the enterprise. And although it gives investors and promoter a 50-50 split of control and profits, it dilutes neither the debenture nor the common stock investments.

Priority securities also come into play when you need to "plug" or equalize differences in contributions among the parties to the deal. I worked with one group of investors who joined with two experienced electronics engineers to buy an electronics firm. They needed $400,000, of which the engineers had only $100,000. But the engineers would constitute the active management of the enterprise, and they and the investors agreed that they should have a 50 percent interest in the company. The corporation issued $200,000 in common stock, half to the investors and half to the engineers. To plug the difference arising from the fact that the investors put up $300,000, capital notes for their additional $200,000 were issued to the investors.

From a financing viewpoint, there are varying reasons why one form of senior or preferred security should be used instead of another. Although debentures and notes are both corporate obligations, there are differences in the eyes of lending officers. Notes require more specialized attention as to varying due dates and also to subordinations, and for this reason lenders prefer seeing debentures on a financing statement. These instruments must be subordinated to senior borrowings. Therefore, almost all debentures are issued with a subordination provision, printed on the face of the bond. Lenders can readily satisfy themselves that, by the very nature of such a security, it is satisfactorily subordinated. Where there are capital notes, however, the lender must obtain a separate subordination agreement from each investor, and if this is required at a later date, requesting it can sometimes cause second thoughts on the part of an investor who, at an earlier time, had willingly made the investment for which he or she received the note. Also, debentures are usually issued in large groups or *series,* each group having a single common due date — much easier for a lender to reckon with, as opposed to notes of varying terms and due dates payable to a number of investors.

Issuing debentures is a bit more costly and time consuming. So if you are involved with only a handful of investors whose subordinations are easily obtained, the use of notes may cause you no further financing problems when you seek to arrange for additional senior borrowings.

Choosing Between Notes and Debentures

The decision to use notes or debentures, on the one hand, or preferred stock, on the other, rests on a different set of criteria.

It should be remembered that preferred stock is not a corporate obligation. From a tax point of view, the corporation frequently benefits by the use of a corporate obligation rather than the use of preferred stock. This is because the obligations bear *interest,* which is tax deductible; the mandatory *dividends* on preferred stock are not deductible. If your corporation is in the 40 percent tax bracket, it costs nearly twice as much money to pay preferred stock dividends as to pay debenture or note interest. But preferred stock *is* a permanent part of capital and lenders therefore view it more favorably than debentures, since there is no fixed due date for repayment.

This same fact — the lack of a fixed requirement for repayment — removes what can be a sword of Damocles hanging over management, particularly during early growth stages when working capital is tight. While the preferred dividend is somewhat more costly, as described above, it can later be eliminated entirely if the corporation does well because of the unrestricted right to *call*, or pay off, preferred stock whenever there is sufficient earned surplus to do so. Further, some preferred stock issued by startup corporations automatically converts to common stock at the time the company goes public.

The 'Thin Corporation'

Tax considerations also influence your investors, making it necessary to pay attention to their personal tax positions when negotiating with them for their money. Some seek only the opportunity to earn more interest than they would at their bank, and they seek ordinary income in the form of interest or dividends. Others look to shelter income, giving rise to what financiers call the "thin corporation."

In the thin corporation, much of the capital comes in return for notes reflected on the balance sheet as "advances from stockholders" or "principals' advances to corporation." Usually these bear little or no interest and carry no due date. Since, however, the absence of such terms may lead your lending officer to construe these notes as loans payable on demand, you must take care to persuade your investors to agree at the outset to subordinate their notes to borrowings from banks or other institutions.

You must step carefully with the Internal Revenue Service, too. As a rule the IRS doesn't balk at 4 or 5 to 1 ratios between stockholder advances and stock upon startup. Thus the corporation may issue stock for 20 percent of investment and corporate notes for the balance. Profits go first to repay the notes, thus enabling the investors to recover 80 percent of the cash advanced as a tax-free return of investment. But they pay taxes on all stock dividends.

If the venture generates no profits but only losses, these may become tax deductible for the investors in several ways. The tax code allows investors in a corporation organized under Subchapter S of the Internal Revenue Code to file as individuals. In this way each investor, not the corporation itself, reports his or her share of corporate profits and losses — an attraction in obtaining investments from people in high tax brackets. In thin corporations, the investor may take the loss only after the corporation fails with no chance for the repayment of stockholder advances. Even then, the investor may take only a capital loss — a limited tax benefit. But in the Sub-S corporation, the investor may take *as a loss against ordinary income* his or her proportionate share of any corporate loss during the year in which it takes place.

This gives the Sub-S investor the opportunity to invest relatively tax-free dollars when the risk is greatest, at the inception of the enterprise. Later, if the corporation prospers, the high-bracket investor remains in good position because the law allows the corporation to elect to report as an ordinary corporation, with no tax liability to the individual investor for undistributed profits. At this point, with profits assured, the investor holds a comfortable position for capital gains.

Chapter 4
Unsecured Borrowing for Working Capital

The simplest way to obtain working capital is to borrow it on an unsecured basis. The mechanics of making such loans are simple, so the costs are low. For these reasons we find that commercial banks — by far the biggest source of this kind of financing — prefer to make unsecured loans to businesses (and to qualified individuals) whenever they can.

Unsecured loans show the following characteristics:

- They impose no lien on the assets of the borrower;
- They are short term *but renewable;*
- They fluctuate according to seasonal needs or follow a fixed schedule of repayment;
- They call for periodic partial or full repayments ("resting the line");
- They give the lender no priority over any common creditor of the borrower;
- They are granted primarily as a percentage of the net current assets (working capital) position of the borrower; and
- They usually require that all principals holding debt of the borrowing company take a subordinate position.

By checking your own situation against the above criteria, you will be able to determine whether your financing needs will qualify for obtaining working capital through unsecured borrowing. If not, you can try some of the other methods of financing described in subsequent chapters of this book.

The first criterion — that the loan involves no lien on the assets of the borrower — actually stands as a definition of unsecured credit. In the financial community, the word *lien* has a specific meaning. A lien represents a priority claim on property. Thus, without a lien, the lender has a *claim* on the property of the borrower but no special *position* among other creditors. Lenders must stand in line with other creditors to satisfy their loans. A lien isolates the security behind a loan — the collateral — for the benefit of the lender.[1]

The Benefit to the Bank

Why do banks prefer unsecured loans if they do not include liens? Because they are easy to handle and cheap to administer. The unsecured loan gives the lender no special place as a creditor, so in granting such loans banks look carefully at general liquidity, overall financial strength relative to the size of the loan, and present ability to repay.

Unsecured loans are short term — technically, at least. Their short-term nature makes them ideal for spot transactions — for example, to cover seasonal shortfalls in cash flow such as those experienced by toymakers described in Chapter 2. Your business may qualify for many types of institutional financing, but if your need is short term, a bank is your best source. Other institutions prefer long term financing and they follow practices too complex and costly to make short term financing practicable. Banks, on the other hand, follow practices ideally suited to unsecured lending to cover short term needs. If, for example, you need two-month, five-month or seven-month financing, you can obtain a loan for the specific term, so long as it is for less than one year.

In business, the more frequent need is for money to cover seasonal shortfalls in cash flow. As described earlier, working capital complements equity capital by covering the fluctuating needs of the business for cash over a period of one year.

In meeting the need for working capital, banks establish unsecured loans on an annual basis and carry them on their books as such — but they handle the transaction with a series of 90-day notes. They advise you that they have established an *open line* of credit limited to, say, $30,000, making that much available to you over a year's time. Some banks send you a letter confirming the establishment of your line of credit; some give you such a letter only if you request it. Some hold to a policy against giving

---

[1]For a more complete discussion of the role of liens in financing, see Chapter 5.

written confirmation, but you can still count on the line if your bank has advised you that it exists. I mention this to reassure those who might wonder about the 90-day notes.

It is important to understand the technicalities behind these short term notes. You must sign a note before you gain access to the money, usually for the amount you actually borrow at the outset even when this amount is less than the maximum of your line. (If you must sign additional notes to gain access to the rest of the line, you may keep a supply of unsigned notes in your office.) There is no harm, incidentally, in signing a note for, say, $20,000, even though you want to use only $10,000.[2] You may use as much or as little of the line as you need, and the bank can hold you responsible for repaying only the funds actually advanced. The note bears a date and stipulates that it comes due on or before 90 days after this date. Some banks prefer to make their notes payable "on demand or on or before 90 days" but this presents no practical difference. The practices of banks using such wording parallel the practices of banks not using it.

The Details

In either case, the 90-day note gives the bank the opportunity to reappraise your credit and, if necessary, call the note. In actual practice, banks operate on the presumption that they need to review your position only once a year. But you must handle things properly, even though renewing a 90-day note is a technicality. You do this by paying the note off in cash or, more usually, by "paying by renewal" — that is, by substituting a new 90-day note for the old. So long as the one-year period of your line has not expired, you may merely sign and present a new note in substitution of the old, which the bank stamps "paid by renewal" and returns to you. Don't take this procedure lightly, however. The bank wants to see you handle the details properly — an important element in maintaining your creditworthiness. Handle the payment or substitution promptly; otherwise the bank may call the loan and you may find yourself unable to secure another and, in the

---

[2]The bank will either give you a cashier's check or deposit the money in your checking account. It is politic to ask the bank to place the money in your account so that the bank will benefit, however briefly, from the deposit. This also simplifies your own bookkeeping.

worst-case scenario, short of cash when you need it most. Most banks send notices about ten days prior to maturity; some don't mail maturity notices ahead of time, so flag your calendar. In either case, act promptly.

Longer Amortization

Most unsecured loans are one-year lines of credit consisting of a series of 90-day notes. The variation on this theme is the loan, also consisting of a series of 90-day notes, that amortizes over a longer period. Under such a loan, the bank agrees to extend the term over more than one year if, by reducing your outstanding balance periodically, you show your ability to repay the loan in full. A one-year line may allow you in effect to keep your loan at the same level for a full year and then repay it all at once. But the amortizing loan is just that: It amortizes, usually through monthly or quarterly payments. Even so, in order to conform to the classic facade of the unsecured loan, the loan may technically consist of a series of 90-day notes.

For example, you might borrow $20,000 unsecured with a verbal agreement to reduce the balance by $2,000 each quarter, the note to be fully paid in 18 months. (Your banker will note the terms of your verbal agreement in your credit folder, incidentally; you should do the same in your own records, to make sure that your understandings coincide at renewal time.) You sign a 90-day note for $20,000 and, at the end of the first quarter, repay $2,000 and sign a new 90-day note for $18,000. Assuming that you meet the payments, the arrangement continues until the end of the sixth quarter, or 18 months, when the remaining balance comes due. By that time your payments total $10,000, so (ignoring interest) you have $10,000 to go. You may find it possible at this point to retire the note with one payment — or you may ask to liquidate the balance with five more quarterly payments of $2,000. Having seen your ability to make good on your commitment, and now looking at a new arrangement which has only a year to run, your banker will most probably accommodate you if your financial picture remains good.

This example illustrates an important aspect of unsecured borrowing — namely that, although the original bank commitment is for a relatively short time, the arrangement can be extended over a longer term by satisfactory performance. As each 90-day note is renewed, the lender observes progress and is therefore able to provide continued funding.

"Resting the Line"

However you arrange it, the unsecured loan satisfies the lender's requirement not to "lock in" its funds like an equity investor. To accomplish this, unsecured lending requires the borrower to demonstrate the ability to repay the loan over a relatively short time. We have seen how the amortizing loan satisfies this requirement. More commonly, businesses use one-year unsecured *open lines* of credit for working capital, and they satisfy the bank's need to see repayment by *resting the line* regularly. To rest the line, the borrower pays off the line entirely or substantially reduces it once a year. Some banks prefer that the borrower rest the line, or remain out of debt, for at least 60 days, but circumstances may justify resting the line for only three or four weeks out of the year. The mere ability to pay down the line, even for a short period, usually constitutes ample proof to bank examiners that the borrower has not locked in the bank's funds but instead uses the money for true working capital purposes, to handle seasonal increases in volume and in inventory.

The borrower usually rests the line at the period of greatest liquidity — that is, following the peak sales period, when inventories drop and accounts receivable pay up, and before the climb begins to the next year's sales peak. Sales usually peak for even the most stable and unseasonal of businesses, followed by relatively slow periods. You should plan to rest your unsecured line during these less active phases of your business cycle, when you have the least need for funds to carry inventory and accounts receivable. (As we will see later, this is also a good time to mark the end of your fiscal year and compile your financial statements.)

The condition of a business frequently justifies the use of both open-line and amortizing unsecured capital loans. Almost every business needs open-line financing for seasonal cash needs. Most businesses can finance normal growth out of retained surplus from the previous year's profit, even when it must rest its line. Sometimes, however, this doesn't do the job — usually for the following reasons:

- You grow more rapidly than your retained profits can handle, and you need a lot more cash during this year's period of least activity than you needed last year;

- You add some new program to your operation; or
- You show an operating loss for the current year but now find yourself on an upward trend.

Combining Unsecured Loans

Under all three scenarios at least part of your need for working capital does not arise from the cyclical nature of your business. Under the first, the solution is to arrange a combination of unsecured loans — one for growth capital, the other for working capital.

For example, assume that your business generates $300,000 in annual sales and that you use a $25,000 open line of credit to handle peak needs during the fall and winter. You plan to rest your line in March, your slowest month. Last year March sales totalled $8,000, but your volume increased steadily thereafter, and this year March sales come to $20,000. This increase requires that you tie up $12,000 for accounts receivable and $6,000 for inventory, or $18,000 in all.

Now suppose that you decide to invest some of the year's profit in equipment and some in a promotional campaign to sustain your growth. If you can show your lender sound reasoning for these decisions, you should have no trouble obtaining a separate amortizing loan of $18,000, payable $3,000 per quarter. Your increased profits will make repayment possible, but you will still need your $25,000 open line, which you have just rested; in fact, you will probably need a bigger open line to finance the larger accounts receivable and inventory necessitated by your increase in sales.

Note that *as you move into your peak season, you must pay down on your amortizing line just as your need for working capital increases because of your business cycle.* Your situation could become untenable if you had access only to the amortizing line of credit. But if you have an amortizing *and* an open line, the combination accommodates both growth and your ordinary seasonal fluctuation. You liquidate the amortizing line out of your increased profits, and you repay your open line during your next slow period.

You have, in short, a sound and realistic banking arrangement. Your banker may not extend such a combination when you first qualify for unsecured borrowing, but if you show satisfactory performance, you will probably secure it when the need arises.

Negotiating with Your Banker

As mentioned earlier, an unsecured loan gives the lender no prior claim or lien on assets. Therefore, to qualify for unsecured financing, your financial picture must show liquidity — that is, relative freedom from heavy debt and pressure from creditors.

Qualification for unsecured credit is usually based on the following:

- Debt to worth ratio;
- Net current asset position; and
- Perceived ability to repay.

The *debt to worth* ratio compares claims against the total equity of the borrower. The lender, having no specific assets reserved to cover the loan, wants to feel that the possibility of a forced liquidation by creditors is slight — and that in any case, you have assets strong enough to cover the claims. Since there are many assets to offset liabilities on a balance sheet, your unsecured lender can still find safety even if debt is several times the worth. How? Because net worth provides a positive buffer after subtracting liabilities from assets. Let's see how this works in the following example:

Assets		
Cash	$ 5,000	
Accounts receivable	35,000	
Inventory	45,000	
Total current assets		85,000
Machinery and equipment (net)	18,000	
Office equipment (net)	4,000	
Autos and truck (net)	9,000	
Total fixed assets		31,000
Prepaid items	3,000	
Deposits	1,000	
Good will	4,000	
Total other assets		8,000
Total Assets		$124,000

Unsecured Borrowing for Working Capital

Liabilities

Accounts payable	$14,000	
Notes and acceptance payable	10,000	
Taxes	4,000	
Current contracts payable	15,000	
Total current liabilities		$ 43,000
Equipment contracts, long term	12,000	
Notes due after one year	25,000	
Total noncurrent liabilities		37,000
Total Liabilities		80,000
Net worth		44,000
Total liabilities and capital		$124,000

Note that although net worth comes to only $44,000, the assets total $124,000, with only $80,000 in claims against them. *Creditors and lenders look to assets, not just to net worth, to satisfy their claims.* In this case, the long-term debt to worth ratio is slightly under 1 to 1—$37,000 in long term liabilities to $44,000 in net worth. This is excellent; banks like debt to worth ratios of 2 to 1 or lower. (You must turn to other funding sources if your ratio is higher than 2 to 1.)

The *net current asset* position is the most specific yard-stick used in analyzing your eligibility for unsecured borrowing. You measure net current assets by subtracting total current liabilities from total current assets. The remainder, net current assets, is more commonly called *working capital.* Taking the figures above, we measure working capital as follows:

Total current assets	$85,000
Less Total current liabilities	43,000
Net current assets (working capital)	$42,000

Banks normally limit their unsecured open lines to 40 or 50 percent of working capital, sometimes venturing a little higher to account for seasonal peaks. Working from these figures, therefore, the example should qualify the business for an open line between $20,000 and $25,000.

Another common yardstick is the *current ratio,* the ratio of current assets to current liabilities—a rough measure of liquidity. For example, a financial statement which shows

$15,000 in current assets to $10,000 in current liabilities yields a current ratio of 1.5 to 1 — an acceptable ratio. A current ratio of 2 to 1 is excellent; 3 to 1 is outstanding (and rarely found in a growing business). Financiers call any ratio of *less* than 1 to 1 — i.e., one which shows less current assets than current liabilities — an inverse ratio. A business showing an inverse ratio does not qualify for unsecured borrowing.

To your lender, your current ratio doesn't mean as much as your working capital position, but lenders check your current ratio first, partly because of custom and partly because of the ease with which they may calculate it.

The Fiscal Year

You can influence what your lender sees by choosing carefully when to end your fiscal year. This date has no effect whatever on the calculation of working capital and net worth, but it does influence your current and debt to worth ratios. We mentioned earlier that the end of your fiscal year should come during your period of greatest liquidity, and now it becomes clear why. Let's look at two financial statements prepared at different times for the same company, the first showing position at the height of the peak season:

Assets		
Cash	$10,000	
Accounts receivable	50,000	
Inventory	60,000	
Total current assets		$120,000
Fixed assets		20,000
Total assets		$140,000
Liabilities		
Accounts payable	$45,000	
Bank loan	20,000	
Accruals and taxes	60,000	
Total current liabilities		80,000
Long term liabilities		18,000
Total liabilities		98,000
Net worth		42,000
Total liabilities and net worth		$140,000

This statement yields a current ratio of 1.5 to 1 ($120,000 in current assets to $80,000 in current liabilities). It yields working capital of $40,000 (current assets of $120,000 less current liabilities of $80,000). This, in turn, shows that the enterprise remains eligible for the $20,000 in unsecured bank financing.

Now let's calculate a statement for the same business several months later, at the time of greatest liquidity:

Assets		
Cash	$ 5,000	
Accounts receivable	25,000	
Inventory	50,000	
Total current assets		80,000
Fixed assets		20,000
Total assets		$100,000
Liabilities		
Accounts payable	$30,000	
Bank loan	0	
Accruals and taxes	10,000	
Total current liabilities		40,000
Long term liabilities		18,000
Total liabilities		58,000
Net worth	42,000	
Total liabilities and net worth		$100,000

Note that fixed assets and long term liabilities remain the same, and so does net worth, at $42,000. Working capital remains $40,000. But in only two months receivables have dropped from $50,000 to $25,000 and inventory has dropped by $10,000. These changes, along with $5,000 in cash, yielded $40,000 in liquidity with which the businesses paid off the bank loan and reduced accounts payable and accruals.

As a consequence, the current ratio is now 2 to 1, an improvement over the 1.5 to 1 ratio yielded by the earlier financial statement. And the total debt to worth ratio has improved from 2½ to 1 to less than 1½ to 1.

Clearly, the second statement, prepared when the business enjoys its greatest liquidity, reflects it in the best possible light.

Lenders use more flexible criteria when judging applications for unsecured credit from individuals or from the proprietors of very small businesses. Because such loans expose the bank only to nominal loss — and because banks recognize that such loans constitute their best means of attracting customers whose needs (and deposits) may grow — lending officers have some leeway to accommodate such borrowers on an informal, personal basis. They hold such loans to a sensible percentage of the individual's net worth, and they must still see the ability to repay the loan within a year or two. But given these factors, the lending officer's personal impression of the ability and integrity of the applicant tips the scales.

The practice of extending unsecured loans, even to individuals, has become prevalent in the modern economy. Banks in the big cities led the way, and others followed in order to compete for customers. I know of one multimillionaire with an annual income exceeding $250,000 who had to pledge a life insurance policy to secure a $25,000 short term loan. In another case, a surgeon with good net worth and income had to put up blue chip stocks as security for a $16,000 loan. Both of these individuals qualified for simple unsecured borrowing with no collateral — but they dealt with old fashioned, small town bankers. Each ended up in the hands of more sophisticated competitors who offered them unsecured loans. These days, almost any professional qualifies for nominal unsecured credit based solely on his or her ability to perform.

Lenders look on applications for a small business loan in much the same way, though they place more emphasis on the financial statement.

Preparing to See Your Banker

Unsecured bank borrowing ranges from nominal loans to those involving hundreds of millions of dollars. For loans of nominal size — say, to $25,000 — you may need to complete only a one-page form outlining your financial position. In recent years banks have settled on a fairly standard form with minor differences to suit their particular needs. For those individuals who function as businesses — attorneys, physicians, sales reps, and independent real estate brokers — the use of this form usually suffices. The activities of such people commonly require only simple bookkeeping, and they don't need an accountant to prepare the bank's form.

Lenders grant loans to individuals on the basis of their information about, and personal faith in, the individual's ability and integrity. The accounting requirements of even small businesses are more complex, making the use of an accountant generally necessary. Banks do little detailed auditing of businesses seeking unsecured lending; the audit usually consists of a check for consistency between the statement submitted by the business and its books. So if your accountant checks or closes your books semiannually or annually and helps to prepare the bank's loan forms, you can be sure of consistency.

Larger businesses must use the services of an accountant who not only audits and closes the books but also prepares periodic detailed financial statements in conventional format. In seeking financing, such businesses attach these forms to the bank's forms, leaving blank those sections calling for accounting information. Bankers review the form for other background information they need to know; they also want the principals of the borrowing company to attest, via their signatures, to the warranties and representations detailed in the fine print of the forms. Since lenders extend unsecured loans without imposing liens on the assets of the borrower, they word this fine print so as to make a misrepresentation of the facts a fraud punishable by law.

Types of Financial Statements

As the size of the credit increases, accounting requirements stiffen. As a rule, even a small business must present financial statements prepared by an outside accountant and submitted on the accountant's stationery; company-prepared statements don't do. I have seen excellent work done by public accountants, and the work of those with good reputations meets with a good reception at the bank. But perhaps unfairly, lenders often give greater weight to statements prepared by certified public accountants on the theory that CPAs undergo a more rigorous licensing process and conform to a uniform and specific national code. Thus the title "certified public accountant" appended to the name of the individual who prepares your financial statements is like the word "sterling" on your silver: a stamp of worth. Furthermore, as the business grows, owners find themselves pondering the benefits of using the services of a prestige accounting firm. There are about a dozen of these, all national—some international — in their operations, with offices in all major cities. Their names appear among those who shepherd public stock offerings, and their reputations prove helpful when a business seeks to establish bank credit in different parts of the country. But you don't need a prestige accounting firm in order to obtain credit with a banker with whom you expect to establish a personal relationship. Many local CPA firms hold the respect of the bankers in their area, and they can call on the services of the prestige accounting firms should a specialized need arise.

Terminology

Not every statement signed by a CPA carries the same weight, however, and it is easy to misunderstand the terminology.[3] CPAs, for example, sign *unaudited* statements, *audited statements with qualifications*, and *unqualified* statements. These terms aren't self-explanatory.

The most widely used form — and quite acceptable in a great number of cases — is the *unaudited statement.* In preparing the unaudited statement, the accountant limits the degree to which he or she checks into the background of the facts behind the figures. The accountant checks the trial balance, possibly makes postings to the general ledger, makes journal entries, and closes the books. He or she probably also checks into the validity of any items not clearly understandable and, having cleared away any questions, prepares the financial statements yielded by these figures.

But — and this is important — the accountant does not personally supervise the taking of inventory or verify the accounts receivable by checking with each customer. This results in an unaudited statement to which the accountant appends the phrase, "taken from the books and records of the company" or "prepared from figures submitted by the company," signifying the limit of the accountant's involvement. Thus an unaudited statement is one in which the accountant does not vouch for the

---

[3]The word "certified," when applied to an inventory, for example, usually means that the accountant has personally supervised the taking of the inventory and verified the prices. But lenders routinely refer to any statement prepared by a CPA as "certified" even if the accountant undertook no personal verification at all.

validity of the books, records, and figures supplied by the company.

Many auditing firms issue an unaudited statement without a *transmittal*.[4] Instead, they merely stamp the phrase "prepared without audit" on the bottom of the balance sheet and profit and loss analysis. I find this practice deplorable; the accountant might as well say, "The less said about this company, the better," for all the good he or she does for the client. In my opinion, the business owner ought to demand that such an accountant splurge on another piece of letterhead for a proper transmittal, if only to make a better impression on a lender.

The Importance of the Accountant

But bankers and other lenders may accept unaudited statements even when you ask them for substantial lines of credit. The presence of an outside accountant creates the assurance that, even if the accountant has not personally verified the facts behind the numbers on the company's statements, he or she could probably uncover — and would report on — any irregularities. The training undergone by CPAs certainly qualifies them to do so, and they worry enough about their reputations, not to mention their licenses, that they don't issue even unaudited statements where they suspect some misrepresentation. Most accountants stand ready to prepare audited statements, which entail more work and expense, for the client who wants to enhance his or her credit. As a rule, lenders want to see an unaudited accountant's statement once a year.

As businesses arrive at what we might call the middle level of their growth — that is, when they pass the beginning stage but have not yet become truly big— they require the *audited statement with some qualifications*. Statements of this type represent a competent and complete audit. They satisfy the requirements of management for information necessary to run the business properly — a function at least as important as obtaining credit. The auditors check every significant facet of the operation,

---

[4] The transmittal is the cover page of the statement, on which the accountant describes the type of audit conducted. The transmittal appears on the letterhead of the accountant, addressed to the company and signed by the accounting firm, not by the individual accountant who did the audit. By custom, the signature is usually rubber-stamped.

preparing statements and notes sufficiently detailed to provide a thorough understanding of the background and composition of the entries. The auditors verify bank balances and make spot checks of accounts receivable, but since they do limit their activities, the transmittal does make certain qualifications. Frequently the auditors indicate this by writing in the transmittal that they have not conducted a "complete" audit, that indeed they did an audit "limited in scope" and that they therefore are "unable to render an opinion."

The Exceptions

But such wording does not do justice to the quality of the audit, so you do well to insist that your accountants prepare a transmittal specifying the exceptions that result in the qualifications — specifying, in other words, what the accountants didn't do. Financiers and lenders recognize the immateriality of many of these qualifications if so specified, and render to your statement the respect it deserves. They know, for example, that your accountant need not verify all receivables one by one because they can get a good idea of the quality of same by postulating the turnover from the total receivables shown in comparison to sales volume. They also know the meaning of certain technical qualifications such as arise, for example, with an unaudited inventory of a year ago whose results your accountant cannot now check.

A good qualified transmittal might read thus:

> We have examined the balance sheet of ABC Company as of December 31, 199-, and the related statements of income for the fiscal year then ended. Our examination was made in accordance with generally accepted auditing standards but it did not include all of the tests of the accounting records and other auditing procedures which we considered necessary, in that, under the terms of our engagement, we did not confirm the customers' accounts by direct correspondence, nor did we test the physical existence or the pricing of inventories.
>
> Because of the materiality of the investment in inventories and accounts receivable in relation to total assets, and as we did not apply generally accepted auditing procedures with respect to the examination thereof nor satisfy ourselves in regard thereto by other means, we are unable to express an independent

accountant's opinion on the fairness of the overall representations in the accompanying financial statements.

The *unqualified audit* is the ultimate in financial reporting. It follows rigid requirements resulting in truly full disclosure. The accountants must supervise the taking of inventory. They verify every account receivable by mail, the return going directly to the accountant's office. They review even items not related to accounting such as correspondence, corporate minutes and legal files to check for contingent liabilities or claims that could affect the worth of the company.

Lenders and investors sue accountants for misrepresentation, failure to disclose, or incompetence when they feel misled or damaged. The threat makes CPA firms very careful in preparing unqualified audits and issuing a statement. Indeed, such statements contain absolutely standard wording in their transmittal. Here is an example:

> *We have examined the balance sheet of ABC Company as of December 31, 199- and the related statement[s] of income and surplus for the year then ended. Our examination was made in accordance with generally accepted auditing standards, and accordingly included such tests of the accounting records and such other auditing procedures as we considered necessary in the circumstances.*

> *In our opinion, the accompanying balance-sheet and statement[s] of income and surplus **fairly represent the financial position of ABC Company as of December 31, 199- and the results of its operations for the year then ended, in conformity with generally accepted accounting principles applied on a basis consistent with that of the preceding year.**[5]*

The words in boldface identify the statement as being wholly audited and without a single qualification. Such a statement is acceptable without question by any lender. It is mandatory in a public issue registered with the SEC. It may be required in a merger or acquisition.

---

[5]Emphasis added.

An unqualified audit costs money, but it often makes sense to obtain one when negotiating with a potential financing source — even one that does not strictly require such a statement. It presents a calling card of the highest quality, and you may decide to obtain one if its cost is not disproportionately high relative to the size and other expenses of the business — if, in other words, you can expect to gain enough to offset the cost.

You must present other information to your lender in addition to a financial statement. This information includes:

- A general description of your business activity;

- Statistics; and

- Forecasts.

In seeking unsecured short-term financing, submit material that tells your story briefly. Don't clutter your presentation with items that divert attention from your main objective. Other forms of financing require a great deal of information, but unsecured lenders streamline their loan procedures and use fewer criteria in judging an application. It helps to include in your presentation a few pictures or catalog pages showing your products, plus letters of interest from potential customers, or purchase orders.

As for statistics, you may need only to include a brief record of your last several years of operation — not complete financial statements but a single spreadsheet of past sales volume and earnings. If your business is new, you should include a simple cost analysis comparing your anticipated sales with expected costs and predicted profit. In any kind of application — that is, whether your business is new or well established — you should include a forecast of future growth and earnings.

Choosing a Bank

A great deal rides on your choice of a bank. Banks vary greatly in their operations, depending on policy, location, past practice, and the expertise of their staff lending officers. In referring to banks I mean full service commercial banks, of course, not savings institutions which accept deposits and call themselves banks but specialize in residential real estate lending. Such banks don't lend to businesses. For that matter, some commercial banks don't do much unsecured business lending, either, sometimes because they can't break old habits, sometimes because they don't have to. You find such banks in towns far away from financial centers; country banks, for example, make crop and livestock loans but may have so little call for commercial unsecured lending that they just don't think in these terms.

But in most cities you find a choice of eligible banks, particularly since the spread of branch banking. Other things being equal, you will probably want to deal with a bank near your office or business. This makes for convenience, and as we show shortly, it also gives certain incentives to the lending officer.

The size of your bank is important. If you run a big business with big financing needs, you probably need a big bank. A small bank may find itself "loaned up" in times of tight money — unable, for example, to increase your credit line just when you need it most, perhaps even unwilling to lend to new applicants at all. But small banks often give their lending officers more autonomy, making them easier to work with. A bank's capital limitations are also important. Banks lend money which primarily comes from deposits made by the public. They also lend their own money — their capital and surplus. The combination of those two items lumped together (*capital*, in financial discussions) determines the size of the loans a bank may make.

Risk Concentration

Generally a bank may not lend more than 10 percent of its capital to any one customer. Since deposits usually exceed a bank's capital by many multiples, this rule ensures against any concentration of public money in any one risk.

Knowing this, you calculate a bank's loan limit with ease. If a bank reports $600,000 capital and $400,000 surplus, you know that it lends to a limit of $100,000, or 10 percent of the combination (which may amount to only about 1 percent of the bank's total deposits and capital, incidentally). Banks make copies of their current *Statement of Condition* readily available, usually in pocket-size forms in the lobby.

You may choose your bank because you like a particular officer, naturally enough. Bank officers vary in personality, preferences, and authority. Depending on their rank, they hold certain automatic or personal approval limits — the maximum loan the officer can grant individually without approval from the loan committee. An assistant vice president might have authority to lend you $10,000, a vice president $25,000, and a senior vice president $50,000. The limits vary with the bank, sometimes reflecting policy, sometimes reflecting the size of the bank. Larger lines of credit must go to the loan committee, of course, but since the lending officer whom you contact carries your application to the committee, you want this individual to become your enthusiastic partisan. The personality and character of the officer plays a big role, in other words, so you may have to try more than one bank in order to find an officer who seems receptive to your activities and enthusiastic about your prospects.

A loan officer may have authority to grant a large loan but may delay doing so after you provide him or her with all the facts concerning your request. Many banks require that all approvals be recorded in the minutes of the loan committee meetings even when the committee itself does not act on the application. As a rule such requirements delay things only one or two days, since most loan committees meet several times a week.

Banks don't make the personal approval limits of their officers public information, so you may have to make an educated guess based on the rank of the officer you contact and the size of the bank. This doesn't mean that you ought to seek out the highest ranking loan officer, who may prove so busy that you don't get the attention you deserve relative to the size of your request. More important, in my opinion, is that you find an officer with whom you can establish good rapport. He or she can always go to the loan committee for approvals beyond the personal limit, and in any case, a good officer in a progressive bank can move up in rank rapidly — just as rapidly, in fact, as your business grows. Such a banker, upon reaching a position of authority, may remember that the two of you started out together, as it were. This enhances your chance to match your growth with your need for adequate working capital.

The Statement of Financing Aims

In talking with you, your banker will ask you what kind of financing you seek. Surprisingly, many seekers of credit become vague at this point. But it's important to give a specific answer to the question. If you don't, your banker may propose an unsuitable loan. At the very least the banker may wonder at your ability to manage your financial affairs. *Lenders respond positively to those who know what they want.* So prepare to answer the following questions:

- How much money do you seek?

- Do you need it all at once? If not, how much will you need at any one time? Will your need build to a peak?

- What do you intend to use the money for?[6]

- Over what period do you need the money? What, in other words, is to be the term of the loan?

- How will you repay the loan? Do you expect to repay it in full after one year or to amortize it with monthly or quarterly payments?

- Where will the money come from for repayment — from a seasonal drop in your need for the money or from projected earnings?

The answers to these questions define the kind of financing you seek. And your ability to enumerate them specifically is vital to your chances of getting the loan.

What is Your Bank Looking for?

Like any other business deal, both parties must benefit when you borrow money from a bank. You know your own needs here, of course, but you must present your lending officer with a picture appealing to the bank's interests, too.

In preparing, remember that banks make their money by lending to others. Loans are earning assets of banks and vital to their growth and financial viability. Banks must put their deposits to work in the form of loans so that banks can pay interest on savings deposits and cover their own overhead. Loans to local individuals and companies generate the highest yield, but banks make other investments. They participate in loans to large national companies at "wholesale" interest rates, and they invest in short term government securities. These placements earn less than loans to individuals and companies, but they are attractive compared to higher risk situations

---

[6]In asking this question your banker wants to make sure that the loan goes to constructive purposes.

offering no compensating benefits. Banks confront a vicious circle: They must lend money to obtain income, but they must attract deposits to make loans — and making loans is one of their best means of enticing good depositors. So when people talk to bankers about loans, their deposits stand as an enticement to the banker to grant the loan.

The savings and checking accounts of individuals comprise a large part of a bank's capital, but banks don't expect businesses to leave their funds dormant. Instead, they expect the business borrower to establish at least a commercial checking account if the bank extends credit.

Checking accounts create deposits for the bank, consisting not only of the balances maintained by the business but the *float*. Float is money remaining in the bank until the checks you have written against it clear the account. When you write a check to a supplier, for example, you deduct the amount from your checkbook, but four or five days may elapse before your supplier receives the check, deposits it, and actually receives your funds from your bank. If your supplier is in a different city, a week or more may go by before your bank must make payment on your check.

Meanwhile your bank has enjoyed the use of the money at no cost, since it pays no interest on commercial checking accounts. If you pay $100,000 in bills each month and your checks take, say, five days to clear on average — i.e., one sixth of a month — your bank benefits from a float representing one sixth of your deposits, or $16,000.[7]

The Benefit to the Bank

Given these numbers, you might find it to your advantage to carry an average balance of $10,000 in your checkbook. If you accumulate funds until the tenth of the month and then pay bills, your checkbook might show $20,000 at its period of highest liquidity against only $2,000 or $3,000 immediately after you pay your bills. If you add this to the

---

[7]If they do a lot of unsecured business lending, big banks perform a special analysis of your average monthly balances in which they weight a standard three-day float against the collection of funds arising from checks from customers deposited in your account. This analysis somewhat diminishes the plus benefits of your own float, but as a rule they still constitute a material factor.

$16,000 float calculated above, you could reasonably postulate that your bank statements will show an average balance exceeding $25,000 despite the fact that, at the tightest period, you might have written checks to utilize practically all the money at your disposal.

Now let's suppose that you seek a $100,000 line of credit. You make a point of telling your loan officer that you expect to maintain an average balance of $25,000 in your checking account. This represents a definite benefit to the bank, which gains anytime a growth business maintains an average balance exceeding 20 percent of its line of credit.

In fact, things look even better for the bank in this picture than you might suspect. I have mentioned the wisdom of resting your line of credit for one or two months a year — say, 10 percent of the year. Your bank earns interest only on money actually borrowed, so it lends and earns nothing while you rest the line. If you borrow the full $100,000 for 90 percent of the year at 6 percent, you pay $5,400 in interest — that is, 6 percent of $90,000, your average annual borrowings.

But you maintain an average balance in your checking account while resting your line because of the nature of business in general and because, in any event, your needs for cash diminish during your slack period. Your balance averages $25,000 during the year. The bank lumps this together with the $10,000 you didn't use while resting your line, and lends the total to someone else. It charges 6 percent on this new $35,000 loan, just as it charges 6 percent on your line of credit. Thus it earns $5,400 from you, or 6 percent of $90,000, and another $2,100 from someone else, for a total of $7,500, or 7.5 percent of your line of credit.

And in lending that $35,000 out, the bank may create another customer for itself.

Another Incentive

If you employ others, your bank sees another incentive to doing business with you. Your employees may come into the bank to cash their paychecks and, perhaps, to open savings and checking accounts whose funds will meet the needs of still more borrowers.

Last but not least, your bank lends you working capital because it has faith in your ability to grow a profitable business. If your company becomes big enough to go public, the bank may earn fees as stock transfer agent and as trustee for your employee pension plan.

In short, every loan may bear fruit for the bank in the shape of benefits derived from a wide range of services on which it can earn fees, whether the business borrower is public or private. As you can see, these relationships benefit both borrower and lender.

Guarantees and Subordinations

Many people confuse *guarantees* with the requirement of collateral for security. For this reason borrowers are sometimes surprised when asked for personal guarantees of unsecured loans. In fact, since unsecured financing gives the bank no security in the form of a lien on collateral, the personal guarantee becomes almost mandatory when the bank lends to a corporation. Loans to proprietorships or partnerships obviously entail the personal liability of the borrowers, but the corporate form isolates officers and principals from personal liability for loans made to the corporation. Therefore banks must ask for guarantees if they want to look to the personal worth of the principals. They ask for personal guarantees for almost all financing extended to privately owned corporations excepting very large firms with a long history of successful operation. They usually do not require personal guarantees from public corporations.

If, when establishing a line of credit, you object to signing a personal guarantee, your banker will say: "You run the business. You stand closer to it and know far more about it than we do. If you don't have enough faith in the business to back it with your guarantee, perhaps we should be reticent about lending our depositors' money to it." The banker has a point.

Actually, most lenders want a business to stand on its own merits. Regardless of the personal wealth of the guarantor, they don't want to finance an undertaking that does not appear feasible. So don't assume that your personal guarantee alone justifies your banker in approving your loan. Instead, in your banker's eyes, you and your business are inseparable, and sometimes bankers seek a personal guarantee for a line of credit far higher than the net worth of the borrower. In such circumstances, to be sure, the personal guarantee means very little. But the lender has another purpose here: It ties the loan to the management abilities of the principal. If the principal leaves the corporation, he or she will notify the bank to terminate the guarantee. By such notice the bank learns of the change in management and may call the loan if the new management does not show the necessary qualifications.

Subordinating Other Loans

Even when personally guaranteed, unsecured financing frequently involves the *subordination* of other loans. Thus in making an unsecured loan the banker requires that other creditors of the corporation — beginning with those principals whose holdings in the entity consist partly of stock and partly of loans[8] — place their loans in a position inferior to that of the bank. As we explained in Chapter 3, the principals of the corporation enjoy certain tax benefits by identifying part of their investment as advances to the entity, but their loans stand as an obligation of the entity just as the bank's loan does. Without a subordination agreement, the loans from principals could hold a priority equal to that of the bank and, in the event of liquidation, reduce net worth. But in fact the investors intended their money to become part of capital, and they identify their advances as loans in exchange for the tax benefits. They did not intend to put their claims first in line before those of the bank from which they obtain unsecured financing. Thus they subordinate their position so that, should problems arise, the bank stands first in line to recover its position.

Let's analyze this by studying the following items from a financial statement.

(Total assets		$200,000)

Liabilities		
Accounts payable	$15,000	
Notes payable, bank	40,000	
Accruals	5,000	
Total current liabilities		$ 60,000
Long term liabilities	40,000	
Principals' advances to corp.	80,000	
Total liabilities		$180,000
Capital stock (net worth)		20,000
Total liabilities & net worth		$200,000

---

[8]Carried on the corporation's books as "principals' advances to the corporation." See Chapter 3.

As you can see, the net worth of this corporation comes only to $20,000, and no bank would advance it the $40,000 loan indicated in the statement solely on the basis of so low a net worth. But by obtaining a subordination agreement from the principals for their $80,000 in advances to the corporation, the bank gains priority as a creditor, making the loan quite proper. In essence, the subordination specifies that the bank and the principals agree to consider the principals' advances in the same light — i.e., as additions to the enterprise's capital, as the principals intended in the first place. At the same time, the principals keep the tax advantages inherent in their position as holders of notes for 80 percent of their investment in the corporation. This, as we have seen, allows them to remove $80,000 in corporate profits tax free, as a return *of* their investment. Of course, the subordination agreement seeks to prevent them from doing so, but only temporarily. As the corporation earns profits and adds to surplus, the bank may recognize other worth to satisfy its claim and release an equivalent part of the advances from subordination. This frees the investors to remove their money from the corporation.

Using Your Credit

Obtaining a line of credit benefits the corporation directly by making additional capital available and indirectly by laying a steppingstone toward even more credit in the future. For this reason it is important to establish *and use* credit for working capital at the earliest possible time. Don't wait until you need the capital; in fact, try to obtain your first modest line *before you need it.* Obviously, you make your task easier if you seek your first credit when you can show a liquid position, no matter how small, because this assures your lender that you haven't used up all of your starting equity capital.

Let's suppose that your business shows $50,000 in capital, consisting of $25,000 in fixed and other assets and $25,000 in working capital. You started this venture with $50,000 in cash. You bought $20,000 worth of fixed assets and have operated long enough to tie up some of your capital in inventory and in accounts receivable. You still have $10,000 in the bank. You have no trouble paying your bills and feel no immediate need for additional cash — *but this is the time for you to apply for a bank line.* Your banker asks why you need the money. You answer that you anticipate an increase in your business shortly as you reach your seasonal peak, and you want to prepare.

A glance at your position shows that you should win approval for a $15,000 unsecured open line. Accordingly, your bank approves the line, informing you that you may have access to the funds once you sign a note. The loan agreement provides that you pay a *commitment fee* — essentially a standby fee to guarantee the availability of the funds, commonly priced about ¼ of 1 percent of your line.[9] Following execution of the documents, the entire line of credit is available.

Drawing Down Against the Line

Usually, the business borrower finds it necessary to use some of the line as soon as it becomes available. But even if you don't need the funding immediately, I strongly recommend that you draw down against your line within a reasonably short time in order to begin your banking history of unsecured borrowing. The bank is not concerned how you use the money; your banker doesn't check to see whether the money sits unused in your business checking account or goes out immediately to pay bills. Your banker wants to know only that you *do* use the money and repay it as agreed.

I once met with a client on a subject which illustrates another aspect of the point I want to make here. The client managed the finances of a growing company and, the previous year, had increased his company's line of credit from $150,000 to $500,000. He accomplished this by showing a remarkable surge of profit and by projecting that, if the company were to take advantage of its growth opportunities, it needed more credit. The company did grow as my client forecast, but his projections proved so conservative that the company's profits mushroomed, and it needed only part of the new credit. The turn of events pleased my client, naturally enough, and he expressed surprise when I recommended that he still bor-

---

[9]Banks charge a standby fee when you don't use part or all of your line — on the theory that if the bank ties up the money for you and you don't use it, the bank can't lend the same funds to someone else and thus loses the chance to collect interest. The standby fee applies to the unused part of your line, payable in those months when you use less than your maximum line: the less you borrow on your line, the higher the standby fee. You may be able to negotiate these fees after a period of successful experience.

row his full line. *"Even if you use if for only one month,"* I told him, *"take the full amount."* The action, I said, would enhance his borrowing history, kept permanently by the bank for its own purposes and — equally important — transmitted to other banks and financial institutions requesting credit information. If my client had stopped at his lesser need, his credit history would have read: "Subject has borrowed up to $275,000 and repaid as agreed." But if he followed my advice, his credit history would read: "Subject has borrowed up to $500,000 and repaid as agreed" — an even more impressive record.

The client reaped one other benefit. He had objected to my recommendation on the grounds that I counselled him to pay interest for a short period of time on money he didn't need. I gave him a simple answer. His loan agreement with the bank carried an informal understanding that the balance in his business checking account would average 20 percent of his line of credit. During the month in which he borrowed the full line, the balance in his checking account averaged 40 percent of the line. This made it possible for him to carry balances below 20 percent during the rest of the year and still maintain a 20 percent annual average. Without the need to borrow all the funds required to carry normal 20 percent balances for the rest of the year, his interest expense dropped. The savings offset the higher cost of that one month — and the business ended the year having shown itself fully capable of qualifying for a $500,000 line of credit.

CHAPTER 5
SECURED WORKING
CAPITAL LOANS

The histories of many growth companies show periods when the companies meet their needs only through *secured financing.* At such times other sources of capital prove unavailable or inadequate, and without secured financing, the progress of many a business success might otherwise come to a stop. Fortunately, the variety and flexibility of secured financing provides the missing element necessary to continued progress.

The Lien

The methods of modern secured financing make it possible to obtain far more capital assistance than was ever considered feasible or even proper in the past. The broadening of this kind of credit stems from the instrument which differentiates it from the unsecured borrowing discussed in the last chapter, the *lien.* Unsecured lending does not involve a lien, but secured lending does, and it gives borrower and lender a wide field over which to range.

As discussed in Chapter 4, a lien establishes a priority claim on specific assets. Given by borrower to lender, a lien isolates the security behind a loan — the collateral — for the benefit of the lender. Needless to say, the borrower does not give liens lightly, and all liens must conform to certain legal requirements as specified in Article 9 of the Uniform Commercial Code. In the past the Uniform Commercial Code differentiated among chattel mortgages, trust receipts, accounts receivable assignments, etc., but now the code, adopted by all 50 states, lumps all liens together under the term *security interest.* The document creating the security interest is a *security agreement* regardless of the type of prior claim it creates. Lenders and borrowers continue to use the old terms in discussing secured lending, of course, but the statutory terminology no longer does.

The UCC sets up several requirements for the creation of a valid security interest. You need a security agreement,[1] first of all — the main memorandum of the loan transaction set forth in writing and containing at least a description of the collateral and the signature of the borrower. Typically the security agreement also describes the transaction, the amount of the loan, provisions for subsequent loans to be made under the agreement, etc. Banks and finance companies ordinarily use standard forms for their security agreements. The security interest becomes valid when it *attaches* — i.e., when 1) the parties reach agreement as to terms and 2) the borrower receives the money. The agreement specifies, among other things, what rights the borrower retains in the collateral advanced as security.

Perfecting the Secured Interest

By itself, however, the existence of a valid security agreement does not give the lender protection in a contest over priority with other creditors, possibly even against a trustee in bankruptcy. As a result the UCC establishes a recording system for determining priorities. The code requires that the secured lender *perfect* the security interest by filing, or recording, a *financing statement* with the appropriate governmental official, commonly the Secretary of State, though this varies with the nature of the collateral. The financing statement — another standard form — describes the collateral and bears the signatures of both parties to the transaction.[2]

This system makes it possible to find out if anyone has filed a security interest on the assets of the borrower — information of great importance to the unsecured lender, who holds no lien and needs to know, therefore, if there are prior claims on certain assets.

Most common creditors are trade suppliers to the borrower. They usually sell on open account, and they set their customer's line of credit according to the customer's worth and payment record. By checking these filings, creditors become aware of liens on certain assets which

---

[1]Unless you execute a *bona fide* pledge transaction, in which the lender actually takes physical possession of the collateral of the loan.

[2]The law allows you to file a security agreement in lieu of a financing statement, but case law shows that a financing statement can't take the place of a security agreement.

would give another creditor prior claim on those assets in case of insolvency. If a secured lender does not protect its interest by recording a financing statement, it stands in no better position than any common creditor holding no claim upon specific assets in the event of insolvency.

A moment's thought shows how this system adheres to basic notions of fairness. The business owner, seeking a loan which may be greater than his or her net worth, gives the lender a prior claim on certain assets. The law 1) recognizes the bargain as mutually agreeable to borrower and lender but 2) protects the common creditor from becoming the innocent victim of the arrangement by 3) giving the common creditor a means of discovering who holds liens on the property of the borrower, so that the creditor may know whether he or she can look to the value of certain assets for the satisfaction of debt. In actual practice most suppliers don't bother to check the recordings, and in any case, the use of liens is now so prevalent, even among large, well-rated companies that they are accepted as commonplace.

Liens have fueled extraordinary growth in the American economy. For example, one of the largest national credit card companies achieved its early growth through the use of secured accounts receivable financing. Motion picture producers frequently assign liens on the proceeds of their films. Airlines, food processors, retail establishments, prime defense contractors — all have used secured financing as an element of growth capital.

The Commercial Finance Company

Accounts receivable financing is the most widely used method of providing secured working capital. Many banks now provide it, but the pioneers of accounts receivable financing were the big *commercial finance companies.*

By custom and — so far — by regulation, banks serve customers in their immediate areas. The big commercial finance companies concentrate on the business client, and they operate nationwide using specialized techniques which broaden the possibilities of finding satisfactory solutions to financing problems peculiar to commerce and industry. The big firms have become veritable "department stores of finance" for business. Some, including Commercial Credit, General Electric Credit, and Walter A. Heller, work with clients in virtually every state in the union. A business in Arizona, for example, may ship to customers in New England and the Middle Atlantic States — and do business with the Los Angeles office of one of the big commercial credit houses.

The differences in the services offered by banks, as compared to those offered by commercial finance companies, arise from the dissimilarities in their aims and their capital structures. As noted in Chapter 3, banks seek to build their deposits as they build their lending activities, and this may influence the fate of your application for credit. Commercial finance companies face no such difficulty; instead, they tap an unusual source of funds to build their supply of lending capital.

Capital Structure

At the base of their capital structure, commercial finance companies have their own substantial investment and net worth, in the form of hundreds of millions of dollars of common stock and retained earnings. Because of this worth and because of the diversity and liquidity of their loan portfolios, they obtain unsecured bank lines at good interest rates.

In the past, a commercial finance company might have access to credit lines totalling three or more times its own capital. Then came the big breakthrough to a new source of capital — long term loans from insurance companies and other institutions. These institutions provide multi-million dollar 12- to 15-year loans covered by notes or debentures. These placements are either longer term than, or subordinated to, current bank borrowing, and they make additional bank lines available which enable commercial finance companies to leverage their capital up to eight times.

In this way they provide a unique route to channel the tremendous accumulations of capital held by such institutions so as to serve the needs of small and mid-sized businesses. Most of the big commercial finance companies organize as public corporations, so they can broaden their capital base by issuing additional stock and thus obtain more institutional placements and bank lines. Indeed, they can supply as much capital to business as business can handle.

Given their objective — to increase the total amount of loans outstanding on which they can earn a profit — the commercial finance companies try their best to find a way to develop techniques to approve credit applications without jeopardizing their capital.

Asset-Based Financing

As a rule, businesses turn to commercial finance companies in the middle stage of growth. Smaller businesses satisfy their needs through modest unsecured bank borrowings, but when this arrangement meets its limits, the techniques of secured financing become necessary. At this point businesses need the variety and flexibility of secured financing as pioneered by the commercial finance companies and offered now even by some banks through what they call *asset-based financing* (although on a more conservative basis than the commercial finance companies). Later, once growth takes a business to a higher level, it will have accumulated sufficient net assets and surplus to qualify for some of the more advanced forms of financing, including new and more substantial unsecured bank credits.

The exceptions to this rule include certain distributorships having little in the way of fixed assets but big-volume sales of standard commodities on short markups. Such firms can achieve excellent profits, but they need substantial sales totals to do so. If they sell standard commodities to creditworthy customers, they may use commercial finance funding on a permanent basis. A coffee broker, a lumber wholesaler, a bulk chemical dealer can achieve annual sales of several millions of dollars, with profits of more than $100,000 on an investment of little more than the annual profit. Large amounts of turnover money, provided by commercial finance companies, make this possible. These funds represent debt far higher in ratio to worth than banks can extend on an unsecured basis. Without them, the borrower would be limited so severely as perhaps to preclude any profit whatever, since the low gross margins of many basic distributorships make it impossible to operate very long at lower sales volumes such as those common among other types of companies.

Certain business activities require secured financing from their very inception, not at a middle stage of development. You would need secured financing, for example, if you were able to obtain the distributorship of an established product with a potential for immediate, sizeable sales to customers placing repeat orders from a quickly revolving inventory. Right at the outset such a business would require secured inventory and accounts receivable financing. In some cases you can achieve a proper gross operating margin only if you buy from your suppliers on cash discount terms; the difference of a point or two on each purchase can represent a big part of your profit. Secured financing can provide the cash, often at a cost far less than the extra profit it creates.

From all of this it should become clear that you need secured financing when your business shows a high ratio between your need for working capital and your worth. And it comes as no surprise that programs of secured financing usually involve big credit lines. For this reason, the leading commercial finance companies and banks prefer loans beginning at about $200,000. Smaller commercial finance companies may start you on a line as low as $50,000, particularly if they see a good chance for growth in the line. At the upper end, commercial finance companies arrange for multimillion dollar lines of credit, some reaching as high as $20 million with bank participation.

Secured Financing Contracts

Most secured financing programs involve detailed contracts. These become necessary because programs such as revolving accounts receivable loans provide high-speed, somewhat automatic handling of substantial sums of money, frequently many times greater than the entire worth of the borrower, who looks to repayment from thousands of customers across the nation. Because the lender deals at arms's length with the borrower, relying on data supplied by the borrower, the contract must cover the diverse aspects of the arrangement in detail. As a result, such contracts, designed to cover a multitude of industries and situations, grow to unwieldy length of boilerplate language. But most of their stock provisions merely recite conditions that a responsible businessperson would take for granted even if they had remained unstated.

As a rule these contracts cover eight items:

1.   *Intent of the parties.* The contract describes the basic arrangement — for example, specifying that the borrower will assign receivables and that the lender will advance money against them.

2.   *Representations.* The borrower describes his or her usual terms of sale and commits to assign receivables which arise from *bona fide* sales with no known offsets or contras, etc.

3.   *Warranties.* The borrower warrants that his or her products or services will be of acceptable quality and promises to stand behind same and replace them if necessary.

4.   *Rights and remedies.* The lender sets out those steps it can take to protect itself against, or recover from, circumstances which place the loan in jeopardy.

5.   *The percentage of advance.* This is usually expressed as the maximum percentage of loan against collateral at any one time — for example, "up to 80 percent of the total collateral assigned." Lenders want the words "up to" here because they may deem certain collateral *ineligible for advance.*[3] Equally important, the borrower wants the same phrase so as to borrow only the amount to meet the business need — and save on interest. The parties to the transaction negotiate the percentage of advance; borrowers differ in their needs, so lenders don't impose the same percentage on all. Naturally enough, lenders try to keep the percentage as low as possible, and they understand perfectly well that certain industries show a higher rate of returns or rejects than others, and so demand more prudent advancing policies. The borrower, on the other hand, wants an advance percentage realistically geared to his or her gross markup. Obviously, a small gross markup calls for a high advance against receivables. Lenders accommodate this need because most industries with small markups involve standard commodities and a high class receivables portfolio. For example, a wholesale lumber dealer generally buys from the mill at a discount which allows for a gross profit of less than 9 percent. The wholesaler, however, must pay the mill before the retailer pays from the other end, and the demands from the mill account for more than 90 percent of the receivables from retailers. Since business in this industry involves very high volumes, even a well-capitalized wholesaler needs financing to carry receivables. As a result, it is not uncommon to find a 90 percent maximum advance, particularly when the wholesaler

---

[3]See below.

can show a list of creditworthy customers.[4] In most industries gross profit margins run between 15 and 40 percent, and maximum contract advances usually fall between 70 and 85 percent of assigned collateral.

6.   *Terms of Contract.* Most financing contracts run for one year, renewable for three years. It pays to look for two items here — the renewal clause and the penalty provision. Usually contracts provide for renewal automatically *unless the borrower gives written notice 60 days before the end of a contract year.* Any notice requirement longer than 60 days is probably excessive and bears changing. It's a good idea to flag your calendar several weeks before the notice deadline date so that, should you want to cancel it, the arrangement doesn't renew automatically simply because you fail to notify in time.

Also, carefully review the penalty provision. Most term financing arrangements provide for penalties if you pay off your loan in advance of the term of your contract. These penalties are important to the lender of secured financing, and for good reason. The lender incurs a cost in analyzing and processing new loans. So the lender wants to spread this cost over the full life of the loan, offset against the full amount of interest expected from the loan; otherwise the lender may stand to take a loss. The penalty protects the lender against the dislocation of substantial funds without earning the expected return. Accounts receivable contracts usually establish the penalty to be equivalent to a prorating of one year's interest. For example, if the lender expects to earn $48,000 over one year (averaging $4,000 per month) and you pay the loan off after only eight months, the penalty could theoretically be four months' interest, or $16,000.

In fact, however, since lenders use secured financing to accommodate *growth* companies, the loan usually increases over time and generates more interest, thus diminishing the penalty due in the event of prepayment. In our example above, if you had paid $48,000 in interest by the eighth month, you would owe no penalty — assuming, of course, that the wording of the contract doesn't specify otherwise. Check to make sure it stipulates that the penalty is applicable on an *annual* basis; if it specifies a *monthly* penalty — $4,000 per month, in our

---

[4]Several industry grading authorities have jurisdiction over the lumber industry, making claims and rejections infrequent and quickly settled.

example — the borrower gets no benefit from increased borrowing and interest, and no cumulative credit toward satisfying the annual minimum requirement. In negotiating your terms, make sure that the contract calls for a prepayment penalty only in the event that the cumulative interest paid falls short of the amount anticipated in the contract. Further, if you present a promising growth potential, it may be possible to negotiate a penalty set at two-thirds of the anticipated annual interest charges. Thus if your lender anticipates interest earnings of $48,000 and you prepay after eight months having actually paid $50,000 in interest, you owe nothing further. If, on the other hand, you prepay after eight months having actually paid only $40,000 in interest, your penalty would be two thirds of $8,000, or $5,280.

7.   *Interest.* Interest rates for receivables financing range somewhat higher than ordinary bank interest for unsecured loans. But it's important to distinguish between *stated interest* and the *actual cost of money.* You pay interest on a secured accounts receivable loan only as you use the money; if you don't use the money, you don't pay the interest. Your contract states interest as a per diem charge, and your loan may fluctuate according to your daily need.[5] In addition, unlike an unsecured loan from a bank, your lender doesn't require that you maintain a minimum balance in your checking account — indeed, doesn't care where you do your checking at all.

It is important to pay special attention to the difference between stated interest and the actual cost of money. A study conducted by the University of Chicago illustrates how a business which uses unsecured bank borrowings at a *stated* interest rate of 7 percent can show an *actual cost of money* of 15 percent. The study calculated the costs of maintaining minimum balances in a checking account, the costs of balances maintained during line-resting periods, and balances built up when receipts from customers bring down receivables. I consider the Chicago study a bit extreme, but I do know that the average bank loan does have an actual money cost at least 25 percent higher than the stated interest cost.[6] On the other hand, secured

---

[5]See below.

[6]This is true for small to mid-sized businesses. As a company grows and lines of credit increase, banking arrangements can be made that bring down the real cost of borrowing considerably.

receivables finance contracts provide for a reduction of cost whenever customer payments come in, as they do, for example, in the most liquid period during the middle of each month. To clarify, we should translate the per diem rates of interest into the more familiar per annum charges — that is, by multiplying the per diem charges by 365. For example, a per diem rate of 1/30 of 1 percent — a typical rate charged by commercial finance companies — converts to 365/30 of 1 percent per annum, or slightly more than 12 percent. This seems much higher than stated bank interest of 7 percent, but as we have seen, a stated interest of 7 percent can represent an actual cost of 9 percent or more. Moreover, since the per diem charge applies only to *cash actually used for that day only,* the comparable per annum charge may turn out less than stated. This would not happen, of course, if the loan remained at a constant level throughout the year. But if you need $100,000 during the tightest period of the month, you may need less — say, $70,000 — during your mid-month period of liquidity, when receivables come rolling in. As a result, a contract charge of 1/30 of 1 percent — that is, about 12 percent per annum on a *stated* basis — may translate into an *actual* cost of money used of about 10 percent of the full line of credit.

The point here is that the difference in cost between secured and unsecured borrowing may turn out to be less than it might initially appear. And as we argued in the last chapter, the important thing is to decide whether the additional financing you seek will yield a greater profit, over and above the money itself.

I once heard this principle put very simply by a wholesale grocer who said, "I look upon money for financing like I look at a No. 2 can of tomatoes. If I can buy it and sell it at a profit, then it makes sense to me."

8. *Provisions for future advances.* Lender and borrower may envision additional, perhaps larger, loans in the future. Ever mindful of priority, the lender wants the later advances to enjoy the best security possible — and the earlier the money can be secured, the better. The provisions for future advances allow this to happen by establishing the priority of the lender as of the date of the original agreement, irrespective of when the lender actually advances money. Thus if the original agreement bears the date January 1, 1994, and the lender makes an additional loan exactly two years later, the provision for

future advances establishes the lender's priority as of the earlier date, protecting him or her against creditors with later claims. This remains true even if the later loan exceeds the earlier. For example, a security agreement for an original loan of only $100,000 may nevertheless have a clause securing future advances up to $500,000.

Negotiating the Contract

Many provisions in a financing contract don't vary at all, particularly those concerning the legal aspects, warranties and representations. You waste time if you attempt to modify any of these, since no bank or institution will consider even slight changes in the legal verbiage. But you can negotiate the contract provisions dealing with the business aspects of the arrangement. You should attempt, for example, to obtain reasonable termination notice requirements and prepayment penalties (sometimes referred to as "minimums" in the contract). You want the contract to base prepayment penalties on cumulative cost as described earlier in this chapter and to give credit for interest already paid during the year. It is very important that the contract set the maximum loan as a realistic percentage of collateral, reflecting the standard gross margin of your industry. Most lenders agree to a percentage proper for the particular industry, so make your case here clearly. Keep in mind the fact that no lender knowingly establishes a financing arrangement which, from the very outset, is unworkable.

Negotiate the interest cost once you have resolved all credit and legal problems, not before. A secured financing lender can agree to a rate only after it understands the situation fully — because only full knowledge enables the lender to judge the risk accurately. Here an important point presents itself — namely that the cost of handling a secured financing arrangement is quite significant. In fact, to a lending institution, the handling costs can equal the cost of its own money.[7]

Interest rates for commercial secured financing range from 1/36 to 1/20 of 1 percent per day—or between 10 and 18 percent per year. And since it costs about as much to

---

[7]A Federal Reserve study found that the leading commercial finance companies make no greater profits on their capital investments than banks do on unsecured loans, despite the difference in interest rates — a fact attributable to the extra cost of specialized handling involved in secured lending.

handle a $50,000 loan as to handle a $400,000 loan, lenders charge higher interest for smaller loans than for larger; otherwise, the handling costs eat up the interest earnings on smaller loans. Loans ranging from $300,000 to $1 million come with interest rates ranging between 10 and 13 percent, depending on the size.[8]

Whatever the interest rate when you start out, you will find opportunities to improve your position down the road. For one thing, at some point the lender will have recovered a good part of its handling costs — specifically, the costs of acquisition and investigation. For another, after establishing a *modus operandi* with you, the lender may find it possible to streamline its ongoing handling procedures so as to reduce cost. Keep your eyes open for a chance to renegotiate.

Participations

Many businesses begin their financing programs with unsecured borrowing from a bank — and then discover a point at which the bank line no longer suffices. Sometimes the bank reaches its maximum loan relative to its capital. More frequently, the business grows faster than its ability to increase its unsecured credit. If a commercial finance company enters the picture at this point, it sometimes becomes possible to persuade the bank to join in the effort on a participating basis.

Assume that a firm enjoys a $200,000 unsecured bank line at 6 percent and grows to the point that it needs another $200,000. The firm's bank can't justify the increase on the basis of the company's financial statement, and it doesn't do secured accounts receivable lending. So a commercial finance company steps in with a participating deal. It offers the business the additional $200,000 at 12 percent and undertakes to administer the whole $400,000 loan. The bank agrees because it will continue to earn service fees and benefit from the (perhaps larger) account balances of a valuable customer. It also spares itself the cost of handling the loan. The business, meanwhile, pays the average of the bank rate and the commercial finance rate. For example, the bank might want 6 percent and the commercial finance company 12 percent; therefore the business would pay 9 percent on a $400,000

---

[8]See below.

credit line — more than it paid the bank alone, but less than it would pay the commercial finance company alone.

Occasionally commercial finance companies initiate such programs so as to obtain more advantageous rates for their own clients — usually when the client has no present bank line but is sufficiently large and sound to justify a participation. Sometimes the commercial finance company brings in a number of banks so as to reduce even further the average interest rate paid by the client. The commercial finance company handles the loan and earns a higher interest rate on its own loan. For example, the Coburn Credit participation involved a $20 million line of credit administered by A.J. Armstrong, a commercial finance company. Of the $20 million, $4 million came from A.J. Armstrong and the rest from eleven banks. The banks earned 6 percent interest and benefited from account balances averaging 20 percent of the line of credit, constantly maintained. This cost, when averaged against the A.J. Armstrong charges, resulted in a cost to the borrower of slightly move than 8 percent on the entire $20 million loan.

Credit Criteria

The revolving line of credit advanced against accounts receivable is one of the most flexible forms of secured financing. These advances — usually 70 to 90 percent of outstanding receivables — fluctuate directly with need. Let's see how things work if we assume 80 percent. If your accounts receivable come to $70,000, you can count on a $56,000 loan. If you expect a $40,000 increase in receivables in the coming month, you can borrow another $32,000 to produce or buy the goods you will sell to create this jump in receivables. Conversely, when your need drops, so does your financing.

With accounts receivable programs, commercial finance companies and banks establish an almost "open" limit on your credit. The higher your sales and receivables go, the more capital they will provide, with relatively little concern for your mounting debt-to-worth ratio. They base their lending on *the quality of the collateral*—your receivables—not on your general financial position. Accordingly, they commonly arrange to audit your books and records, examining your financial statement against your journals and general ledger — your books of original entry. The audit may also entail checking inventory and equipment visually to see that your financial statement fairly reflects them. The investigator will want to see that your office systems are efficient and that your detail records are up to date — important items since the lender must depend on your handling.

The audit of your accounts receivable will be most important of all. Here the main concerns are:

1.   *Concentrations.* There are risks, exclusive of the inability to pay, that impair your collateral. Your debtors must pay their bills for you to qualify for accounts receivable financing, and you can't show too big a part of your receivables concentrated in a few debtors or, worse, one debtor. Accounts receivable lenders do business like insurers in this respect; they want to spread their risk. Even if your one big debtor enjoys an AAA-1 credit rating, there are risks other than financial inability to pay that may impair the collateral. These risks, described below, increase when there is a debtor concentration. Normally, if a firm sells to thousands or even hundreds of different customers, no concentration problems arise. And it is not uncommon to show a few major customers so long as none of their individual accounts exceeds 10 percent of your total receivables. Even a single customer who represents as much as 20 percent of your receivables may not sour things if this debtor is creditworthy and the rest of the debtor list is conservative and diverse.

2.   *Debtor credit.* Lender and borrower should have a common interest here. Since a receivables loan may exceed the net worth of a company by several multiples, the lender wants to see that the borrower does not accept orders from poor credit risks. But the lender's credit criteria are no stricter than the borrower's should be; it's bad business to be careless about customer credit whether you use receivables as collateral for borrowing or not. The lender retains the right of recourse against the borrower with receivables financing because this type of financing, even if secured by collateral, is still a loan which the borrower must repay whether the collateral liquidates properly or not. But the right of recourse may prove meaningless if the borrower's losses through debtor credit exceed net worth. This makes it all the more crucial that the borrower's customer portfolio show a creditworthiness consistent with good business judgment.

3.   *Rejections and Offsets.* The auditor will study customer remittance advices and debit memos, as well as

the borrower's own credit memos, to see whether debtors take excessive deductions in paying their invoices. A few deductions always arise from billing errors, but these are not important. More significant are deductions arising from faulty merchandise or from a failure to provide agreed-upon services. Debtors have the right to offset claims against any amount owed. These claims can build up before the debtor asserts them, so a high rate of rejections — more than 2 or 3 percent — can seriously reduce the real value of an accounts receivable portfolio.

4. *Contra Accounts.* Whenever a firm sells to another firm *from which it also makes purchases,* a contra situation exists, and your invoices to that company constitute a contra account. Since your customer has the right to deduct what you owe from what he or she owes to you, the lender can't begin to guess what the customer may or may not pay you. Accordingly, the auditor will compare the names of your creditors on your accounts payable ledgers against the names of your debtors. A contra account becomes ineligible for advances under a standard financing plan. If this presents a significant problem, you can sometimes arrange with your contra names to agree that neither of you will take offsets against the other but will pay in full. The lender may make receivables from such a contra eligible for financing.

5. *Turnover and Collection Ratio.* The turnover of accounts receivable in a business will vary according to industry practice. Payment terms range from seven days in the food industry to 65 to 75 days in the health care industry (because of the complexities of medical and hospital insurance billing). If accounts receivable of a particular company follow the norm, lenders find it acceptable. The norm is expressed in terms of *turnover.* If, for example, accounts receivable average 30 days (one month) before they are paid, the turnover is 12 times (12 ×) per annum. Because some customers pay more slowly than others, a company which bills on terms of 30 days quite frequently may have receivables remain outstanding an average of 45 days which would create an 8 times (8 ×) turnover. Obviously, the health care industry would have less than a 6 times (6 ×) turnover since the average receivable remains outstanding from 65 to 75 days. It is therefore important that the operating margin be sufficient to include the interest cost of financing these longer terms. The lender will recognize standard industry prac-

tice and, as long as the receivables perform according to that practice, consider them eligible collateral.

The *collection ratio* provides a unique qualitative analysis of accounts receivable. Its significance arises from the fact that only cash collections are used in the computation of a collection ratio; credit memos do not count as receivables collections. The collection ratio is obtained by taking the total sales of one month and dividing that figure into the total cash collections of the following month. Therefore, if your sales for one month come to $50,000 and your collections for the following month are $40,000, your collection ratio would be 80 percent ($40,000 divided by $50,000).

Actually, a collection ratio representing only one month's sales does not give an accurate picture. This is because sales fluctuate month by month, usually according to peak and low seasons. When sales increase, they will outpace collections. For this reason collection ratios are usually computed over a six-month period. Six months of sales are divided into six months of cash receipts — taking figures used for cash receipts from a month subsequent to the month of the billings. Thus if you total six months' sales receipts from January 1 through June 30, you must divide that total into six months' cash receipts from February 1 through July 1. Here is an example:

Month	Sales	Collections
January	$ 80,000	——
February	60,000	$ 75,000
March	90,000	60,000
April	100,000	75,000
May	80,000	90,000
June	50,000	80,000
July	——	70,000
Total	$460,000	$450,000

In the example above the collection ratio is 97.83 percent ($450,000 divided by $460,000).

On a continuing basis throughout the year, the sales of each new month are added, and the sales of the oldest month are dropped. The cash receipts are treated similarly in that the new month is added and the old dropped, so that at all times only six months figure in the computation.

The most important aspect of the collection ratio is its demonstration of a *trend*. Ideally the perfect collection ratio is 100 over a six month period, but because of bad debts and customer deductions, this is usually not achieved over a six-month period. As sales build up to peak, the ratio drops — say, from 98 percent to 96 percent. But after the peak season there will come months when you collect more than 100 percent of the previous month's billings. The use of the six month average eliminates the seasonal fluctuations and, in a well run business, usually stays rather close to 97 or 98 percent. Whenever the six month average reflects a downward trend, it flashes a danger signal, and both business operator and lender will want to determine the specific cause of the downtrend.

6.   *Agings.* The aging report presents the most detailed picture of the accounts receivable portfolio. It lists each debtor alphabetically and spreads the outstanding account according to its age, following these categories:

- Current;
- One to 30 days past due;
- Thirty one to 60 days past due;
- Prior past due.

Here is an example of a segment of a typical aging:

	Total A/R	Current	1 to 30 Past Due	31 to 60 Past Due	Prior
Alpha Markets	$ 1,200	$ 1,200			
Baker Industries	400				$400
Cohen & Reilley, Inc.	11,000	9,600	$1,400		
Daylen Corp.	7,500	6,000	750	$750	
Everts Inc.	4,200	4,200			
Foods Chain	3,000	3,000			
Gringo Enterprises	350		350		
Hopping Co.	2,700	2,100	600		
Sub totals	$30,350	$26,100	$3,100	$750	$400

Open receivables in the prior column — i.e., those more than 90 days old — are generally ineligible as collateral. You gauge the standard complexion of the aging by comparing the *first two columns* — i.e., current and one to 30 days past due. If, for example, the receivables totalled $200,000, of which $160,000 was either current or one to 30 days past due, this percentage would be 80 percent.

Any aging which shows 80 percent or more in the first two columns reflects an excellent position. Seventy five percent may be acceptable; much lower might not.

7. *Consignments and Allowances.* If you can, try to eliminate consignments and allowances from your picture before you seek receivables financing. Consignment sales virtually preclude the possibility of arranging receivables financing. Consignment does not represent a final sale, so the practice creates no true receivable with which to secure financing. An exception exists for those industries in which consignment represents almost the entire established trade practice. For such industries lenders determine the usual returns on consignments and deduct the return percentage from the collateral at the outset, advancing against the rest. If, for example, a magazine publisher showed a general return of 30 percent of consigned copies, a lender might advance against 80 percent of the remaining 70 percent, which would be equivalent to 56 percent of the assigned collateral.

Products sold subject to allowances — such as advertising allowances, cumulative quantity discounts and the like — create a somewhat similar problem. The lender will require that all such allowances be deducted from the assigned receivables, and the advances will be made against the net residual value.

Detail Handling and Dominion

These days the Uniform Commercial Code makes it much easier for lenders to demonstrate *dominion* over collateral. In the past, when a lien specified *shifting stock* — for example, inventory flowing into receivables after sale — the borrower had to account for all changes in the collateral; otherwise the creditor would lose secured status. Now the law allows a *floating lien,* which specifies *classes* of collateral without regard to their changing contents. The lender still wants to police the collateral to protect against fraud by the borrower, of course, usually by keeping *schedules of assignment* executed by the borrower and *payment in kind.*[9]

The collateral of a receivables financing program consists of the invoices covering sales to the customers of a business. Batched together — usually daily or weekly — these

[9]A discussion of these requirements will also explain the general operating procedures of accounts receivable programs.

are listed on the schedule of assignment, a form provided by the lender. The listing requirement is as streamlined as possible, commonly calling only for the debtor name and the dollar amount of the invoice. The schedule is dated and signed; it is also totalled, and this total represents the entire batch of invoices then assigned to the lender as security for the loan.

Collateral Account

The total amount of each schedule assigned adds, therefore, to the *collateral account* of the borrower which has been pledged (or assigned) to the lender. The borrower then requests the amount of funds needed from the lender, who advances the funds so long as the amount remains within the limit of the percentage stipulated in the basic contract. Along with the schedule of assignment, the lender usually requests a copy of each invoice and some proof of shipment such as a bill of lading or a copy of a delivery receipt. These forms are ordinarily part of the invoice set and related documents which come together while the borrower prepares customer billings, so it takes no more work to make copies for the lender. In fact, the lender makes every effort not to impose additional costs on the borrower; it is usually acceptable merely to attach a copy of the sales journal to the schedule of assignment, in lieu of making a detailed listing on the schedule.

When remittances are received from customer-debtors, the *exact check* must be given to the lender — which is what is meant by payment in kind. The debtor check must be given to the lender; it is not permissible to deposit it in the borrower's bank account, even if the borrower immediately issues another check to the lender in exchange for same. But as you will see in the explanation of *availability financing* below, this is actually not a cumbersome process.

The practical effect of receivables financing shows up in a simplified example. Assume that the borrower assigns $100,000 in receivables on a contract allowing financing on 80 percent. This entitles the lender to 80 percent of each remittance received from debtors; the borrower would theoretically retain a 20 percent equity in the remittance to be received from the customer. If the borrower receives $40,000 in remittances, the borrower forwards it to the lender. But the borrower could request 20 percent, or $8,000, from the lender. This is called *return of equity.*

As this example shows, all remittances go to the lender, but receivables financing does not freeze the funds of the borrower, who can immediately call for the return of its share of receivables as payments come in. In actual practice, remittances come in continuously, and the borrower assigns new invoices and calls for advances or returns of equity — which brings us to the next item, *availability financing.*

Availability Financing

In accounts receivable financing there are two interrelated fluctuating controls — the *collateral account* and the *cash loan account.* Each is maintained as a running balance which fluctuates as the result of detail transactions. The collateral account changes as follows:

- When invoices are assigned, the collateral account increases.

- When payments come in from customer debtors, the collateral account decreases *in the amount of the bill being paid* — not necessarily in the amount of the cash received. If, for example, the debtor owes $500 but pays $450 because he or she claims a $50 credit for damaged goods, the $450 wipes out the entire receivable — so the collateral reduces by $500.

- When the borrower issues a credit memo, the collateral account reduces because the credit memo reduces receivables.

The cash loan account changes as follows:

- When the lender advances cash to the borrower, the cash loan account increases.

- When remittances come in from debtors, the cash loan account decreases.

- When returns of equity are made to the borrower, the cash loan account increases.

The collateral account reflects *the daily total of security pledged by the borrower.* The cash loan account reflects *the daily total of money lent to the borrower.* The borrower gets a complete picture of these accounts once a month on a form known as the *account current,* as shown in the accompanying table, which illustrates the actual working of a receivables financing program. The "Available" column gives the borrower key information — how much he or she may borrow at any given time. The table assumes that the program opens with an initial assignment of $100,000 in invoices.

The table is keyed with numbers to illustrate various types of transactions as follows:

1. On February 3, $100,000 in invoices are assigned, reflected as a transaction under the "schedule" column, and added to the total collateral. Assuming that the contract limits advances to 80 percent of the total assigned, the borrower has $80,000 available but as yet has not taken an advance.

2. The next day, February 4, the borrower takes an advance of $60,000, which increases the loan amount by that sum. Since the availability was $80,000, there remains $20,000 available.

3. On February 7 the borrower assigns new sales invoices in the amount of $25,000. This increases the collateral to $125,000, of which 80 percent would be $100,000—making the total available now $40,000.

4. On February 8 the borrower calls for $30,000 in additional cash. This increases the cash loan to $90,000 and leaves $10,000 still available.

5. On February 11 the borrower receives debtor remittances in the amount of $40,000 and forwards the money to the lender. This reduces both collateral and cash loan by a like amount — but it *increases availability* to $18,000.

6. On February 12 the borrower calls for a $12,000 return of equity; $6,000 remains available.

7. On February 14 the borrower assigns $20,000 in new invoices, increasing collateral. Availability increases to $22,000.

8. On February 15 the borrower calls for $7,000 out of availability.

9. On February 16 debtors pay $25,000 worth of invoices. But one debtor claims a deduction of $3,000 for a shortage in shipment, so the borrower receives only $22,000 in cash. The cash loan reduces by $22,000, and collateral reduces by $25,000. But despite the customer deduction of $3,000, availability increases to $17,000 because of the remittances received.

Secured Working Capital Loans

No.	Date	Adv. by Lender	Assign Sched.	Cash Receipt	Rec. Debit	Collateral	80% Advance	Cash Loan	Available
1	2/3		$100,000			$100,000	$ 80,000	—	$80,000
1	2/4	$60,000				100,000	80,000	$60,000	20,000
1	2/7		25,000			125,000	100,000	60,000	40,000
1	2/8	30,000				125,000	100,000	90,000	10,000
1	2/11			$40,000	$40,000	85,000	68,000	50,000	18,000
1	2/12	12,000				85,000	68,000	62,000	6,000
1	2/14		20,000			105,000	84,000	62,000	22,000
1	2/15	7,000				105,000	84,000	69,000	15,000
1	2/16			22,000	25,000	80,000	64,000	47,000	17,000

As this series of transactions shows, an availability program—which is a true *revolving loan*—presents the most flexible type of financing possible. The borrower calls for money only as needed and pays interest only on money used, as reflected in the cash loan balance column, on a day to day basis.

Eligible Collateral

You must take one more element into consideration when computing daily availability—the qualification of *eligible* collateral. Receivables more than 90 days old are usually ineligible for advance, as are contras, receivables in dispute, and big concentrations of receivables from one debtor. The lender supplies the borrower with a list of these ineligibles periodically; the borrower subtracts the total from the collateral balance before computing the availability.

Because receivables financing frequently constitutes a high ratio to the net worth of the borrower, the lender imposes certain monitoring functions on the borrower. For example, the borrower must submit regular financial statements prepared by an outside accountant. From time to time the lender's field auditors conduct detailed examinations at the lender's place of business, auditing from the financial statement or trial balance to the books of original entry and subsidiary ledgers and spot checking detailed collateral records such as the individual customer accounts receivable ledgers. The lender also makes regular analyses of the cash collections and trends in receivables turnover, customer claims for rejects and shortages, etc. In addition, all secured lenders conduct a continual *verification* program by mailing what appear to be routine accountant verification statements to debtors selected randomly. If such debtors reply that the receivables are incorrectly stated, the lender so advises the borrower and adjusts the collateral account accordingly.

You might conclude from all this that receivables financing interferes with customer relations, but it doesn't. Almost all receivables financing proceeds on a *non-notification* basis, which means that the customer never learns of the existence of the financing arrangement. The invoices sent to the customer bear no telltale mark, and the debtor mails all remittances directly to the borrower or to a *lock box* at the borrower's bank. The lender doesn't even endorse the debtor checks forwarded by the borrower. Instead, the borrower's name is endorsed on the debtor checks under an arrangement which permits them to be deposited into the lender's account. When verifications go to debtors, they appear on the standard forms of an accounting firm, in the name of the borrower —as if part of a routine audit being made by the borrower's outside accountant. As a result, customer relations go on without disturbance.

Bulk Handling

To certain clients, lenders extend the use of a *bulk handling* receivables financing arrangement. Under such arrangements, the lender does not require detailed listings or journals in connection with the schedules of assignment. The schedules themselves are special short forms containing a warranty that the mere adding-machine tape used in totalling the invoices to be assigned accurately represents an increment of *bona fide* receivables. If the borrower receives large numbers of remittances monthly, the borrower may sometimes deposit them in his or her own bank, usually in a lock box account for the benefit of the lender. Obviously, the borrower must have a fair net worth and show a reasonably good financial condition to qualify for bulk handling. The borrower must also have financial statements prepared quarterly and supply monthly receivables agings to the lender. By spot checking these agings in regular auditor visits, by correlating the audits with a good verification program, and by making careful analyses and comparisons of the quarterly statements, the lender may exercise sound credit judgment on a bulk account.

Old Line Factoring

Factoring is another way of obtaining working capital in ratio to accounts receivable. Technically, however, there are several material differences between factoring and receivables financing. Most important, factoring shifts credit risk to the factor. Factors don't lend against receivables; they actually *purchase* the outstanding receivables without recourse to the client. Thus the factor assumes the risk that the debtor may fail to pay.

But if the factor buys an invoice covering the delivery of faulty merchandise, the factor can charge back the *reserve account*[10] of the client, because the contract between factor and client carries warranties invalidating the sale covered by such an invoice.

Factoring is the oldest form of what we now know as commercial finance. It began more than a century ago when the founders of what is now James Talcott & Company sold Scottish woolens to manufacturers in the U.S. As the manufacturers grew and increased their output, their needs for woolens increased, but the mills in Scotland refused to extend higher levels of credit to their faraway customers in a relatively young country. So Talcott, which had firsthand knowledge of its customers, agreed to purchase the American accounts receivable of the Scottish mills and thereby assume the credit risk. From this beginning the practice of factoring grew until it became, of itself, a substantial industry.

Credit Information

Since it deals primarily with accounts receivable, factoring shares most of the credit criteria and contract provisions of receivables financing. The differences in the two techniques clearly show why factoring has its own special advantages with respect to certain industries. Indeed, factoring so influenced the growth of such industries as textiles, apparel and leather that today it remains almost basic to these industries.

Textile converters who sell to garment makers face the problem of supplying to customers who, though capable of buying in large volume, show big fluctuations in their worth depending on the success or failure of each year's designs. With such customers, ordinary credit-checking services are inadequate and too slow to report material changes. To counter this, factors keep their fingers on the pulse of certain industries. By handling a number of clients in a particular trade, they observe, on a daily basis, the payment patterns of debtors in that trade. They quickly detect any material changes in payment practices, and exchange credit information freely among themselves. Not only do they make direct telephone queries to one another, but the representatives of the factoring companies in New York in particular lunch together at least weekly and exchange information and outlooks. Their clients benefit because such activities enable the factors to

---

[10]See below.

do the greatest possible volume of business without risk of bad-debt loss.

The factor also serves an important function when the client cannot easily obtain credit information about debtors or evaluate it if available. For this reason some Japanese trading companies, giants in their own right, use the services of factors to take credit risks for their U.S. offices. The Japanese companies frequently rotate key personnel between Japan and their foreign offices. The executives, thrust into local economies with which they are not familiar, use the credit services of factors — even without actually borrowing from them — so as to limit the risk of bad-debt loss on big orders.

European manufacturers also make wide use of factors. They submit to their factors all orders received from U.S. customers. Once the factor checks, or okays, the credit, the factor issues a *maturity guarantee* to the bank of the European manufacturer stating, for example, that the factor guarantees to pay to the bank 90 days after invoice the entire face value of the invoice covering shipment of the order. The factor collects directly from the U.S. customer and assumes the credit risk. Meanwhile the bank, located near the European manufacturer and knowing the manufacturer's ability to perform, frequently advances to the manufacturer a large percentage of the working capital needed to complete an order. In this way a financing device based on the creation of an account receivable indirectly yields production financing for the manufacturer.

The extension of guarantees by factors is not limited to international transactions. Frequently factors help clients to make key raw material purchases by issuing payment guarantees. All suppliers accept the payment guarantee of the factor, and by performing this function, the factor enables the client to make excellent buys, to assure the delivery of raw materials in sufficient quantity to fill order backlogs, and thus to earn a profit far in excess of the cost of the factor's services.

Maturity Purchase Procedure

The detail handling procedures under a factoring arrangement are quite streamlined when you consider that the factor assumes credit risk. Prior to shipment, the client submits a list of orders received from customers. The factor checks these orders and agrees to buy the invoices and assume the credit risk. Actually, the client doesn't submit every order from each customer because the factor, in checking out a first order from a new customer, *sets a line* for that customer. Until notified otherwise, the client knows that the factor will continue to buy all invoices up to that limit at any one time.

When shipments go out, the client lists the covering invoices on a schedule and, assuming that all items fall within the lines set by the factor, the factor agrees to buy them on a *maturity date.* This establishes a contract between factor and client for a purchase at a future date reflecting standard industry billing practices. For example, in the end-of-month billing practice prevalent in the softgoods industry, all billings up to the 25th of one month come due after the 10th of the following month. Most of the remittances come in between the 11th and the 20th of the month, so the factor sets the 20th of the month following shipment as the maturity date and agrees to pay on that date the cash purchase price for all invoices *factored* up to the 25th of the previous month.

Advances

The client does not automatically receive any money at the time the invoices are factored because a *future* purchase is involved. But the client has the right to request and obtain funds if needed. In other words, the client can draw an advance against the money the factor has promised to pay on the maturity date. This advance can run as high as 90 percent of the total purchase price; in fact, under special circumstances a factor may occasionally *overadvance* — actually advance more than 100 percent of the purchase price. When done, of course, the practice reflects a close relationship between factor and client, and acknowledges that such exceptions are feasible. Advances are actually loans at interest slightly above bank rates, strictly on a pure daily cash basis over the period from the date of the advance until the maturity date. The loans are automatically repaid on the maturity date out of the factor's purchase price of the now-mature invoices. It is important to note that the factor pays in full for the purchased invoices on the maturity date *whether or not the factor has received payment for same from the debtors.*

When the client assigns schedules of invoices, factors create a *client reserve* on their books. This reserve consists of funds due the client from the factor. If the client requests no advances before the maturity date, the reserve consists of almost 100 percent of the value of the factored invoices, payable in cash to the client on the maturity date. If the client takes advances, on the other hand, the reserve consists of the difference between the total due on future maturity dates and the amounts borrowed on advance. The factor may offset against this reserve any debtor claims of faulty goods received or improper billings. The factor may not, of course, offset any bad debt losses from debtors.

Notification

Because the factor assumes full credit risk and must therefore take responsibility for followup and collection, the factor must be in direct contact with the debtors of the client.

The whole process, in other words, is on a *notification* basis. All invoices bear a legend stating that they have been assigned and that payment must go directly to the factor. Statements are issued monthly under the name of the factor and go directly to the debtors. In those industries in which factoring is widespread, notification is accepted without question as a standard procedure. (The federal government accepts assignment readily on government contracts, and in fact — in the Assignment of Claims Act — actually insists on notification.) Even so, in certain industries a few firms do not accept assignments, giving rise to problems with the usual factoring arrangement.

The positive side of the coin is that full notification presents many cost-saving opportunities to business firms.

Since the factor keeps detailed records of every debtor of every client, the client need not staff a credit department, an accounts receivable bookkeeping department, or a statement and collection department. The factor lends money on advances at close to bank rates, and when you consider that the factor supplies all these services — and absorbs all bad debt losses as well — all for charges usually ranging between 1 and 1½ percent of the value of the invoices assigned, you see why the arrangement enjoys such popularity.

Hybrid Factoring

In California, at the end of World War II, a form of factoring developed which was something of a hybrid between receivables financing and old line factoring. The factor did credit checking for the client but did not make non-recourse purchases over such a broad range or to the extent or limit of the old line factor. Also, the factor handled debtor accounts on either a notification or a non-notification basis.

The hybrid factor provides a service for smaller accounts which don't need enough money to qualify as clients of the big national commercial finance companies. Necessarily, interest rates run higher in hybrid factoring because the handling costs go up in ratio to the quantities of funds employed by individual clients — usually from $10,000 to $50,000 at most.

Hybrid factoring does not utilize the maturity-purchase arrangement offered by old line factors. Credit information is always made available to the client, but schedules are often assigned without prior credit approval. If this is done, the factor rates the schedule and marks all unacceptable accounts, usually with the initials "D.R." (for *department risk*). The factor makes advances but charges the client reserve for unpaid debtor accounts, usually after 90 days. On the other hand, under hybrid factoring, schedule advances (with the exception of a nominal reserve) are paid as soon as the schedule is processed; there is no necessity for interim loans prior to the maturity date, so the client pays no loan interest charges. The factoring fee — usually 2 to 3 percent of the total face value of the invoices assigned — comes out of the schedule advance. In fact, a business doing a volume of up to $300,000 probably could not perform the same functions for less cost and still get the benefit of the working capital advanced against assigned invoices.

Loans on Warehousing

Like accounts receivable, inventory is a current asset which generally fluctuates in ratio to the activity of the business. Therefore, borrowing programs coordinating with inventory movement represent a valid form of working capital financing. Since most inventories consist of commodities that are somewhat standard in nature, they qualify as collateral for secured lending. *Warehousing* is an arrangement whereby inventory which is to be used as collateral for loans is *physically segregated* and placed under the control of a third-party warehousing agent. The presence of a segregated inventory is disclosed to suppliers as described below.

Warehouse Advance Criteria

The percentage of advance is negotiated on the total amount of collateral placed in the warehouse. This percentage is always based on the *cost* of the goods involved, although if freight and other charges (such as duty, in the case of imports) are significant, they can be added to the price of the items to obtain *landed cost,* or the total delivered cost laid down in the warehouse. Most important in the mind of the lender is that the borrower should have a reasonable cash investment in the inventory. This is required not only as a possible buffer against loss but also because the requirement of even a nominal cash equity on the part of the borrower will restrict excessive inventories. For example, if an arrangement were made for loans of 75 percent against an inventory of sheet aluminum, one of the limiting factors would be how much money the borrower could provide to fund his 25 percent equity. If the borrower had $50,000 for this purpose, the financing of 75 percent would be limited to $150,000, resulting in a total inventory of $200,000, of which the borrower's 25 percent would equal the maximum of $50,000 he had available for this purpose.

Usually, however, the maximum loan is set on the basis of sound business principles. The chief consideration is the annual turnover, which should be normal to the industry and also prevent the cost of financing the inventory from outweighing the profit to be made from sales. Generally, slow-moving inventories are justified only where there are higher gross markups on sales to compensate; chinaware, which turns over only two or three times a year, is a good example. On the other hand, low-markup items such as foodstuffs, paper, or metals should have a fast turnover, sometimes as high as 10 to 12 times a year. Probably an average inventory turnover is about five times a year; therefore, for example, the maximum inventory loan should be one fifth of the cost of goods sold annually. Let us postulate an aluminum baking-pan manufacturer with sales of $1 million per annum, of which the cost of aluminum in the product is 60 percent of selling price. Annual cost of goods sold would be $600,000. On a five times turnover, maximum inventory loan would be one fifth, or $120,000. Actually, the limit might be set to accommodate seasonal fluctuations — for example, setting the limit during the slow season at $90,000 but during the peak season at $150,000. When set, these limits are known as the *inventory line.*

As we mentioned earlier, in addition to the line, the other limiting variable is the *percentage* of advance against cost. This is usually governed by the estimated ease of disposal in case the lender must liquidate the collateral, which in turn is established by the market for the collateral itself. The highest percentages of advance are made against true commodities such as coffee, cotton, and vegetable oils which are actually traded on the world commodity markets daily. The lender knows that the market for these items is so widespread as to make it practically possible, in an emergency, to dispose of them through a few telephone calls. For this reason advances on true commodities can run as high as 95 percent. Rated immediately below these are standard raw materials such as brass, paper, standard pipe, and lumber on which inventory advances can run as high as 80 percent. Once again, the criterion of disposal is important. For example, standard plywood sheets, which have a widespread use, nevertheless can require as much as a 25 percent discount in order to move quickly in a distress situation; therefore a lender will be reluctant to advance more than 75 percent on cost against a plywood inventory. Framing lumber generally falls into the same category and, because of its bulk, is a good example of an item for which the element of *landed* cost is important. Douglas fir lumber which costs $78 per MBM in Oregon, where it is milled, may cost $102 in San Diego because of freight charges. Since these charges determine the local market, a lender may advance $75 per MBM in San Diego on the same lumber on which he could lend only $55 per MBM in Oregon.

Public Warehousing

Many financial inventories are stored in public warehouses established as ordinary storage facilities by independent companies engaging in the warehousing business for the profit they make on their services. They do indeed profit from the special functions they provide for the financial industry, but originally these warehouses stored and handled goods for clients not having such facilities of their own. For this reason, besides general storage depots, there exist lumber warehouses, cold storage warehouses for perishables, and so on. Whatever its type, the warehouse serves a valuable function for financing purposes. As a disinterested third party with no affiliation with the borrower, the warehouse operator can demonstrate dominion for the lender and segregation of pledged inventory. Trade suppliers do not assume that warehoused inventory is an unencumbered possession of a company being financed. The law assumes that a creditor will check the customer's premises for assets before extending substantial credit, and any such check would not reveal inventories located elsewhere. Further, as agent of the lender, the warehouse operator takes certain steps clearly establishing the fact that the lender behaves like a secured lender, qualified to have an inventory financing arrangement properly interpreted.

When goods go into storage in a public warehouse, the warehouse operator issues a *warehouse receipt* which may serve as collateral for inventory financing when presented to a financial institution. Under instruction from the lender, the warehouse operator controls the release of goods from its custody, retaining responsibility for the safekeeping of all goods in custody, including coverage for fire loss as demonstrated by an *insured receipt*. Warehouse operators provide periodic physical inventory reports to both lender and borrower, at nominal cost, and they maintain complete records. A public warehouse can often receive, store, and ship inventories more economically than many firms can on their own premises.

Field Warehousing

For some businesses, the storage of inventory in a public warehouse at a distant location presents problems of cost and inconvenience. This is particularly true for manufacturers who must process raw materials into finished goods before shipment, or for other businesses which must pack a variety of items from inventory to fill orders.

Such firms find *field warehousing* an excellent alternative. Under this practice the borrower sets aside part of its own premises as a field warehouse and gives control over the area to a third party company. The major field warehousing companies run offices in most U.S. cities, but they can render their services in any location. These companies — among them Lawrence, Hazlett, and New York Terminal Warehouse — are recognized by financial institutions for their competence and financial responsibility.

Whereas public warehouses often originated as storage depots, field warehousing companies formed specifically to provide dominion and control in inventory financing, and they perform a valuable service to lenders and borrowers.

Ostensible Warehouse

Field warehousing satisfies the legal requirement of dominion in a unique way. As we have seen, the law gives trade suppliers the opportunity to discover any secured financing arrangements between a business and its lenders. One acceptable way to satisfy this requirement is to establish an *ostensible warehouse* on your own premises — on the theory that a prudent supplier would visit your premises and actually see the field warehouse before extending credit. Actually, few suppliers take the trouble, and the use of field warehousing is so prevalent among many fine large companies that sophisticated suppliers accept it readily.

To establish an ostensible warehouse, you set aside a clearly delineated area on your own premises — a separate partitioned area, if possible, although a chicken-wire barricade will do. Some businesses — for example, lumber yards — designate everything except their office area as an ostensible warehouse. You draw a simple plan of the area, usually on a piece of 8½ by 11 inch paper, and post it near the warehouse entrance to show the approximate limits of the field warehouse. You execute a sublease of the warehouse section of your premises to the warehousing company, usually for $1 per year. You post a few metal signs of nominal size around the warehouse identifying the goods inside as the property of the warehousing company, and you designate one of your own employees to act as field warehouse manager. You transfer this employee to the payroll of the warehousing company, which bonds the employee and bills you for the wages the employee earns. In this way you incur no additional expenses, and in fact, the employee's warehousing duties may take so little time that the individual remains free to continue his or her other duties for your business. But the arrangement enables the warehousing company to take full responsibility for the stored inventory, issuing *bonded warehouse receipts* to the lender and performing certain services for the borrower, including the issuance of monthly inventory reports showing movement and balances. The cost of the service is nominal, based on a fraction of 1 percent of the inventory in the warehouse.

Warehouse Release Methods

Both field and public warehouses follow essentially the same operational procedures. As mentioned earlier, when goods go into the warehouse, the warehouse manager issues a receipt and the lender will advance funds to the borrower. At this point the warehouse manager, as agent of the lender, controls custody. This makes it necessary to establish methods of removing the goods from the warehouse — usually by one of the following techniques:

- Pre-delivery payment;
- A blanket release; or
- Minimum hold.

The lender has the right to choose the method so, as the borrower, you should attempt to negotiate the method best suited to your operation. Once lender and borrower agree, the lender issues a written *delivery instruction* to the warehouse governing future releases until changed.

If the lender requires *pre-delivery payment*, the warehouse manager must receive full payment for the goods before releasing them. The payment may be in cash or in the form of an assignment of receivables created from shipment of the goods to be released. It may also take the form of loan proceeds from new warehouse receipts issued as additional goods from suppliers go into the warehouse. Whatever its form, the payment goes directly to the financing institution, which advises the warehouse manager how much to release.

The *blanket release* is more flexible. Under this system, the delivery instructions stipulate that the warehouse manager may release uncompensated releases up to a certain limit, termed the "blanket." For example, a blanket of $25,000 means that the warehouse may release, on request from the borrower, up to $25,000 in goods at cost.[11] As releases approach the limit of the blanket, the warehouse manager issues a *confirmation of*

---

[11]Note that goods go into the warehouse and appear on receipts at their true cost, and they keep the same basis throughout their stay in the warehouse.

delivery to the lender. The lender, meanwhile, receives payment from the borrower either in cash or in assigned accounts receivable. The lender signs the confirmation of delivery and returns it to the warehouse manager. This *reinstates* part of the blanket. Using the same $25,000 blanket in our example above, let's assume that the borrower has obtained releases of $10,000, $8,000 and $5,000, leaving only $2,000 open on the blanket. The borrower pays $18,000 to the lender, who in turns signs the first two confirmations of delivery and returns them to the warehouse manager. This reinstates $18,000 of the blanket, which, added to the $2,000 previously available, gives the borrower $20,000 to work with.

The *minimum hold* is the most streamlined releasing procedure. Here the delivery instructions allow the warehouse manager to release goods on request from the borrower, provided that the total value of the goods in the warehouse does not fall below a certain figure. If the value does drop to this minimum, the warehouse temporarily "closes" to the borrower. The minimum hold procedure works best when the borrower needs frequent releases — and delivers new merchandise to the warehouse with equal frequency. The procedure works best, in other words, for businesses with a consistently high inventory that turns over rapidly. Obviously, if inventory drops, the borrower has fewer accounts payable due to suppliers, and thus more funds with which to reduce the inventory loan from the lender. Under these circumstances, the lender could issue new delivery instructions to the warehouse manager specifying a lower minimum hold, since the lender needs less collateral to justify a lower loan.

Inventory — or Floating — Liens

The Uniform Commercial Code greatly expanded the scope of secured financing. Before its development, a lender perfected a security interest in property only by showing specific exercise of dominion over the collateral, and if the borrower gained dominion over the property, the lender's security interest became of doubtful validity. This greatly frustrated the needs of commerce. Banks had to police their collateral elaborately, for fear that the borrower would commingle proceeds from sales with other funds and give rise to the threat that the security agreement might be ruled a fraud against unsecured creditors. The hard and fast rule was that the borrower had to account for all proceeds arising from the disposition of any collateral. The lender, meanwhile, found it very difficult to get a valid security interest covering large quantities of shifting stock.

The Uniform Commercial Code changed the picture by allowing the lender to take a security interest in inventory and its proceeds — inventory meaning all items held for sale, present and future, in a business with a rapid turnover of stock. Also, the lender's agreement may state that the security agreement covers inventory *whenever acquired.* This obviates the necessity of drawing up a new security agreement every time fresh inventory comes in, and the necessity of accounting for each piece of inventory as it shows up. The proceeds clause in the security agreement extends the security interest automatically to any proceeds of the sale by the borrower. The borrower may deal with the collateral proceeds in any manner he or she wishes, without threatening the secured position of the lender.

This arrangement preserves the legal status of the lien, but from a credit point of view, the lender commonly includes certain procedures and reporting requirements in the agreement with the borrower. Normally the lender wants to receive periodic sales and collection information, as well as periodic inventory reports, to ensure that the outstanding loans remain adequately secured by inventory or receivables.

The borrower may reinvest the proceeds in new inventory since the bank's security interest covers all inventory, past, present and future. As long as the value of the collateral remains sufficient to cover the obligation, the credit position remains satisfactory to the lender.

Future Advances

Another concept validated by the Uniform Commercial Code is a provision for *future advances* in a security agreement. A future advances clause provides that obligations covered by the security agreement shall include advances of money or other value given by the lender in the future. The collateral secures all such advances even though lender and borrower have not agreed, at present, that they be made.

The combination of an *after-acquired* and a *future-advances* clause produces a *cross security* or *floating lien* agreement under which collateral acquired at any time may secure advances whenever made. Such an agreement allows the two parties to engage in continued financing over an extended period without renegotiating the original security agreement. The bank's right to a security interest in all proceeds suffers no impairment under such an agreement.

The floating lien finds its greatest utility in financial arrangements involving manufacturing and sales of inventory. It does not apply to any security interest based on possession of the collateral by the lender — for example, goods in a warehouse over which the lender has dominion.

Lenders consider the same credit criteria for inventory lien financing as for warehousing loans. But because inventory liens provide looser control, lenders tend to advance against smaller percentages of liened inventory than against warehoused goods. On the other hand, since the lien can extend across all the inventory of the borrower, including inventory still in the manufacturing process, the total collateral can be higher with an inventory lien.

For example, an inventory of warehoused lumber in a furniture factory could warrant a 75 percent advance. The same lumber could warrant only a 60 percent advance as part of an inventory lien made to the same furniture factory. But since the factory adds value to the lumber in inventory by making it into furniture, the manufacturer builds up collateral with which to secure the lender, so the total advanced in both cases might well end up the same.

Categorizing Inventory

It is important to analyze the general mix of inventory by categorizing it as raw materials, inventory in process, and finished goods. The analysis allows the lender to determine an optimum safe advance, and without such an analysis, lenders tend to be conservative. Raw materials usually command the highest advance as a percentage of value, since the lender may recover it intact for resale. Inventory in process commands much less because the raw material is no longer standard or wholly recoverable. Finished goods command a greater advance, but since the manufacturer wants to ship them as quickly as possible, they usually don't figure highly in an inventory lien. Thus, in the example of the wood furniture manufacturer, a lender might establish the advance according to the following table:

Secured Working Capital Loans

Category	Advance (%)	Cost Total	Advance
Raw materials	70	$ 90,000	$63,000
In process	40	50,000	20,000
Finished goods	60	25,000	15,000
Total		$165,000	$98,000
Advance against total			60%

This type analysis shows that the lender advances an average of 60 percent against inventory. The lender will check the category mix periodically to see if it remains the same.

Conservative lenders prefer warehouse financing to inventory liens. Borrowers prefer the inventory lien because it is less cumbersome, although it commonly justifies a lower advance. In some cases a *combination of lien and warehousing financing* best serves the interests of both parties. Under such an arrangement the raw materials go into a field warehouse, and a lien covers the rest of the operation. The materials in the field warehouse command an 80 percent advance, and the inventory in the rest of the operation a 60 percent advance. This gives the borrower a 70 percent advance, on average — a higher advance than a lien alone would justify.

Liens work better, however, where the inventory consists of many diverse items or of large quantities of low-cost items, because of the impracticality of field warehousing. Also, it should be obvious that keeping in-process items in a field warehouse would be virtually impossible, so that here again, the lien emerges as the only alternative.

The borrower must submit a detailed physical inventory to the lender in order to create a lien, and usually semiannual inventories thereafter. In the interim, a monthly *designation* usually satisfies the requirements of dominion and control. The following is an example of a designation:

Jones Manufacturing Co.
Inventory Lien Designation

Beginning inventory March 1		$280,000
Purchases, month of March		90,000
Sales-March	$150,000	
Inventory cost of goods sold	× 50%	(75,000)
Ending inventory March 31		$295,000

Certified correct from our records (signed and dated)

Note that the interim designation reflects summarized book figures, to be corrected at the end of any month during which a physical inventory takes place. Each month the loan adjusts up or down to conform to the new designated total. If the designated total reduces, the borrower must repay the percentage advanced against the higher total of the previous month. If it increases, the lender increases the loan, subject, of course, to the inventory line limit.

Chapter 6
Secured Growth Capital Loans

In Chapter 2 we distinguished growth capital from working capital by describing the function of each. Working capital borrowing usually reflects business cycles and the loan reductions come from annual liquidations, but the repayment of a growth capital loan comes from profits of a program extending several years into the future.

The difference between growth capital and working capital also shows up in the collateral used to secure such loans. As we have seen, the lender of working capital finds security in assets which turn over rapidly and fluctuate seasonally — i.e., in *current assets* such as inventories and receivables. The lender of growth capital, on the other hand, finds security in collateral which remains unchanged in the possession of the borrower — i.e., in *fixed assets* such as machinery and equipment.

Chattel Mortgages

The chief instrument used in establishing the lien required by the lender of growth capital is the *chattel mortgage.* The term no longer appears in statutory language, but lenders continue to use it as a matter of custom. A chattel is any piece of personal property, and it becomes collateral for a loan in much the same manner as real property becomes collateral for a mortgage. The chattel which stands as collateral for the loan remains in the borrower's possession until the borrower defaults on the obligation, in which case the lender resorts to the remedy of *repossession.* The chattel mortgage calls for the borrower to repay the loan over a fixed period with regular — usually monthly or quarterly — payments.

The security agreement between lender and borrower creates the chattel mortgage by identifying the chattel which stands as security for the debt. To *perfect* the security interest, the lender must file a financing statement documenting the transaction at the appropriate public office specified in the commercial code of the state.

Lenders usually use standard forms drawn specially to meet the legal needs established by the Uniform Commercial Code. Any creditor wishing to know whether specific chattels are encumbered may inspect the files of the public office handling the filing. If the lender fails to file the chattel mortgage in that office, it can have no effect with regard to other lenders.

A *future advances* clause, inserted in a chattel mortgage, gives the instrument great flexibility. Such a clause states that the chattel stands as security not only for the initial loan but also for later loans unanticipated at the time of the initial loan. Where no such clause provides for future advances, such advances become unsecured. The legal theory in chattel financing is that the chattel secures a single loan and that, as the borrower pays this loan down, he or she gradually frees the chattel of its burden as security. Thus funds advanced after amortization begins become *unsecured* loans in the absence of a future advances clause.

For example, assume a chattel mortgage of $120,000 payable over four years at the rate of $2,500 per month. At the end of two years (ignoring interest) the unpaid balance stands at $60,000. At this point lender and borrower agree to increase the loan by $25,000 to cover an unanticipated need for growth capital. The circumstances and the present value of the collateral justify the new cash advance, but without a future advances, or *fluctuating,* provision in the financing agreement, the new loan becomes unsecured. This fact alone could interfere with the lender's making the new accommodation.

Fluctuating Chattel Mortgages

Lenders design some loan arrangements to fluctuate so as to accommodate the unexpected. For example, I once arranged the financing of a computer leasing company, using the hardware as the chattel security. The borrower assigned to the lender the $8,000 monthly lease income on the equipment to obtain a six-year loan repayable at $3,000 per month. The lease income would have repaid the lender faster than required, but the original chattel mortgage contained a fluctuating provision. So the lender lent $5,000 a month back to the borrower for operating expenses. Legally, each time the borrower received another $5,000, the transaction constituted a new loan which could not have been secured without the fluctuating provision in the original chattel mortgage.

As an alternative, a chattel mortgage may call for an amortization less than that required to retire the loan over a given period of time. This arrangement accommodates a business whose financing needs do not parallel a straight-line reduction of the chattel mortgage. To see how this works, consider the example of a business seeking to borrow $90,000 for three years to build a new factory with efficiencies expected to yield additional profits of, say, $150,000 over the same period. The borrower demonstrates a reasonable certainty that the new factory will generate higher profits, but it will take a learning period in the new facility. Therefore the additional profits will not begin to be realized until after the first year. Put another way, *the funds to repay the loan will accrue during the second and third year.* Meanwhile the business owner must rely on existing cash flow to finance the loan during the first year.

To accommodate this need, the chattel mortgage specifies an amortization which does not parallel the term of the loan — for example, a three-year loan with a five-year amortization. Under such an arrangement the borrower must have repaid the entire loan after three years, but until that time sends the lender *a monthly payment calculated as if the loan were a five-year note.* To be specific, each month the borrower repays 1/60th of the loan amount, not 1/36th (ignoring interest). Clearly, at the end of three years the borrower's monthly payments total only 60 percent of the loan, and the borrower still owes 40 percent. The borrower repays that 40 percent in one lump sum, known as a *balloon.*

Chattel Loan Balloons

Balloon payments appear gimmicky to some people, but the financial community considers the balloon payment an acceptable procedure when tailored to the needs of a particular business.

On the other hand, lenders and borrowers arrange some balloon loans with full knowledge that the borrower cannot repay the loan in full at the end of the term. Usually they structure such transactions to satisfy certain requirements of the lender.

A basic precept in lending holds that risk increases with the length of the loan term. Long-term business loans are considered riskier because the lender must forecast the borrower's creditworthiness farther into the future, with all the uncertainty that the future holds. The lender of first mortgages on real estate, by contrast, forecasts a basic stability in the long term housing market, notwithstanding the real depreciation in some local markets in recent years. But the lender who deals with businesses contends with the uncertainties of changing technology, markets, and competition. New equipment, for example, may render obsolete even well maintained older equipment, so lenders making equipment chattel loans generally project only three or four years into the future, after which they take another look at the safety of their security. By the time the lender takes this second look, the borrower will have repaid a substantial portion of the loan, thus giving the lender additional security. If other aspects of the borrower's operation appear satisfactory, the lender renews the loan, perhaps on an easier basis.

Liquidity Requirements

Lenders have their own requirements, particularly with respect to the liquidity of their portfolios — an important point for the borrower of growth capital to remember in negotiating a loan. Usually these *liquidity requirements* are imposed on lenders by banking regulations, indentures to debenture holders, or agreements with investors. By liquidity requirements, lenders refer to the *average* terms of the outstanding loans in their portfolios. The average stands as a measure of the collectability of the portfolio, reflecting the precept that risk increases with the term of a loan. If, for example, a lending institution adheres to a liquidity requirement of 180 days, the institution could liquidate half of its portfolio in six months — since the *average term* of all loans is 180 days. As a practical matter, because most lending institutions do the bulk of their lending over very short terms — e.g., 90-day lines at banks, or monthly receivables financing by commercial finance companies — they can also take longer paper, usually with terms from two to seven years, so long as the average doesn't throw the portfolio beyond the institution's liquidity requirement. Most equipment loans range from two to five years, but some go six and seven years. Most lenders make fewer seven-year than five-year loans, and they lean toward the shorter-term opportunities when they approach their liquidity limit. When this happens, the borrower must find other institutions with more flexibility.

For these reasons, the borrower who goes into a lender's offices with a demand for unrealistically long-term financing may ask for the impossible. If the longer term financing is not available, the same final result may be obtained by requesting shorter term financing with a balloon — in the expectation that the lender will renew the loan as a new transaction if all has gone well when the balloon payment comes due.

Credit Criteria

Unlike secured current asset financing, where the primary credit emphasis goes on the quality of the collateral, sound secured growth capital lending pays more or less equal attention to several criteria:

- Justification of the loan purposes;
- Value of the collateral; and
- Cash flow or source of repayment.

As a rule, if you can demonstrate that growth capital will generate production efficiencies, cost savings or increased markets, the expected enhancements of profits and worth justify a financing program. Machinery and equipment may stand as collateral for the borrowing, but you may not wish to limit the use of the funds themselves to purchasing additional equipment; indeed, you may use the funds for any general business purpose as long as it promises the possibility of success. If, for example, you borrow $50,000 (secured by equipment) for an advertising campaign expected to yield profits far beyond the expenditure, you can justify the loan just as easily as you would if you intended to use the money for new equipment. Normally a simple description of the purpose of the loan and an explanation of the way you expect to attain the benefits will suffice for most small or mid-sized applications. If, however, you seek a growth capital loan of $500,000 or more, you must prepare a more thorough explanation as part of a detailed cash-flow projection.[1]

Evaluating Collateral

Every item in the fixed asset category of your balance sheet has worth, but not every item qualifies as collateral for growth capital borrowing. Leasehold improvements, for example, are ineligible, and special patterns, molds

---

[1]See Chapter 11, "Private Placements."

and dies — whatever their cost — command little credit since they may have limited value outside of your business. But standard machinery and equipment — i.e., production, handling, office machinery and even rolling stock — are highly acceptable, depending on condition and *local* resale value. Location has some bearing on value; equipment located in a remote area may require costly shipping to dispose of it. Equipment auctions draw good crowds who pay top prices in Los Angeles but few bidders in, say, rural Utah.

An *appraisal* is usually required to establish the loan value of used equipment. There exist certain companies whose entire business is making such appraisals; their estimates frequently are acceptable. But because most such companies work for insurers or on behalf of litigants, some lenders prefer appraisals from auctioneers whose primary work is to dispose of the equipment they appraise; most lenders work with a few local appraisers with whom they have had previous experience. You can get the names of these appraisers from lenders with whom you hope to establish a relationship.

Appraisers arrive at three different evaluations:

- *Replacement value* — the cost of purchasing new equipment in today's market, to replace the used equipment being appraised;

- *Sound market value* — the going value of a piece of used equipment if purchased from a dealer or if sold to a willing buyer; and

- *Auction or liquidation value* — the present distress value of the equipment, as is, if sold under the auctioneer's hammer.

Insurers want to know about replacement value and sound market value. Lenders want to know about auction value. But replacement value and sound market value play an important role in your negotiations with a lender even so; the appraiser usually lists them along with the auction value, and they serve a good psychological purpose. If a lender notes, for example, that the auction value is considerably lower than the sound market value, the lender will feel more confident about the realistic possibilities of disposal. The following appraisal totals — submitted to me by a large machine shop as I wrote this chapter — stand as a good example of the comparisons here:

Replacement value	$1,267,515
Sound market value	$828,307
Auction value	$472,481

These numbers seemed typical of a business purchasing big-ticket pieces of equipment over a period of years. It interested me to note that the balance sheet of the machine shop listed the depreciated value of the equipment at only $295,630, or far less than the auction value. This had come about because the machine shop took accelerated depreciation, and it meant that the shop could actually borrow more than 100 percent of the book value of its equipment.

You often find a fairly standard relationship between auction value and depreciated book value — an important thing to know if you wish to estimate the auction value of your equipment before obtaining an appraisal. If your business has existed more than five years and has taken normal depreciation on its equipment, the *net* book value of this equipment *after* deducting depreciation is usually roughly equivalent to the auction value, assuming equipment in decent condition.

Loan Ratios to Appraisals

Lenders occasionally make spot advances in fairly high ratio to the cost of individual pieces of newly purchased equipment, but more often they advance growth capital on the security of all of the equipment owned by a business. As a rule the advances run between 25 and 75 percent of the book value, depending on the auction appraisal. Very simply, you should be able to obtain a loan at least equal to auction value appraisal — since your lender should come out whole if forced to dispose of the equipment on short notice.

With going businesses, however, lenders usually advance from 100 to 150 percent of auction appraisal. Here again we see evidence of the principle of *limited-future forecasting*. Assume that you arrange a three-year loan for $120,000 with equal monthly payments of $3,000 plus a $12,000 balloon. Assuming an auction value of $100,000, your lender thus makes a 120 percent advance. In approving the loan, the lender judges that your business will probably continue on an even keel for at least a year, by which time you will have reduced the loan by $36,000 (ignoring interest), leaving a balance of $84,000 — *less than auction value* of the equipment even if you factor in 12 months of depreciation.

Clearly, the lender has a comfortable cushion and may approve your loan without violating conservative lending principles.

Guaranteed Appraisals

In some instances you may have difficulty convincing a lender to rely sufficiently on an auction appraisal to approve a particular financing program. This difficulty can arise, for example, when you and the lender operate in different cities and the lender has little knowledge of conditions in yours, or when the lender has no familiarity with the chattel equipment and no contacts among auctioneers who could dispose of it in the event of a default.

Sometimes it happens that the lender simply can't act fast enough to suit the borrower with an urgent need for a loan. A *guaranteed appraisal* can overcome these difficulties. Under a guaranteed appraisal, the auctioneer promises to purchase the chattel equipment for a specified price upon demand from the lender, with payment going directly to the lender.

When the credit applied for is somewhat marginal, a guaranteed appraisal can provide additional comfort to induce a fence-sitting lender to act favorably. Usually the guarantee decreases as the loan amortizes. Assume, for example, a three-year loan of $400,000 amortized at $100,000 per year, plus a $100,000 balloon. To cover the loan, the auctioneer issues a guaranteed appraisal promising to buy the equipment, upon demand from the lender, for $400,000 now, $300,000 at the end of the first year, $200,000 at the end of the second year, and $100,000 — i.e., the amount of the balloon payment — at the end of the third.

The lender sees that this promise puts the auctioneer on the hook for the loan. Since auctioneers hold liquidation sales as a matter of course — and since auctioneers don't put their guarantees on the line without being familiar with the equipment and its value — the lender has confidence in your loan.

To be sure, the borrower pays for a guaranteed appraisal via a fee running to several percentage points of the guarantee. But when you consider the risk shouldered by the auctioneer and the resulting benefit to the borrower, the arrangement is quite fair. Auctioneers perform such services for relatively modest charges fully confident that, should push come to shove, an auction — from which, don't forget, they will make their usual fee — will make them whole.

Cash Flow Requirements

Once they establish a good purpose for your loan and see ample security, all lenders ask one more question: Where will you get the money to replay the loan? Lenders don't like to own equipment; it's not their business. Despite all their legal protections and their hedges against foreclosure, lenders don't approve applications if they think, from the outset, that a forfeiture is likely.

The cash flow of a business equals profit plus non-cash expenses such as depreciation. Many credit analysts figure profit before taxes because they feel that, if profits fall, so will taxes, and in any case taxes paid in previous years can carry forward against a loss year to provide a cushion.

In any event, analysts always add depreciation back onto profit in computing cash flow because depreciation is a non-cash expense; it is a bookkeeping entry that does not remove dollars from the company coffers. Thus a business with a $30,000 profit and depreciation totalling $12,000 actually has cash flow of $42,000.

The lender looks at this number in calculating your ability to repay a loan. Out of cash flow come all sums required for the repayment of indebtedness, including new debt and existing installment contracts for purchased equipment. These are the only significant items, since all operating expenses have already been deducted in arriving at cash flow. And the lender should approve a loan if the total of these items — plus the amortization requirement of the new financing under consideration — does not exceed the *demonstrated cash flow*.

If the financial statements reflecting current position do not show a sufficient cash flow, you must show how the new financing program will provide the extra increment. You can accomplish this by detailing your cost figures to compare present and future operations reflecting production efficiencies, or by providing a marketing analysis showing how your increased sales will create profits by increasing gross income and spreading administrative expenses.

Discount and Add-On Interest

Although many chattel mortgage loans carry simple interest, some lenders use *discount interest* or *add-on interest.* As first practiced in England, the lender deducts, or discounts, interest when funding a loan. Thus on a $100,000 loan at 6 percent for one year, the lender deducts $6,000 in full payment of one year's interest, advancing only $94,000 to the borrower. In this way the bank receives $6,000 income on an actual loan of $94,000, or 6.38 percent interest. For short terms such as one year, and particularly for loans with no amortization, the difference is slight. But when the borrower makes regular monthly payments over the life of the loan, the effective cost of interest changes considerably.

If you have ever financed the purchase of a car through a bank, you have made use of a type of discounted loan — with a slight difference. Your lender didn't discount interest on your car loan; it added interest onto the amount advanced.

Take, for example, an auto loan of $18,000 over three years at 6 percent. The bank charges $1,080 in interest for each of the three years, or $3,240 in all. But the bank adds the interest cost onto the loan, so that the total face value of your loan comes to $21,240.

Now look at this closely. The original amount of principal advanced to you in cash was $18,000 but — since it will be repaid down to zero at the end of three years — the *average* loan balance during the life of the loan would be $9,000. On that balance the bank earns $1,080 each of the three years, which is obviously 12 percent, not 6 percent, on your loan.

As a matter of fact, once you factor in amortization, the bank's earnings come closer to 11 percent on such a loan, but even so, it's easy to see why banks make these loans, even though their handling costs are higher than those involved with an unsecured line of credit. It costs money to evaluate the collateral, to make equipment chattels, and to process the monthly payments. An add-on rate of 6 percent compensates the lender for these costs and provides an adequate return on a loan involving good-quality chattel. Some very prime situations may qualify for add-on interest as low as 4 percent; others require 7 percent or more. Sometimes — for example, for consumer financing involving relatively low face amounts — the add-on rate goes as high as 10 percent.

Conditional Sales Purchases

The purchase of production equipment and other physical assets on a time-payment basis is now a commonplace practice in American industry. The seller accepts a nominal down payment and makes delivery upon the execution of a *conditional sales contract*. Legal ownership of the property remains with the seller until the buyer makes all the required monthly payments over the term of the contract, usually 12 to 36 months. Because sellers use this technique to stimulate sales, we discuss it again in a later chapter[2]. For now, let's look at the conditional sales contract as a form of financing.

Conditional sales contracts differ from other forms of financing in three ways:

- Conditional sales contracts usually require no legal recording.

- The seller retains title under a conditional sales contract, whereas under other forms of financing the buyer holds title subject to forfeiture.

- A conditional sales contract almost always gives the lender *recourse to the seller.*

The third point explains why a business owner who has obtained financing from a bank on one piece of equipment sometimes can't get the same bank to finance a second, similar piece of equipment. Only one difference exists between the two transactions — namely that the business owner bought the first piece of equipment from a machinery dealer and the second from a manufacturer with surplus stock. But the second gives the bank no "dealer recourse," making it impossible for the bank to finance the transaction.

Because lenders don't want to own equipment through the forfeiture of a contract, the presence of a machinery dealer in the picture, whose day-to-day activities keep him or her in the machinery market, is necessary to the lender. This is true whether the transaction involves new or used equipment, and explains why, even if you make a

---

[2]See Chapter 8.

very good buy on a piece of machinery at an auction, you may have more difficulty financing the purchase than if you pay 30 percent more for the same machinery from a dealer. To be sure, dealers may be on recourse on contracts many times their net worth, but it is not solely the repayment guarantee that the lender seeks. Rather, the lender wants assurance that, in the event of forfeit, the dealer — who is well qualified to do so — will step in to resell the equipment elsewhere. This fact occasionally gives rise to an unusual practice wherein a business which desires financing on existing equipment, and which also requires additional new equipment, sells some of its equipment to a dealer and repurchases it on a contract that includes the additional new pieces desired — the entire transaction being financed by an lender on the basis of the dealer recourse.

Leasing

The technique of *leasing* qualifies as a basic method of equipment financing even though it involves no borrowing. Under a leasing arrangement the financial institution owns equipment which it leases to a business firm for exclusive use over a period of years. Originally leasing involved only very large items — for example, the leasing of railroad cars and engines to railroad companies by equipment trusts. IBM made the leasing of big mainframe computers standard practice in the computer industry, and the U.S. Shoe Machinery Corp. leased special machinery. From such beginnings a broad industry evolved which leases such diverse things as aircraft, trucks, office machines, traffic barricades, turret lathes, motel furnishings, display equipment, offshore oil rigs, and a host of other items.

Instead of lender and borrower, we have here a leasing company, *the lessor*, and its customer, the *lessee*. The usual legal requirement for dominion doesn't apply because the law does not consider the lessor a lender. Instead, the leasing company must show only that it is the actual owner of the equipment of which the lessee has exclusive use — accomplished by affixing a nameplate or label to each piece of leased equipment identifying the leasing company as owner of the equipment.

The proponents of leasing argue that it:

- Facilitates the purchase of needed equipment;

- Releases funds which the lessee would otherwise tie up in owning fixed assets;

- Gives the lessee certain tax advantages; and

- Improves the lessee's financial statement.

The first two of these reasons are obvious, and since the funds of the leasing company replace those of the lessee invested in certain pieces of equipment, working and growth capital are made available in much the same way as by the other methods of equipment financing, such as chattel mortgage lending.

Tax Advantages

The possible tax advantages depend on the facts of each leasing transaction, and tax and case law in this field change constantly. Leasing companies don't trumpet the tax advantages of leasing, but there is no question that the practice accrues benefits to many lessees. Even so, the breadth of the tax aspect prohibits a full discussion in this book. For our purposes, the benefit of leasing to the business is that the lease payments become a tax-deductible item — unlike, for example, the payments made to amortize a loan to purchase the same equipment. The lessee may also purchase the equipment at the end of the term for a fraction of its value and continue to use it or, perhaps, even sell it at a profit taxable as a capital gain.

Some leases qualify for tax writeoffs almost automatically — for example, equipment required for a particular project with a known finite period of usage, such as construction machinery needed for building a dam. Defense contractors lease production machinery for particular application to specific contracts, most commonly on cost-plus contracts. The practice gives the contractor a much better writeoff than ordinary depreciation.

As a rule, leasing contracts qualify for writeoff when the term matches the normal life span of the underlying equipment. I have seen acceptable deductions, for example, involving leased supermarket equipment set up according to the normal life span of the item, usually four to eight years. The lessee made varying lease payments — higher early in the term and lower later — but the total of the payments did not change and the lessee obtained the full tax benefit.

We will see shortly that yet another tax benefit accrues when you use leasing as a tool of business finance — the possibility of *deferring* taxes and freeing up more money to use for growth and retained surplus before you must square away the tax liability.

Credit Criteria

Leasing companies look to many of the same credit criteria as chattel lenders — the intrinsic value of the equipment, the purpose to which the lessee intends to put the equipment, and the lessee's cash flow.

Like lenders, leasing companies don't want to repossess equipment, so they make doubly sure that lessees have sufficient cash flow to cover all annual payout requirements including the new lease. Cash flow consists of net profits plus depreciation, but since lease payments are deductible, leasing companies compute cash flow *before* taxes.

In other respects the standards for financial strength are much the same for lessees as for borrowers. When a lease involves specialized equipment of limited general utility, however, the leasing company may demand more-than-ordinary creditworthiness. On the other hand, leasing companies seem to have easier credit criteria when the leased equipment has widespread use.

Almost always, financing equipment through leasing makes it possible to advance a higher amount relative to collateral value than any other technique. Indeed, you may achieve almost 100 percent financing with a purchase-lease. The lessor retains ownership and need not demonstrate a priority of claim against other creditors; nor does the lessor bog down in any legal proceeding such as a foreclosure in order to repossess the equipment. The lessor remains in position to repossess the property whenever the lessee doesn't meet the conditions of the lease, without challenge to the claim. These liberal practices arose in the early days of leasing, when only substantial lessees engaged in the business, and they have carried over into the entire field of leasing.

You may lease equipment from specialized leasing companies and, nowadays, from a number of the major commercial finance companies and banks with leasing subsidiaries or divisions. It is interesting to note that in their leasing divisions, lending institutions — which may restrict chattel loans to 60 to 75 percent of fair market value (i.e., 100 to 125 percent of auction value) — follow the higher advancing practices of the leasing industry. This leads us to what is probably the biggest advantage of leasing: the benefits that accrue from freeing up working capital.

Purchase-Lease Fund Availability

In a typical purchase-lease contract, lessor and lessee agree on the term, the amount and frequency of payments, the equipment, and other items. The lessor issues its own purchase order for the equipment and pays in full when the lessee accepts delivery. In effect, the arrangement commits the lessor to making a 100 percent advance on the market price of the equipment. As a consequence, the lessor usually requires that the lessee put up a *lease deposit,* usually the first month's rent plus one additional month's rent for each year of the life of the contract.[3] The lessor may view the deposit as a reserve, but however you analyze it, the lessor still makes an advance of about 90 percent of *market value* on the equipment — a high level compared to other methods of equipment financing.

Let's look more closely at the advantages of leasing. It costs more money to lease than it does to make an outright purchase for cash, and it may well cost more to lease than to finance a purchase through a bank loan. But a cash purchase *ties up cash for the life of the equipment;* purchase loans do the same thing, although more slowly. And in all cases the buyer pays an *opportunity cost* — i.e., the loss of opportunity to make a profit on the capital freed up by leasing. Put another way, buying equipment for cash or through a loan saves some money on the financing of the purchase — at the expense of investment opportunity.

For a business making a fair return on capital investment, the opportunity cost may prove substantial. For example, take a company with a capital investment of $100,000 and annual sales of $500,000. Net profits, after all expenses, come to 5 percent of sales, or $25,000. The profits represent 25 percent of investment, and the company needs only the use of new capital in order to grow; that is, it expects to show the same 25 percent return on *the next* $100,000 it invests in its operations.

---

[3]Thus a five-year lease, for example, might call for a deposit equal to six months' rent.

With that in mind, the company leases $100,000 worth of equipment for five years, with payments of $20,000 per year. The equipment produces goods selling for $500,000 each year, with net profits coming in at the expected $25,000. Over the five years the profits reach $125,000, but there's more to the story — namely the extra profit derived from the money *not* spent on an outright purchase.

In the first year this freed-up capital amounts to $80,000 (i.e., the difference between the cost of an outright purchase and the lease payment, or $100,000 less $20,000). Freed-up capital totals $60,000 in the second year, $40,000 in the third, and $20,000 in the fourth. The company puts this capital to use, earning $20,000 in the first year, $15,000 in the second, $10,000 in the third, and $5,000 in the fourth — *in all, $50,000 that the company would not have earned without leasing.*

Most of the earnings advantages of leasing come from the fact that a leasing program frees up capital during the early stages of the contract. A study in the *Harvard Business Review* analyzed the advantages in detail, as shown in the following table. The study assumed a five-year leasing contract, a full cash purchase, a 75 percent bank loan at prime interest, and an installment plan with a nominal 4.5 percent add-on — all on equipment costing $100,000.

Method	Year End	Excess Freed Cash Through Leasing
Cash Purchase	1	$79,026
"	2	58,999
"	3	39,913
"	4	21,773
"	5	4,580
75% bank loan	1	20,466
"	2	16,591
"	3	13,369
"	4	10,805
"	5	8,900
Installment purchase	1	20,281
"	2	15,424
"	3	10,241
"	4	3,121
"	5	−3,236

Clearly, in the early going, leasing frees up valuable capital, and it makes sense to lease when you expect a good return on such funds.

Sale-Leasebacks

Purchase leases involve new equipment, as a rule, but it is also possible to lease equipment not purchased from a machinery supplier. In such cases, the prospective lessee sells the equipment to the leasing company, then *leases it back* for its own use. The technique frees up capital — namely the money gained from the sale of the equipment to the lessor.

A variety of situations qualify for this technique. For example, a user of hot-forming exotic metal presses designed and built his own presses, sold them at cost to a leasing company, then leased them back. In mergers and acquisitions, the buyer often has a leasing company purchase the equipment of the company being acquired and then lease it back to the acquiring company. In some instances, a going business may sell all of its equipment to a leasing company and then lease it back. As a rule such transactions do not yield as high an advance on the equipment as do purchase-leases involving new equipment. But they often do equal the advance obtainable through chattel mortgage borrowing.

Leasing Terms

Most leasing contracts range in term from two to eight years; longer leases cover special situations and call for lessees of substantial financial stature. Leases running less than three years are rare except for automobiles. Most leases involving items that depreciate quickly — for example, office furnishings — run three years. Leases on computers and other automated office equipment usually run four years. Most industrial leases run for five- to eight-year terms.

Once the term of the lease expires, the lessee may:

- Buy the equipment at a *residual value* stipulated in the leasing contract; or

- Renew the lease at a reduced payment.

The first gives the lessee the option to buy the equipment at a price substantially discounted from the original cost. There are no fixed practices by which to arrive at residual values, although they do not vary widely as a rule. The usual residual value is about 10 percent of the original value. The lessee who buys equipment at residual value does so for a fraction of its real value at the end of the lease, but under current tax law, a lease contract stipulating the terms of sale at the end of the lease may strip the leasing company of the depreciation incentives which make it possible to give lessees favorable rates.

Such stipulations may deprive the lessee of a different advantage — the deductibility of lease payments. Tax law distinguishes between lease and purchase contracts, and the Internal Revenue Service gives careful scrutiny to deductions for lease payments on contracts which, in the government's opinion, look too much like purchase agreements.

In this connection, the *renewal option* stands out as the alternative with real economic value to the lessee. Most renewal options call for payments running between 2 and 5 percent of the original purchase price per year.[4] Thus a $100,000 five-year lease requiring payments of $12,000 per year might call for renewal rates of $3,000 per year after completion of the original term. The renewal option runs for one year at a time, so exercising it doesn't "marry" the business to an old piece of equipment just when the market serves up a better, more modern replacement. Many business owners find renewal terms so favorable, and the payments so low, that they don't consider exercising their purchase option.

Leasing Rates

Leasing terms vary widely — naturally enough, since this form of financing extends into situations of varying risks and amounts. The traditional and most generally used format is the add-on charge, usually from 4.5 to 7 percent. As we have seen with chattel mortgages, you multiply the contract term in years to get the total charge. For example, a 5 percent add-on for a $100,000 five-year lease would total $25,000 (five times $5,000), and the payments would total $125,000. From this figure you deduct the lease deposit to yield the remaining balance. Usually the lessor quotes the add-on as a separate increment to the

---

[4]Indeed, they often begin at 5 percent the first year and drop to 4 percent the second, 3 percent the third, and 2 percent thereafter.

contract; sometimes, however, the lessor quotes the rate as a percentage of the equipment cost per month — for example, 2 percent of equipment cost per month.[5]

Some leasing companies, when dealing with substantial leases to highly rated companies, write their leases on a simple-interest basis, usually ranging from 7 to 9 percent simple stated interest — not much less, in actual cost-of-money terms, than the more conservative add-on. There exist a few additional sources of lease financing which are unusually inexpensive, but these apply to special situations involving leasing operations of big companies with substantial taxable income. Such companies go into leasing because, by owning and depreciating the equipment they lease, they may reduce their taxes. The tax savings allow for very favorable rates running even slightly below 6 percent *actual* — as opposed to *stated* — interest. But 1) the lessee must demonstrate considerable financial strength, 2) the equipment must be new and of widespread utility, and 3) the leases must run to $100,000 and up. Such leases generally offer no purchase option, since that would defeat the reasoning which makes the arrangement available on such an attractive basis.

The Purchase Option

Let's look again at the materiality of the purchase option. As I noted earlier, most leases make the renewal option so attractive as to eliminate the advantages of purchasing the equipment at the end of the lease, and in any case, the lessee avoids investing in the purchase of equipment which is probably obsolescing rapidly. Even so, some business managers worry about finding themselves unable to purchase their leased equipment should they choose to do so. Others say to themselves, "After I've practically paid for the equipment by completing the lease, I might as well own it."

There are satisfactory answers to both positions. Actually, no leasing company wants to end up with aging equipment in its possession. Leasing companies make money leasing equipment, not using it to manufacture or distribute things; nor do they want to remove equipment and embark on an uncertain quest for a new lessee or buyer. Approached once the lease ends, a lessor may

---

[5]At 2 percent per month, the rate would roughly equal a 5 percent add-on.

make a sale. I have known special cases where the lessor allowed the lessee to negotiate a purchase midway through a lease contract. Clearly, you can't foresee such possibilities (or provide for them in the lease contract, since doing so would strip away the facade of the lease — i.e., the terms under which the contract becomes valuable to both lessor and lessee, and keeps Uncle Sam at bay.) Besides, most business managers realize the dangers in becoming "equipment poor," absorbing their profits in building up an inventory of equipment, as it were, some of it perhaps incapable of continuing to earn a profit. Pride of ownership can make for poor management, in this sense. By opting to renew a lease or, later, to purchase the equipment, the lessee may continue to use the equipment as long as needed and still benefit from the other advantages which made it a good idea to execute the leasing contract in the first place.

Balance Sheet Advantages

The two major forms of growth capital financing — chattel mortgage borrowing and leasing — provide special opportunities to restructure the balance sheet of a financial statement so as to reflect the position of the business advantageously. They also illuminate why I consider it so important to distinguish between working capital and growth capital.

In Chapter 2 I argued that working capital accommodates the cyclical needs of business over one year. Thus the need for working capital is typically short-term, and lenders offer working capital loans for renewable terms of one year or less. As a result, the balance sheet shows these borrowings under *current liabilities* along with all other monies due in one year or less.

But if you intend to borrow working capital over a period of several years, it helps to set the loan up differently — not, for example, as a series of renewable 90-day unsecured notes but rather in such fashion as to allow you to show only *the first year's indebtedness* under current liabilities on your balance sheet.

In our analysis[6] of financial statements to determine creditworthiness, we saw the significance of the *current*

---

[6]Chapter 4.

ratio (i.e., the ratio of current assets to current liabilities) and the *net current asset position* (i.e., current assets minus current liabilities). *These two indices change* when you substitute leasing and chattel mortgage financing for current borrowing, as the following three balance sheets of the same hypothetical business show.

The first balance sheet shows a $250,000 unsecured bank line, of which $180,000 was needed to finance additional equipment:

Assets

Cash	$ 40,000	
Accounts receivable	160,000	
Inventory	120,000	
Total current assets		$320,000
Machinery & equipment (net after depreciation)		$450,000
Other assets & prepaid items		80,000
Total assets		$850,000

Liabilities

Notes payable, bank	$250,000	
Accounts payable	60,000	
Total current liabilities		$310,000
Other liabilities		70,000
Total liabilities		$380,000
Net worth		470,000
Total liabilities & net worth		$850,000

The current ratio on this balance sheet is barely 1 to 1, and net current assets — i.e., working capital — appears to be merely $10,000. But look what happens to the balance sheet if the company arranges for a $180,000 five-year chattel mortgage loan. Since the company must repay only one fifth of the loan per year, only $36,000 shows up as a current liability. Moreover, since $180,000 now shows up as the chattel mortgage loan, current liabilities consist of the $70,000 in the unsecured bank note plus $36,000 due this year in payment on the chattel mortgage loan. The new balance sheet appears as follows:

Secured Growth Capital Loans

Assets

Cash	$ 40,000	
Accounts receivable	160,000	
Inventory	120,000	
Total current assets		$320,000
Machinery & equipment (net)		$450,000
Other assets & prepaid items		80,000
Total assets		$850,000

Liabilities

Notes payable, unsecured, bank	$ 70,000	
Current portion, chattel mortgage note	36,000	
Accounts payable	60,000	
Total current liabilities		$166,000
Chattel mortgage loan	$180,000	
Less current portion	−36,000	
		$144,000
Other liabilities		70,000
Total liabilities		$380,000
Net worth		470,000
Total liabilities & net worth		$850,000

As you can see, the net worth remains the same at $470,000, but the current ratio improves from 1 to 1 to a healthy 2 to 1, approximately. The net current assets position improves, meanwhile, from $10,000 to $154,000 — on both counts, a big improvement.

Now let's see what happens if the company substitutes a $180,000 sale and leaseback for its chattel mortgage loan in the same amount. To compare the new statement to the two above, let's assume a book value of $180,000 for the equipment involved in the loan and now sold and leased back.

As the following table shows, the transaction eliminates the chattel mortgage from the statement altogether, and it removes the book value of the equipment from fixed assets:

Assets

Cash	$ 40,000	
Accounts receivable	160,000	
Inventory	120,000	
Total current assets		$320,000
Machinery & equipment (net)		$270,000
Other assets & prepaid items		80,000
Total assets		$670,000

Liabilities

Notes payable, unsecured, bank	$ 70,000	
Accounts payable	60,000	
Total current liabilities		$130,000
Other liabilities		70,000
Total liabilities		$200,000
Net worth		470,000
Total liabilities & net worth		$670,000

Net worth remains the same, but the current ratio improves to 2½ to 1 and net current assets increase to $190,000. And in substituting a lease for the chattel mortgage, the business ends up with a debt-to-worth ratio far lower than it showed in either of the two earlier arrangements.

As a matter of fact, however, leasing doesn't always stand out as the better alternative to chattel mortgage financing. Lenders and the bigger accounting firms now insist on adding footnotes to financial statements indicating the presence of leasing contracts and the obligations to pay under same. Pressure is mounting to show one year's lease payments under current liabilities. This would make the second and third of our examples reflect identical current ratios and working capital positions. Some proponents of leasing argue that one year's lease payments ought not to appear under current liabilities for the same reason that rent on leased office or factory space doesn't. However, equipment leases do require the business to make payments on a current basis just as chattel mortgages do, and bankers and financial institution analysts tend to treat the obligations in the same manner. Thus the distinction between leasing and chattel borrowing blurs when it comes to the balance sheet; leasing creates no realistic improvement over chattel mortgage borrowing on the balance sheet. But either technique does improve on the kind of open-line unsecured borrowing illustrated in the first example above.

CHAPTER 7
PACKAGE FINANCING

The foregoing chapters of this book have covered elementary and intermediate techniques of business finance. Before moving ahead to more advanced and specialized procedures, it may be wise to review the basic techniques in the context of familiarity with every variation so far described. Now that you have been presented with a number of alternatives, you should begin to think about how to select the financing methods best for your specific business needs.

This is particularly true when you must use more than one tool of finance. And here we return to the distinction made in Chapter 2 between short- and long-term capital requirements. Taking a slightly different approach, you should be able to determine whether what you seek is best obtained on a secured or unsecured basis. If your needs are high in ratio to your worth, secured financing will be the indicated route to take, particularly if the increased growth and profits anticipated will justify the higher cost of such financing. On the other hand, you should consider unsecured borrowing first if your statement will justify it to the extent that your needs are properly met. Many situations can be satisfactorily accommodated by a single unsecured bank line, based on the criteria described in Chapter 4. This is particularly true of needs that develop during the early stages of a business when a modest amount of money is needed. It is also true much later in the game, when a company has achieved a strong financial condition.

Unsecured Combinations

There are a number of instances where the single unsecured bank line of credit, extended on the regular 90-day renewable notes, may be unsuited to the needs of a business. As was mentioned earlier, this type of credit line is appropriate for a cyclical fluctuation over a one year period. Because of the requirement for an annual "resting" of unsecured 90-day note lines, you must be confident that, during your yearly slack period, you can function with reduced outside financing. In many instances this is true; in others, only partly true. If the latter is the case, the financing need should be broken down into its short-term and long-term components.

A typical situation would involve the usual requirement for financing yearly buildups to peak sales activity — plus a specialized need for specific funds to purchase equipment (or enlarge a selling operation, launch a new promotional campaign, etc.). The specialized need is justified by expectation of greater profits; however, several years of profits will be required to repay the financing of the project.

It is obvious that such an increment of the total financing program must be arranged, not as 90-day renewable note credits, but as a term loan.

Let us say that a distributor requires a total of $136,000 credit for all his needs, and that his statement qualifies for an unsecured credit in this amount. Included in this requirement is an expenditure of $36,000 for new material handling and packaging equipment which will take several years to pay for itself. The proper approach would be to ask the bank for an unsecured line of $136,000, broken into two loans. One loan, in the amount of $100,000, to cover peak seasonal needs, would be structured on 90-day notes with paydown for at least one month during the slack period. The other loan would be covered by a $36,000 term note, payable over three years at the rate of $1,000 per month.

Total Requirements

If the total financing requirement of such a situation is somewhat in excess of the total unsecured line the bank feels it can grant, the desired end may be achieved by suggesting that the $100,000 open line be set up for seasonal fluctuations on an unsecured basis, but that the equipment purchase increment of the loan be switched to a secured transaction by use of a chattel mortgage note.

Another combination which would still maintain the unsecured borrowing position would be to arrange with an outside leasing company of a purchase-lease contract for the new equipment. If the company qualifies for the $100,000 unsecured credit, the bank should have little concern about the lease arrangement because the encumbered asset — the new equipment to be purchased — would not have been part of the company assets to which the bank looked in granting the unsecured credit.

Secured Combinations

When management realizes that its financing needs are so diverse and so large that the proper solution is the use of secured financing, more complex combinations are possible. These combinations extend to a number of asset categories for collateral.

Some of the usual package financing combinations are:

- Receivables financing and warehouse lending;
- Receivables financing and inventory lien financing;
- Receivables financing and chattel mortgage lending (and possibly plus inventory or warehouse financing);
- Any of the above in connection with letters of credit for imports.

You will note that, regardless of the combination, the presence of receivables financing is a necessary element in the package. This is because the lender will want to have some dominion over the ultimate source of repayment of the loans — usually the accounts receivable. Moreover, this requirement also provides the most flexibility for the borrower as, by using proceeds from receivables assignments, the revolving aspect of inventory financing can be expedited. This is demonstrated in the following examples:

- *A field warehouse with 70 percent advance on lumber, plus an 80 percent advance on accounts receivable.* The warehouse loan has a maximum of $150,000 and a $25,000 release blanket. When lumber is released from the warehouse, the blanket is reduced in an amount equal to the cost of the released lumber. But the reductions are quickly reinstated by proceeds from accounts receivable financing, so that the warehouse can continually be drawn from. For example, if $10,000 worth of lumber at cost is released from the warehouse, the 70 percent loan against it would amount to $7,000. To repay this amount from receivables financing would be simple. The $10,000 cost value lumber would be marked up, e.g., 15 percent, and sold to a customer for $11,500. An 80 percent advance on the customer invoice would make $9,200 available, obviously providing more than the $7,000 required to reinstate the warehouse release.

- *An 80 percent receivables financing program packaged with a $250,000 maximum loan against a 60 percent inventory lien and a three-year chattel mortgage of $72,000.* The mortgage is to be reduced $2,000 per month. The company for which this package is arranged averages sales volume of $75,000 per month. An analysis of the cost of goods sold reveals that the products of the company contain a cost of materials averaging 50 percent of the selling price. Since there is a 60 percent advance against the inventory lien, it is decided that an amount equal to 30 percent of sales (60 percent advance × 50 percent of selling price) will be required to repay the lender for his advance against the inventory which has been converted into sold merchandise. Therefore, on sales of $10,000, the amount of $3,000 (30 percent arrived at as described above) would be withheld from the 80 percent receivables advance of $8,000. On the monthly volume of $75,000, it can be assumed that 20 percent or $15,000, will become available monthly from a return of equities arising from receipt of customer remittances — $2,000 of which the lender will be authorized to deduct for monthly amortization of the chattel mortgage. Purchases of new inventory will be financed by the revolving inventory loan arrangement and, as you can see, the normal functioning of the accounts receivable financing program will automatically repay the inventory loans and the monthly chattel loan amortization.

Leverage

A specific case, covering a program arranged for one of my clients, provides an interesting illustration of package financing. My client had the opportunity of buying carloads of imported carpet wool on the East Coast for resale in original cartons to carpet manufacturers in the West. His entire gross markup was only 7 percent, yet he was able to do an annual volume of $800,000 and make a profit of $30,000 per year *on an investment of only $7,500.*

To obtain the distributorship, a $50,000 letter of credit[1] was dangled under the Eastern wool importer's nose. We arranged with a New York bank to provide the letter of credit for 15 percent cash margin — the $7,500 which constituted the entire cash investment in the deal. A bank in Los Angeles agreed to advance 85 percent of *landed cost* against the wool if placed in a public or field warehouse. Since this warehouse loan was against landed cost, it not only provided a takeout of the letter of credit loan from the New York bank, but also virtually financed the cross-country freight cost.

A Factoring Arrangement

To save establishing an accounts receivable bookkeeping department, a notification factoring arrangement was made on an 85 percent advance basis (which provided more than enough to repay the 85 percent of cost warehouse loan because of the 7 percent markup of cost to selling price). The Eastern importer would ship a freight carload, then present the invoice and bill of lading to the New York bank. Since a carload of wool would be invoiced for about $42,000, there was always ample coverage in the $50,000 letter of credit; therefore the New York bank would pay the importer upon presentation of his draft, then forward the order bill of lading to the Los Angeles bank, which would use this as authority to the railroad to release the wool to the local warehouse. The warehouse, in turn, would issue a warehouse receipt against which the Los Angeles bank would advance 85 percent to the New York bank to repay its letter of credit payment to the Eastern importer.

The $7,500 originally put up as margin remained intact with the New York bank to provide for the unadvanced 15 percent increment of cost of the wool in warehouse, and the letter of credit was constantly reinstated by repayment with funds obtained from the warehouse loan. Working capital (and ultimately, the profits) came from return of equities from the factor as customers paid their bills.

In summary, here was a beautifully flowing financing program which, on a revolving basis, used two $50,000 bank credits turning over a sufficient number of times to create

---

[1]See Chapter 9.

an $800,000 annual volume. From this resulted a profit of $50,000 before financing cost. The cost of all the financing was $20,000 and, although this was the major expense of the operation, it was really quite a bargain considering that it made possible a $30,000 yearly profit on a $7,500 investment — a sweet little return of 400 percent on capital!

CHAPTER 8
TIME SALES FINANCE

Installment selling in business has contributed massively to increased sales volumes. Not only have installment contracts constituted the great majority of transactions in certain fields, among them the auto industry, but their use as a selling tool continues to spread over a broad range of activities. This is particularly true of "big ticket" items — goods or services whose cost runs from $200 up to several thousand dollars. From home appliances and pianos, the list stretches to such diverse items as carpeting, dental work, communications systems, mink coats, raw land sales, etc. A new color camera, which sold poorly in retail stores at $200, became a fast-moving item when promoted by a direct-selling force for $276 on a 36-month contract — one of many products which didn't reach its true potential until offered on a time-payment basis.

Carrying the Paper

The success of installment selling has been reinforced by its wide acceptance, both among consumers and businesses. In earlier days people believed it prudent to save in order to make purchases, but the modern buyer tends to see a greater benefit in using the item purchased while paying for it. In such an atmosphere the growth of installment selling — and of the concomitant requirement for financing of time sales — has resulted in the development of a massive segment of the financial industry.

It takes a great deal of money to *carry the paper*—to finance the installment contracts. Very few businesses, including many very substantial firms, are in position to do this for themselves. Businesses frequently advertise that they "carry their own paper," but this is only partly true. The customer may have contact only with the selling firm (through arrangements described below), but there is almost always a financial institution in the background.

Funds for financing installment contracts come from the following sources:

- Consumer finance companies;

- Industrial banking and general finance companies;

- Rediscount divisions of commercial finance companies;

- Banks.

The choice of the source of funds often influences the type of arrangement between the seller of the goods and the financial institution. For this reason it makes sense to look into these formats in some detail.

Outright Purchase of Consumer Paper

As the name implies, consumer finance companies primarily deal in contracts of sale to individuals. This group includes the "small loan" companies whose ubiquitous branches represent giant national companies in a highly competitive field. These companies spend large sums for advertising in the quest for potential customers, and they have found an excellent source in business firms which make time sales to consumers.

In many ways the business which makes an installment sale serves merely as a referral agent for the small loan company. Once the business concludes the sale, it puts the customer into direct contact with the finance company that approves his or her credit. Thereafter, the consumer makes all installment payments to the finance company on a *direct collection* basis.

For a small business generating nominal amounts of installment paper, the consumer loan companies may offer the only funding source. There are both advantages and disadvantages to their use. Generally, they involve very little cost to the seller, who makes the sale, transfers the paper to the loan company, and has no responsibility for followup, collection, or otherwise servicing the contract. Moreover, the finance company usually pays full value for the paper. It hopes to earn the carrying charge in the contract and, if it is attractive, may even kick back a small percentage to the dealer. For the finance company there is always the additional possibility that the purchaser may eventually find it difficult to carry this contract along with other obligations, giving the finance company the chance to *flip over* the customer into a debt-consolidating conventional small loan — the main business of the consumer finance company.

On the negative side, the business loses continuity of contact with the customer, thereby possibly losing the opportunity to make additional sales in the future. The buyer may also lose some enthusiasm for the purchase when completing the credit application or signing additional papers. Some customers balk when they learn they must deal with an outside finance company on a direct collection basis, even though they might be perfectly willing to enter into installment contracts at the dealer's premises.

Dealer Reserve Purchasing

The use of small loan companies for installment contract financing is primarily a contract-by-contract arrangement. Each deal is viewed on its individual merits; the emphasis goes on the credit of the individual consumer.

Frequently, however, it is more desirable to work within the framework of a more standardized overall arrangement between dealer and fund source when the individual consumer credit, although significant, is not directly evaluated by the lender. A number of institutions provide this type of financing, pioneered by the *industrial banking firms,* many of which, such as Morris Plan banks and *thrift and loan banks,* accept savings deposits from the general public under state charters and regulations.[1]

Also in this category are many general finance companies which have their own funds and do not take public deposits. In some larger cities banks make dealer arrangements for assignment of consumer or commercial installment contracts, but as a rule the specialized industrial and general finance companies which make this their chief business provide a broader, more flexible service. These lenders concern themselves with the stability and reputation of the dealer and with the reliability of the goods or services he or she sells on installment contracts. Such lenders often allow the dealer to write contracts on premises; if the dealer knows the customer's credit, the dealer can easily get the new contract approved by submitting a short credit application form to the lender. This makes it unnecessary to bring the customer into contact with the lender, or to have the customer visit the offices of the finance company.

[1] A list of many of these institutions can be obtained from the American Industrial Bankers Association, 813 Washington Building, Washington, DC 20005.

In many cases the arrangement involves *indirect collection;* the customer sends payments to the dealer, who in turn remits them to the lender. In other cases, the customer receives a payment book calling for installments to go to a bank or finance company — which is quite different from having to deal with the finance company in signing the contract in the first place.

Installment contracts are purchased by specialized lenders, usually on a continuing arrangement covered by a basic agreement with the dealer. The purchase may be on a recourse or non-recourse basis. There is, however, generally recourse to the extent of the *dealer reserve* held by the lender. This reserve is created at the time the paper is purchased by the lender. The lender agrees to purchase installment contracts at a specific price below the full value of the contract — i.e., at the *discounted amount.* If, on the other hand, the dealer has added sufficient carrying charges to justify the lender's handling of the contract (including a reasonable profit to the lender), the discounted price will probably be the full amount of the dealer's sale to the customer, prior to the carrying charge.

A number of considerations determine how much the lender's discount varies above or below the fair value of the contract, exclusive of the carrying charges. We will go into this matter more thoroughly later.

The Dealer Reserve

After agreeing on the purchase price, the lender advances the entire payment with the exception of the dealer reserve. This reserve, which may be as small as 5 percent (but can be much larger depending on the relative risk quality of the paper and its underlying collateral), is usually held until the customer pays the contract balance in full. Thus the reserve, as a percentage of the contract price, increases as the contract pays down. For example, a dealer might sell $100,000 of installment paper for full value, with a 5 percent or $5,000 reserve. When this batch of contracts pays down to a total of $25,000, the original $5,000 reserve, if undiminished, stands at 20 percent.

From the lender's position there is some justification on the premise that the most creditworthy customers pay the most promptly — and even prepay in some cases — so that the residual outstanding contract balances will have had the "cream" removed and should call for a larger reserve.

Under this method the reserve does not automatically reduce, and the lender can hold the entire amount until all contracts are paid off. But there can be some modification. In a continuing relationship the dealer usually agrees to substitute new good paper for any contracts which turn sour; in return, the lender frequently agrees to repay part of the reserve to the dealer before all contracts fully pay off, particularly if the lender considers the remaining reserve adequate. It is also possible for a dealer to enter into a prior agreement with the lender on this subject. Envisioning a continuing relationship with frequent assignments of new contracts, dealer and lender might agree that the lender will hold 5 percent reserve on all new contracts but that, as customer payments come in, when the reserve held against all the unpaid contracts of this dealer reaches an average of 20 percent, no further reserves would be required. The total reserve remains at 20 percent, and the lender regularly remits overages. Normally, such an arrangement gives the lender the right to hold all reserves in the event of a termination whereby the takes no further new contracts.

Time Sales Contract Requirements and Rates

Before going into the last major category of installment financing, we should examine the lender requirements as to the paper to be financed. Too often I have seen companies which have gone into installment selling on a basis which precluded proper financing. It is understandable, of course, that a business thinks primarily of increasing sales when it embarks on an installment selling program and, for this reason, does not build into the program satisfaction of potential financing requirements. But the financing source must make its normal profit and conform to all legal requirements when it steps into the shoes of the business whose contracts it assumes. It is necessary, therefore, to cover the following points:

- Are the carrying charges sufficient to provide for the financing cost?

- Are the down payment, contract term, and repayment acceptable on sound industry principles?

- Does the contract include an acknowledgment of receipt of the goods or services in good order?

- Does the form of contract conform in every way to legal requirements?

The first point appears obvious, but it is surprising how many installment programs do not make provision for ample financing cost.

Usually the cost is covered by the carrying charges — in the installment selling field, usually stated as the *time sales price differential.* The use of a "differential" instead of an interest charge is interesting. In legal theory a difference exists between what you can buy an item for with 100 percent cash and what you pay on the installment basis. Assume, for example, that you want to sell a large lot of mixed steel sheet and strip. You might propose to sell the lot in increments, which might take several months. But a purchaser asks for a price on the entire lot. You respond that he can buy it for $40,000 — $10,000 down and $10,000 each month for three months. The buyer counters with an offer of $35,000 cash on the spot, and you agree.

The time sales price differential in this example is $5,000, but it is the result of a difference in the deal itself, not a function of interest. And the law usually agrees that a time sales price is different from a cash price. California, for example, puts a 10 percent limit[2] on annual interest rate chargeable to the consumer on certain contracts. But the state does not consider a time sales price to be interest; for example, it allows a 10 percent time sales price differential — equivalent to nearly 20 percent interest — on the same contracts. The seller, of course, must be consistent; he or she must be willing to sell goods for cash at a price which would be exactly equal to the installment contract price less the differential.

The Prime Incentive

As we will see shortly, it is sometimes possible for the business to make a profit on the financing itself. But since the prime incentive for the adoption of an installment contract program is usually to derive more profit from increased sales, the first consideration is to make sure to cover the financing costs. Time sales price differentials work the same way as add-ons,[3] and they usually vary

[2]In recent years the California interest rate limitation has been indexed so that, when prime rates increase, the maximum rate increases. Time sales differentials remain unregulated.

[3]See Chapter 6.

from 6 to 10 percent per year. Sales of industrial equipment, such as lathes and presses, to commercial users stay close to the 6 percent level. Sales of lower priced items to consumers generally call for a 10 percent add-on differential because of the extra handling cost of the smaller contract. Normally these differentials will be all that the financial institution requires as discounts. In fact, as mentioned above, there may be room for a kickback to the dealer. For example, one of my clients sold an intercommunication and hi-fi radio system to homeowners for $600 cash. Under an installment program he received a $60 down payment, leaving a contract balance of $540. The installment program was a three-year contract with 10 percent time sales price differential ($54 per year × 3) of $162. The total time contract called for $702 ($540 plus $162) to be repaid in 36 equal installments. These contracts were assigned to a specialized lender who was satisfied with 9 percent on this kind of transaction; so he rebated to my client 1 percent of the differential, or $16.20.

It may be wise to talk to potential financial sources to predetermine what discount they require. Then, if you wish to embark on an installment selling program, you can take this information into consideration.

'Packing'

Some firms do not add the entire discount to the differential, as they may have provided for some of the financing cost in their basic selling markup. This is particularly true with companies selling almost entirely on the installment basis. Such companies are little concerned about their cash sales price, since they expect practically no cash sales. But they must establish a cash price in order to add legally the time sales differential. So they *pack* a good part of the financing discount cost into the cash price and — as a selling point — show the time sales differential as only a very nominal charge. The distributor of a a widely sold automatic camera which originally retailed in camera stores for $200 followed this procedure. The distributor switched to direct selling on an installment basis, at a higher cash price — $240, packing in $40 for financing. To the new $240 cash price the distributor added a $1-per-month carrying charge for 36 months, or $36 — a differential calculated to create no resistance whatsoever on the part of the customer. But combined with the $40 packed into the cash price, the technique gave the distributor an ample $76 to cover financing costs for the three-year contract. The distributor adhered to the new $240 cash price and, of course, the company was delighted to sell its camera at that price to the few purchasers who preferred to pay cash.

The second area to clarify in advance concerns the length of time the contract is to run and the amount of down payment. These must reflect the size of the transaction and the anticipated useful life of the product being sold.

It is obviously improper to sell a two-year supply of a particular type of goods on a four-year contract. The commodity sold should certainly provide benefits considerably beyond the time at which the installment contract has been paid in full. A piece of industrial equipment can be placed on a two- or three-year contract; some substantial machinery contracts run even longer. Home study courses sell on 12- to 18-month contracts; somewhat permanent home improvements can be placed on three- to seven-year contracts. Automobile finance contracts are generally limited as to years, but mobile home installment contracts — originally governed by the same limits — have now been found satisfactory by lenders to be placed on contracts of seven years or more.

The Down Payment

The down payment and monthly installments reflect the substantiality of the contract and the value stability of the product sold in several ways. Ideally, most contracts call for a 25 to 33⅓ percent down payment, but this standard is frequently waived. Down payments of 10 percent are fast becoming acceptable to many financial institutions, particularly if the dollar amount seems sufficient to represent a stake which the customer will not want to abandon. Some contracts call for no down payment, but the seller must carry these at least until the purchaser builds enough equity with monthly payments to make the contracts acceptable to a lender.

On balance, the length of contract, monthly installments, and down payment are interrelated. A modest contract must be of fairly short duration. Otherwise the monthly installments will be too small to handle economically.

Finally, the contract must conform to all local state requirements and must include elements on which lenders will insist. The lender wants to see evidence of receipt of the goods purchased and an acknowledgment of the obligation on the part of the buyer to pay the full amount of the contract. The legal requirements which are also important to the lender (who now stands in the shoes of the sell-er) include proof that the customer has received a fully executed copy of the contract, a stipulation that the type shall be large enough and easily readable, a specific delineation of the time sales price differential, etc.

Rediscounting

The methods we have described for financing time sales — through the use of small loan offices and general and industrial banking institutions — place the handling of the contracts almost totally with the fund source. These methods are used by most firms at the inception of their installment selling programs and, whereas the subsequent use of industrial banking companies may provide the ideal answer on a continuing basis, there is another arrangement to which certain businesses turn — the *rediscounting* of their own time sales finance operation.

Rediscounts are provided by some of the larger banks and commercial finance companies. Rediscounting is a procedure whereby one financing agency finances another — on a secured basis — by the method of assignment or reassignment. A small finance company can obtain additional funds by rediscounting collateral originally assigned to it by its clients.

With the growth of installment selling this arrangement now extends to business firms which create a continuing flow of time sales paper through their own merchandising operations. The early cases of this kind involved operating companies which established captive finance companies, wholly owned subsidiaries formed for the purpose of acting as a finance company for the time sales paper generated by the operating divisions of the parent company. The finance subsidiary would be given a cash capital of its own and would make arrangements with outside financial institutions to obtain leverage borrowing.

In the financial industry there are some purists who insist that a rediscounting arrangement is only possible with a separate finance company, and not with a financing division of an operating company. This reasoning reflects the fact that a subsidiary is a separate corporation — a specific legal entity engaged solely in financing, whereas a division of an operating company is not. But recent experience has resulted in outside financing institutions treating both in the same manner in a rediscounting arrangement. I will therefore discuss the topic as equally applicable to both.

The outside financial institutions originally preferred rediscounting a corporate subsidiary entity because the corporate form — restricted as to withdrawals of its cash capital by subordinations from the parent — gave assurance of the continuity of the buffer equity which is desired in rediscounted paper. But it has been realized that, in a properly structured rediscount providing for such equities through limitations on the percentage of advance, even a noncorporate division cannot create new paper without having some equity in same. Moreover, since the parent company may be required to guarantee the rediscounting of a finance subsidiary with modest capital, the differentiation fades even more. In such cases the outside financing source will be looking toward the tangible worth of the entire company.

Rediscount Lines

The overall limiting factor in a rediscounting arrangement is the *maximum rediscount line* — a line of credit established as a ratio to the tangible worth of the applicant. Where a corporate subsidiary is capitalized with an original cash investment of, say, $100,000, the tangible worth is that same amount. When, however, a rediscount line is sought for a mixed financing and operating company, an analysis must be made primarily to determine the liquid assets, eliminating such items as leasehold improvements, good will, receivables from affiliates or officers, and so on.

Once the tangible worth has been determined, the line is set. Normally, the line is initially established on a very conservative basis — for example, a ratio of 1 1/2 to 1 (that is, a $150,000 rediscount line to $100,000 tangible worth). After confidence is established in the arrangement, the line will be periodically increased so that ratios of 3 to 1 or even 4 to 1 can be achieved. Obviously the use of such a leverage — where $4 can be obtained for every $1 invested — is one of the chief attractions of a rediscount arrangement.

Another limiting factor in a rediscount is the percentage of advances made against the time sales paper. Here arises a very important difference between regular accounts receivable financing and rediscounting. As described in Chapter 5, the advance against receivables is a percentage of the collateral — i.e., the face value of the assigned invoices. Proper rediscounting, however, cannot postulate advances strictly on collateral; instead, the rediscount must realistically relate to advances against cash equity in the paper. The reasoning behind this policy is based on the makeup of the time sales paper itself.

Let us take, for example, the sale of a water softening equipment package for a $1,000 cash price on a three-year contract with an add-on time sales price differential of 10 percent. The differential is $300 ($100 $\times$ 3 years) and, when added to the cash price, results in a total contract of $1,300. This contract is assigned to the outside financial source which becomes the prior lien holder of $1,300 in collateral. But the $300 differential is unearned at the outset, and — more important — it represents no investment whatsoever on the part of the seller. Therefore, if an 80 percent advance were made on the total value of the contract, this advance — $1,040 — would actually give the seller more than his entire investment and profit in the contract.

As mentioned above, the rediscount requires some cash equity on the part of the assignor. As a general rule the level at which cash equity begins is determined by subtracting the add-on and seller's profit from the face value of the contract. Assuming the net profit on the $1,000 sale to have been $60, the seller would have $940 in direct cost and overhead (also a valid cost) in the transaction. Most financial institutions recognize that they must advance costs so that the seller can continue doing business at the same level, but they don't go so far as to advance the profit. Instead, the seller should receive profit as a return of equity which develops from the payoff of the contract by the customer. Moreover, as mentioned above, it is also felt that the seller should have some investment in each contract so that he or she has a positive interest in the full payment of the contract by the customer. This creates an incentive to screen customer credit carefully as, in event of nonpayment, it is the seller's equity that is first lost.

A Typical Arrangement

In a typical arrangement, the operating company would assign the sample contract described above to its captive finance subsidiary or division for a price which would eliminate the unearned time sales differential, and also in many cases, less a nominal financing discount of about 5 percent. In other words, the financing entity would acquire $1,300 in collateral for $950 as follows:

Total face value of contract		$1,300
Less: unearned add-on	300	
internal financing discount	50	350
Cost to captive finance company		$ 950

The captive finance company, now the assignee of the contract, in turn reassigns it to the outside financial institution which, on a rediscounting basis, may, for example, advance 80 percent against the $950 cash equity of the captive finance company, or $760. At first glance, an advance of $760 may not seem high against $1,300 in collateral. But let us analyze the transaction further to obtain the true picture.

First of all, the $300 add-on represents no investment by the seller, as we have said. There was probably $60 net profit earned by the operating company in the sale which is reflected by the contract. Therefore the company has an actual investment of $941, which, after subtracting the $760 advanced through rediscounting, results in the final investment in each such similar size contract being $180. As you can see, the rediscount ratio here is slightly better than 4 to 1. With $100,000 cash equity to work with, there would be over $400,000 available through rediscounting.

This brings us to an even more remarkable fact. In the above example — which represents a fairly conservative advance from the outside financial institution — you can see that a $180 investment by the captive finance company can create collateral in the form of time sales contract paper amounting to $1,300. This is a ratio of over 7 to 1. Therefore, on a rediscount basis, you can create more than $700,000 worth of paper with only a $100,000 investment!

Starting a Rediscount with Paper

Because of the requirement that, in a rediscount, you must have some equity in the paper, a certain amount of cash is allocated to a captive finance division or subsidiary. Generally, a minimum of $100,000 is advisable, although I have seen rediscounts begin with hardly half that amount. The possession of sufficient unused cash for this purpose makes it possible to begin the program with relative ease. But if retained earnings or funds from available credit are insufficient, the starting of a rediscount may still not be precluded.

Most captive finance operations are found in companies which have begun their installment selling by discounting their paper with outside financial institutions, as described earlier in this chapter. Not only does the company gain valuable experience this way, but also, as the contracts pay off, reserves become available to provide a return of earned equities. As a result, the operating business can begin to hold some of its own paper, rather than discounting all of it on the outside. At the same time a working credit and collection department can be initiated, sometimes with only one qualified employee, so that when the time comes to go into a full-scale rediscount, the source of rediscounting funds will be satisfied with the internal credit controls. It is true that, prior to obtaining a rediscount arrangement, it may only be possible to carry 25 percent or less of the paper generated while the other 75 percent or more must continue to be discounted with outside finance companies to provide a steady flow of working capital. But the relatively minor portion of the paper which is retained will have 100 percent of its equity provided by the operating business. It is through this equity in paper that the possible inception of a captive finance rediscount can be created.

No Investment

Suppose, for example, a retailer of pianos created new paper at the rate of $40,000 per month on three-year installment contracts. Approximately $10,000 would be represented by the time sales differential which, since it would be an unearned financing charge at the time of original sale of the pianos, would represent no investment on the part of the retailer. If the retailer carried 25 percent or $10,000 of the paper, it would have a theoretical equity of about $7,500 as the result of deducting the unearned financing charge. But this total would not consist entirely of out-of-pocket cost. The gross profit would probably have been approximately $3,000, consisting of net profit plus overhead which might be spread over the other sales, once monthly breakeven point was passed. Therefore if, out of the $40,000 new paper created each month,

$30,000 were discounted with an outside financial source to provide continuing working capital, the retailer could carry the remaining $10,000 with a cash investment of $4,500 per month.

To maintain such a program for one year would appear to require $54,000, but this amount would be provided not only by retained profits during the year, but also by the conversion of unearned financing charges to earned income on the contracts being carried. (Three-year contracts held for one year actually earn considerably more than one third of the financing charge for that year, as the greatest amount of interest is earned in the early part of any installment contract. This can be demonstrated by *the rule of 78;* in the example being used here, about $7,000 interest would be earned during the first twelve months following inception of the retailer's program of retaining 25 percent of its own contracts.) Furthermore, some of the equity can be provided through reporting income from the retained contracts on a cash basis for taxes, thus deferring payment of taxes until the rediscount has been established.

Now, let us suppose the above program has created $120,000 in retained paper at the end of twelve months. Adjusting this face value for customer monthly payments received, and for the unearned time sales differential, a rediscounting source might advance between $60,000 and $70,000 as a loan against the paper. True, this is too small a line for the financial institution to entertain for a rediscount on a regular basis; but it can easily be shown that this was created by retaining only 25 percent of the retailer's contracts. Obviously, once begun on a basis of involving 100 percent of the retailer's contracts, this rediscount would represent a loan of about $400,000, which will certainly qualify as to minimum requirements. The problem of which comes first, the chicken or the egg, has been solved. The rediscount is established as sufficiently large on an early potential basis; and the first advance of $60,000 to $70,000 will provide the retailer with sufficient cash to satisfy its equity requirements in making the potential of a $400,000 rediscount line an actuality.

Cost and Profit in Rediscounting

Usually, the basic incentive for establishing a captive finance company is to facilitate growth of sales on an installment basis. The primary benefit sought is the enhancement of profits from volume increases. Many businesses have found that, if they present a standardized financing package in all their markets, their representatives do a better selling job. A standard financing package integrated into a national merchandising plan usually becomes possible only with a captive finance company in the picture. Also, other types of businesses, particularly retailers and distributors, find that carrying their own paper maintains a closer contact with customers, resulting in continuing sales on a repeat basis.

But there is the additional incentive of making profit from the financing itself. There are a number of well-known illustrations of this possibility — for example, GMAC, the captive financing operation of General Motors, which turns in a very healthy financing profit.

The earnings which truly arise from the financing activity itself depend on a number of variables. To make a realistic analysis, the rediscount should be equated against the cost of discounting paper with an outside fund source. In other words, if you postulate a 5 percent discount as the basis on which your captive finance company purchases paper from your operating divisions — but an outside source would purchase your contracts at face value less only the time sales price differential — you are not realistically earning an extra 5 percent (of course, the opposite can be true if your paper is being discounted beyond the differential)

Usually, the financing profit arises strictly from the excess of add-on income earned in comparison to the cost of money and handling. It is therefore a netting out of the following variables:

- Time sales price differential (add-on);
- Handling cost;.
- Rediscount interest cost.

As has been mentioned previously, the add-on can run from 6 percent to 10 percent per year, depending on the commodity sold and the category of customer. Most consumer goods carry the maximum add-on of 10 percent, yielding the captive finance company an income of approximately 20 percent interest on its money. (Actuarially, it is slightly less, but this is offset by the fact that money borrowed in a rediscount is never 100 percent of the face value of the paper.)

The physical handling of the paper — preparing payment books, entering payments, checking credit and making collection followup — can cost 1 to 3 percent of the contract sale price. Where the handling cost is higher, the add-on is usually higher to compensate for the added expense. Finally, the cost of rediscounting funds will vary from 6 percent to 12 percent, simple interest, depending on the source of funds and the application itself.

Taking the high range of figures — both income and expense — a typical consumer sales rediscount with 10 percent add-on would have gross income of 20 percent interest less costs of 15 percent (interest 12 percent plus handling 3 percent) for a net profit of 5 percent on volume. With the leverage of four times or more obtained in rediscounting, this earning rate could lead to a yield of 20 percent net profit per annum on investment.

There is, of course, one further cost factor involved — bad debt loss. Customer credit loss in rediscounting is usually not as significant a factor as it might be in an ordinary operating business. Not only is a captive finance company run according to the more prudent credit policies of a typical finance operation, but the receivables, instead of being on an open account basis, are covered by a contract of conditional sale. Facing the possibility of repossession, a customer will make strong efforts to avoid losing the equity created through making a down payment and subsequent installment payments. A fairly conservative reserve for bad debts would be about 1½ percent (which a rediscounting source of funds will want to see reflected on your balance sheet). You can frequently carry higher reserves for tax purposes.

Rediscount Credit Criteria

Earlier in this chapter we briefly mentioned certain criteria related to individual contract credits. Whether the customer is a commercial account or a consumer, normal credit precautions are expected in ratio to the size of purchase. The down payment and total term of contract must be sensibly proportioned to the commodity sold, its usage and depreciation. The financial institution supplying rediscount funds will want to satisfy itself that your method of processing individual credit applications is sound and normal. But after checking these elementary requirements, emphasis switches to a major extent to the quality of the overall portfolio, as reflected in the monthly aging.

In time sales financing, the basis of advance against eligible collateral is a *contract aging.* The determination of eligibility of collateral differs slightly from the method used in accounts receivable financing as described in Chapter 5. Receivables are aged according to the number of days past due from the due date; time sales contracts, however, are aged on the basis of the number of payments missed per the terms of the original contract. No purpose is served by setting forth the date of the last payment received, or the number of days it is past due. The status of the entire contract is much more meaningful. Therefore a typical time sales contract aging would appear as shown in the table on the following page.

You will note from this aging that the entire unpaid balance of the contract is placed in the column which correctly reflects the status of payments. If one payment were two months late and the other payments followed at regular monthly intervals, the entire contract is still running two months behind its scheduled repayment terms. Generally, the outside financing institution will make a rediscount advance on all collateral represented by contracts with customers who have missed no more than two payments.

The above eligibility requirement sometimes causes problems which arise with customers who, although they may fall a few months behind because of temporary reverses, are later able to pick up and maintain a schedule of steady monthly payments.

'Two-Thirds of Contract'

Some financial institutions will still classify such accounts as ineligible, but others can be induced to advance once again on what is known as a *two-thirds of contract* provision. This provision allows a formerly delinquent account to reestablish its eligibility if it reaches a payment schedule that is two thirds of the original contract terms — and if a recent steady payment history has been demonstrated.

To illustrate, let us take a $3,600 contract, payable in 36 equal monthly installments of $100 each. The customer makes three payments, reducing the unpaid balance to $3,300, then misses the next four.

A Typical Time Sales Contract Aging

Name	No. of payments made	Original contract amount	Monthly installment	Date of contract	Current	Missed one payment	Missed two payments	Prior (missed more than 2 payments)
Alberts	18	$ 1,080	$ 30	3/93	$ 540			
Baker	15	3,600	100	7/93		$ 2,100		
Chase	2	1,800	50	8/94	1,700			
Dean	4	900	25	5/95		800		
Everts	15	1,800	50	6/93	1,050			
Fox	3	720	20	9/93				$ 660
Green	1	2,880	80	10/94	2,800			
Hoyt	5	1,440	40	5/94	1,240			
Jones	5	1,800	50	3/94			$1,350	

At this point the account would be ineligible for advance. But conditions improve and the customer continues the monthly payments. When he has made five such payments, the account once again becomes eligible for a rediscount advance.

Why? The original contract called for twelve payments to be made each year — one each month. The customer made three payments, missed four, then paid five consecutive months — which accounted for the twelve months of the first year. The contract called for twelve payments, and, since the customer had made eight, he had returned to a position of being within two thirds of original contract terms. The remaining unpaid contract balance was therefore again eligible for advance.

Other than the difference in determining eligibility, the handling of a rediscount arrangement with an outside financial institution functions in very much the same way as does accounts receivable availability financing. The explanation and table in Chapter 5[4] on the use of an availability line can be consulted for additional information.

Floor Planning and Trust Receipts

Many companies which sell on an installment basis function as distributors of such standard items as refrigerators, television sets, machine tools, compressors, etc. Such distributors perform no processing of their inventory, merely stocking it for resale in its original form as purchased. These firms frequently have the availability of *floor planning*, or *flooring*, as a means of financing the inventory bought for resale. One of the earliest uses of flooring — and now certainly the most widespread — was the financing of automobiles and trucks for the retail dealer by the creation of trust receipts. From that beginning, flooring has spread to major appliances and the other items mentioned above. It should be noted that flooring is only found where the inventory consists of specific items of major individual value which are easily identified and, because they are standard brand merchandise, turn over quickly in a widely established market.

Although flooring is another form of inventory financing, we cover it in this section because it usually occurs with

[4]See pages 86 to 89.

installment selling. The institutions which supply flooring credit — banks and specialized finance companies — do so only if assured of the opportunity of financing the installment paper generated by the business. In other words, few lenders do floor planning unless they see some time sales financing in the picture.

The parties to a flooring arrangement are generally 1) the supplier, 2) a bank or finance company, 3) the dealer and 4) the customers. Originally the dealer held the items owned by the bank "in trust" as evidenced by trust receipts. More recently, under the Uniform Commercial Code, the dealer enters into an agreement with the bank whereby the bank takes a security interest in all inventory of the dealer. The term inventory is all inclusive, covering all items the dealer holds for sale, present and future. This agreement further provides that all proceeds from the sale of the financed inventory must go to the bank, less the dealer's profit.

The result is that the dealer pays for only a very small percentage of the cost of the inventory, yet retains a good percentage of the profits arising from the sale. The bank pays the cost of the inventory directly to the supplier, rather than to the dealer.

In practice, it works like this: The dealer orders the inventory from the supplier by presenting evidence of the financial arrangements with the bank. The supplier ships the goods to the dealer and sends the invoice to the bank for payment. When the dealer sells the goods to the public, payment is made in one of two ways — cash or *chattel paper,* that is, a note coupled with a security interest in the goods. According to the agreement with the bank, the dealer must either pay over the cash or assign the chattel paper to the bank within a very short period, usually three days. The bank generally prefers to get chattel paper, due to the attractive interest it can collect on the obligation.

A sample transaction proceeds as follows: Supplier sells a car for $9,000 to the dealer, the bank paying 90 percent ($8,100) and the dealer $900. The dealer marks up the car $1,500 and adds finance charges of $2,000, selling the car for a deferred payment price of $12,600. The dealer keeps its investment in the car ($900) and its markup ($1,500) and turns the remainder (usually in the buyer's chattel paper) over to the bank. The bank earns the interest on the payments from the consumer.

The bank is generally well protected in this arrangement, as its security interest also extends to all proceeds of the sale of the inventory. Thus, if the dealer takes a trade-in as part payment for a sale, the bank has a secured interest in the trade-in under the original security agreement.

Under the Uniform Commercial Code, the filing of a *financing statement* by borrower and lender takes the place of the earlier intent to engage in trust-receipt financing. The transactions are covered contractually by a security agreement. But some of the elements of trust-receipt financing are retained because flooring is still a trust arrangement and the secured collateral originates in a *tripartite* or *three-cornered* transaction. There should always be three entities involved — the outside supplier, the borrower, and the lender. The borrower then resells the collateral in the manner described above. The lender may advance funds directly to the outside supplier, or may provide a *sight draft envelope* for the supplier to present to the bank for payment with the invoice, shipping documents and receipts included. In this three-cornered transaction the borrower receives the goods in trust while the lender's lien has come into existence simultaneously with the purchase.

CHAPTER 9
INTERNATIONAL FINANCE

The jet age and the post-World War II global economic recovery set the scene for unprecedented growth in international trade. Manufacturers and distributors seeking larger markets found many opportunities in foreign lands. Other firms in numerous fields — retailing, electronics, plywood, metals, etc. — realized that, in order to be competitive in their costs, it was necessary to consider importing raw materials or finished goods. But this recognition presented a unique problem: how to meet the specialized financing requirements of international transactions. Few business professionals possessed experience in either importing or exporting. Information, previously very limited, had to be expanded and disseminated. As a result of the demands of quickly expanding international commerce, however, knowledge of import and export finance became available — and, with it, the fact that almost every business expecting to compete successfully must be aware of the potential of global trade.

Importing

A large segment of import trade is handled by specialized importers or *import brokers*. These firms, which have made a business of importing merchandise for resale, are usually well versed in the special methods involved as a result of stratified experience. To the business community as a whole, however, the procedural requirements and financing techniques connected with importing seem so esoteric that only the daring will exercise the initiative required for beginning their own importing activities. Yet the import side of the picture, with its ultimate credit risk localized in the U.S., truly does not present such a difficult or complicated proposition.

Import financing can be obtained from banks and, to a far lesser extent, from the major commercial finance companies, a few of which maintain special international departments. Specialized commercial finance companies can offer certain advantages in larger importing programs — particularly those involving standard commodities — but early aspirations in import financing can probably be much more readily accommodated by commercial banks.

It is not our purpose to go into detail relative to the broad field of importing; rather, we are primarily concerned with arranging for the specialized financing requirements which importing can create. Certain foreign suppliers, primarily in western Europe, ship to their regular customers in the U.S. on an open-account basis. Obviously, you need no specialized financing when you are fortunate enough to make import purchases on such a basis. But this is the exception rather than the rule. By far the majority of import purchases must be made on a cash basis. To satisfy this requirement, yet still protect buyers who must pay cash for their purchases in a foreign country, sometimes before they receive their goods, the *letter of credit* provides the best solution.

Letters of Credit

In international trade, an L/C generally refers to an irrevocable bank letter of credit. Conforming to international banking conventions, a letter of credit is a standardized document which guarantees payment by the issuing bank of the amount of money stipulated. Once issued, it cannot be canceled prior to its stated *expiration date.* When funds are called for against a letter of credit by the payee, or within the banking chain involved in the processing, this is known as *drafting* against the letter of credit. The right to draft is subject to a group of limitations, normally referred to as *specifications,* spelled out in the letter of credit itself, which can be either quite simple or very complex. As an elementary example, you might obtain a letter of credit from your local bank in St. Louis, Mo., to use on a pleasure trip in western Europe. Since it is centrally located in your itinerary, you have the credit forwarded to the Bayrischer Vereins-Bank in Munich. The only requirements for drafting are that you appear at the bank in Munich, identify yourself, and request the money, up to the maximum of the letter of credit. By so doing — and if the expiration date you yourself set has not passed — you will immediately be handed the cash.

Letters of credit for commercial transactions are more complex — but there is one common attribute of all L/Cs. If the specifications are fulfilled prior to the expiration date, the payee can expect immediate cash payment. For this reason, irrevocable bank letters of credit, issued by banks of the leading nations, are recognized all over the world. For the American importer a letter of credit is the gilt-edged calling card which can expedite purchase orders placed with foreign suppliers. The foreign shipper knows that, as soon as he has complied with the L/C requirements, he can immediately draft his cash payment, usually at his own bank. In fact, there are even further advantages intrinsic to the use of letters of credit. Take, for example, the case of a manufacturer in Japan (where the use of L/Cs is practically mandatory for purchase orders from foreign buyers) who receives a $100,000 letter of credit payable upon shipment of 50 special photographic lenses. The manufacturer requires some operating capital to produce the lenses for this order. He therefore applies to his bank in Japan, which, with firsthand knowledge of the manufacturer's ability to produce, and with an irrevocable bank letter of credit in its possession, may lend up to 75 percent or more of the face value of the L/C prior to shipment. In this way, letters of credit become also a potent source of ready working capital.

Letter of Credit Specifications

Because the financing source of import financing — the bank or institution which opens the letter of credit — shares many of the risks to which the importer is exposed, the importer must know how to structure his L/Cs properly in order to obtain financing. The important structural elements are as follows:

1. *Maximum Amount.* A letter of credit is not necessarily limited to providing payment for one order or for one shipment. For this reason the maximum amount may be set up for several months' future requirements. This is particularly true where there is competition for scarce merchandise or in cases where a seasonal output of a supplier is contracted for on an advantageous basis. For example, a credit which is opened for $100,000 maximum limit might cover payment for shipments of $25,000 per month for four months. If the total maximum limit is not used prior to the expiration date, the balance is canceled.

2. *Expiration Date.* The expiration date is a very important control because the cancellation privilege inher-

ent in most undelivered purchase orders is denied in the irrevocable letter of credit. Since a letter of credit is a contingent liability, the expiration date serves as an escape valve should the supplier be unable to fill the orders in a reasonable time. Normally, therefore, most letters of credit carry an expiration date 60 to 120 days after the opening date.

3. *Purchase Description.* The purchase description is, of course, the definitive part of the L/C. As in any purchase order, it is important to specify exactly what is being bought. The quantities and descriptions should be described in detail. If there is insufficient space on the face of the L/C, a detailed purchase order may be attached.

4. *Base Terms.* The base terms in a letter of credit transaction describe general standard arrangements. These arrangements are identified by abbreviations recognized throughout the world of commerce. There are several components which vary within the basic terms — i.e., freight, insurance, customs and duty. The base terms describe who pays for the cost of these components — buyer or seller. Let us take the case of a U.S. importer, located in Los Angeles, who purchases radios from a Japanese manufacturer in Tokyo who will ship from the port of Nagoya. If the base term is *f.o.b.*[1] *Nagoya,* or *ex dock Japan,* the shipper will be responsible only for seeing that the shipment is loaded aboard a ship at Nagoya; the American importer must pay for ocean freight, insurance, duty, and customs broker charges. In the opposite condition, when the Japanese manufacturer pays for most of the costs involved, the base terms would be f.o.b. Los Angeles, duty paid. Of course the individual elements are subject to bargaining between importer and exporter, so there are many varied combinations; however, there are two basic arrangements for which there is common terminology. Generally, f.o.b. indicates that the foreign manufacturer is responsible only for the cost of getting his goods aboard a ship at a port in his country. The other frequently used term is "CIF" (which stands for customs, insurance and

---

[1]Literally *free on board.*

freight), indicating that all costs are borne by the exporter, except for the import duty. Unless the base terms state "duty paid," the importer is responsible for payment of import duties.

5. *Documentation.* The documentation stipulations are fairly standard, calling for papers necessary to insure smooth processing of the shipment to its ultimate destination. Most documents are called for in triplicate or quadruplicate and primarily include on-board ocean bills of lading, consular invoices, and commercial invoices and packing lists.

6. *Insurance.* Insurance may be paid for by the shipper or by the importer, although the importer more frequently bears this cost. Regardless of which party bears the cost, it is important to the importer to have proof of the existence of such insurance. Normally the importer obtains a blanket marine policy which requires little or no advance deposit. These policies can be obtained from your customs broker, which presents the added advantage of convenience because the reporting and charges required under the policy can be handled — transaction by transaction — by the customs broker while performing the other duties of clearing the port and processing through customs. For the protection of the importer, and to satisfy most financial institutions, marine policies are written to exceed the invoice value, usually stated as 110 percent to 120 percent of value, because of varying duties and other costs which may be intrinsic in the import. In fact, in recognition of this circumstance, marine policies are the only types of insurance which can be written for more than 100 percent of specifically known value.

7. *Inspections.* Many imports require inspections for protection of the buyer as well as his source of funds. Since letters of credit can be funded to the shipper merely on presentation of documents, the importer must either have confidence in his source, or appoint an inspector in the country of origin to check quality and quantity. Overseas purchasing agents can frequently perform this function, and some countries, like Japan, also provide official inspection agencies if requested. Further, there are certain categories of imports requiring specialized inspections before they will be admitted into the U.S. Meat, flower bulbs

and plants require U.S. Department of Agriculture inspection and approval; canned goods must have been processed in canneries which meet the requirements of the U.S. Department of Health, Education, and Welfare. In the case of substantial orders, particularly those involving technical or quality requirements, specialized inspection organizations such as the Societe Generale de Surveillance (SGS) can be used since their inspections are respected by banks worldwide.

8. *Shipping Variations.* One of the controls written into letters of credit is stipulation of how shipments may be made. The standard L/C form asks if transshipments will or will not be allowed, or if partial shipments may be made against the total order. The latter clause bears careful consideration under certain circumstances. Usually, if the order involves major items such as trucks or automobiles — or standard commodities such as grain, lumber or metals — partial shipments present no problem. On the other hand, if items are ordered as a total of balanced assortments, serious trouble in the financing can develop. For example, an importer of chinaware from Bavaria might order 100,000 assorted pieces of dinnerware, the totals of each piece being determined by the usual assortment which the importer sells to his domestic customers. Under a partial shipment permission, the Bavarian factory could ship 10,000 coffee cups and back-order the saucers, which would probably hold up all the importer's orders from his customers, thus preventing creation of accounts receivable meant to provide liquidation of the letter of credit financing. Of course, partial shipments could still be allowed so long as each partial shipment contained a stipulated assortment.

9. *Payment Terms.* While drafting against a letter of credit always produces full cash payment, the L/C can stipulate various payment dates relative to the completion of a transaction. The payee actually completes the transaction by conforming to the stipulations of the letter of credit. Thereafter, the letter may be drafted according to various cash payment terms, of which the following are some examples:

- *Cash upon presentation of documents.* This form of immediate cash payment upon conforming to L/C stipulations is quite prevalent.

- *Cash ex dock at destination.* The payee can draft when the goods are taken off the ship at destination and hence come under control of the importer's customs broker. Automobiles are frequently handled in this manner.

- *Ninety-day drafts.* Here the time lapse begins immediately upon conformance to the L/C by the payee. The seller presents his documents to the foreign bank, ninety days after which he is guaranteed to receive cash payment. Because there is banking responsibility for this payment, the seller has a gilt-edged receivable against which he can always arrange financing. Meanwhile, the importer can benefit by having a lower cost for his own financing and also by having three months' leeway in coming up with the full payment of the draft.

Obtaining Letters of Credit

Most letters of credit, even those obtained through other types of financial institutions, are physically opened by banks. The major commercial banks have international departments for this purpose; banks without such specialized departments can still provide letters of credit by working through their major correspondent banks. As mentioned previously, a few of the leading commercial finance companies open letters of credit for their clients and, although they use banking channels for this function, the client needn't worry with this detailed aspect of the transaction.

There are, in fact, several important differences in the approach of the specialized finance companies as compared to that followed by commercial banks. Knowledge of these differences will help you to determine which financing source is best for you. Banks usually restrict their role to paying the amount stipulated in the L/C — the purchase price to be paid to the foreign supplier — and do not cover the other costs, which, including duty, can be quite substantial. An L/C covering $10,000 in purchases of Japanese woodenware from the manufacturer, for example, can require $4,000 additional for freight, insurance and duty. When the bank calls on the importer to pay the letter of credit draft, the importer also faces the problem of paying the customs fees and duties for the goods imminently arriving at his or her port.

A commercial finance company, on the other hand, will compute *all* the costs, including duties, and arrange a financing program to cover them. In fact, most commercially financed international credits will be combined into a complete package including domestic financing of the inventories and receivables. In contrast, banks are prepared to begin with a modest program, yet are fully capable of handling the largest requirements.

Banks treat smaller letter of credit requests in a manner similar to their handling of unsecured borrowings. With a $5,000 L/C, the banker primarily counts on the client's ability to pay it when the credit has been drafted. But — and this is important — banks extend themselves farther with letters of credit than with ordinary unsecured credits, for several reasons. Letters of credit relate to specific transactions with finite short-term liquidations (usually at the time of draft) so they are easier to control. Even though the approval may be made partially on the lines of unsecured credit criteria, each letter of credit creates a secured transaction with underlying commodities as collateral (see below). Also, letter of credit business occupies a favored position in the eyes of most sophisticated bankers. The fees earned are not handsome (ranging from 1/4 of 1 percent to 1 percent of the face value of the credit) but there are side benefits. Banks handling large volumes of letters of credit may frequently enjoy deposits of foreign banks involving funds which have been drafted. Moreover, as there are always other banks involved in the process (the bank which opens the credit plus the bank to which it is forwarded) new inter-bank relationships are created with foreign banks which can reciprocate when their own customers enter into transactions requiring the services of an American bank.

Letter of Credit Line

For the foregoing reasons, you will probably find a receptive atmosphere when you apply for bank financing of a letter of credit program. Companies which have reached their maximum limits of unsecured bank borrowing can still obtain an additional *letter of credit line.* For example, a firm selling wholesale meat to restaurants and markets purchases Australian lobster tails and boned beef from a specialized importer. The firm perceives a larger market for boned beef which can be combined with the suet and waste from its restaurant cuts to produce an acceptable grade of ground beef. A survey reveals that it may obtain what it needs at a definite cost saving by dealing directly with the Australian shippers on a an L/C basis. Even though the meat wholesaler is at his maximum line of $50,000 unsecured credit with his bank, he is agreeably surprised to learn that the bank will grant him an additional $40,000 letter of credit line. With his fast turnover, the meat wholesaler picks up an additional $400,000 volume per year at a good level of profit.

The same credit availability will prevail should an application be made to a bank by a business which does not already have an unsecured line but intends to use its line solely for importing on a letter of credit basis.

Lender Criteria

In establishing a letter of credit line the lender judges several criteria. As we have mentioned, small applications win approval simply on the basis of the qualification of the borrower for unsecured borrowings in the same amounts. Beyond this level the lender bases its decisions on:

- *The foreign source of the goods being purchased.* It is a matter of great concern that the foreign supplier have a reputation for dependability. Inspections can sometimes be spotty, and the importer must be assured not only of proper counts inside master packing cases, which cannot all be opened for checking, but also as to consistent quality. The source should be checked with any trade references supplied, through international Dun and Bradstreet reports, and with foreign banks in the local area. Branches of foreign banks in the U.S. cooperate in supplying this information. If sufficient information cannot be obtained about a source whose products are in demand, the importer should use the services of a reputable foreign buying office. These offices charge about 5 percent of the purchase for their services, including inspection, and can sometimes save their entire cost by negotiating a better price with the supplier.

- *The ready market for the goods.* When products are first introduced into this country, their salability may be questionable, but a bank will usually open up a modest letter of credit if the project is feasible. When moving into more substantial credit levels, however, the lender will want to see more positive evidence that the goods will have ready utilization. Purchase orders from customers are, of course, the best indication; the lender prefers to open credits for goods against customer orders, rather than for products to be placed into inventory for future resale. Of course, if a manufacturer begins to import a material to use in its fabricating process, to replace a domestic material already being used, the indication of utilization is definitely present, subject to the quality of the import being demonstrated in actual production.

- *The commodity rating.* Letters of credit create, as we have mentioned, a secured lending transaction. Therefore, the underlying collateral is of definite importance. This becomes increasingly significant as large levels of credit are utilized. The risk rating of underlying collateral is more closely related to broad commodity classifications when letters of credit are involved because true commodities have almost worldwide standards of value. Coffee, wheat, soybean oil, tin, etc., are true commodities. Not only can they be sold, under forced liquidation conditions, by making a few telephone calls, but they will bring prices listed daily in the newspapers. True commodities, therefore, can be viewed as having a collateral value of close to 100 percent of the purchase cost. Other commodities such as plywood, skein wool, steel strip or hardboard also have an immediate disposal market, but because they respond to local supply and demand, can have a collateral value of 70 percent to 85 percent of the purchase cost. Other standard items, such as transistor radios, skis, tulip bulbs, cameras or cutlery, respond even more to local disposal pressures and their collateral ratings vary from 50 percent to 70 percent of purchase cost. To all these rating-levels must be applied a further factor to reflect the usual range of price fluctuations. Most commodities have a historical pattern of price fluctuations over particular time periods.

The time which must elapse from the opening of a letter of credit to the date the lender is repaid is the time swing to be considered. If, for example, a letter of credit were opened for the purchase of skein wool, over a 60 day time swing, and wool has historically demonstrated a two-month price fluctuation never in excess of 5 percent, the basic collateral value determined for this commodity need only be hedged 5 percent against possible price changes. The resultant net collateral evaluation will determine the margin requirement for the letter of credit financing program.

Margin Requirements

When initiating modest letter of credit financing, a bank relies primarily on its client's ability to repay. Therefore the credit is opened as a 100 percent contingent liability of the bank, backed by its client's creditworthiness. This principle cannot be extended beyond the limits of good banking judgment. Import financing can develop into substantial leverages — where the contingent liability of the lender to make good the letters of credit as drafted may be many times the worth of the client borrower. Somewhere along the line, therefore, the lender must seek a buffer against loss — i.e., *a margin requirement.* Stated simply, the margin is the buffer (or safety difference) between the lender's commitment on a letter of credit and the collateral evaluation — the amount the lender feels it can recoup if required to make a forced liquidation of the underlying collateral.

When a margin requirement is established, it must be deposited before opening the letter of credit. For example, if a credit line is arranged which calls for a 20 percent margin, a letter of credit for $100,000 will require a $20,000 cash margin. As you can readily see, the lender still provides a five-to-one leverage in the credit. Basically, all letter of credit transactions are created because of a requirement for virtual cash in advance payment by a foreign supplier. If, in the example cited above, the importer had to come up with the entire $100,000 out of its own funds — and then had to tie up this money for two or three months while awaiting shipment — a far greater financial hardship would be created, as compared to having only $20,000 tied up during this period.

The amount of margin required will depend on several different considerations. Once again, we encounter different treatments at various levels of size of credits. When credit requirements exceed the modest level where no margin is required, the borrower is apt to find that banks will first tend to apply a standard margin, rather than one specifically allocable to the underlying collateral. These standard margin requirements usually vary from 15 to 25 percent. As the credit levels move into a more substantial range, however, a definite margin arrangement must be set.

In the foregoing section we have discussed collateral evaluations of various types of commodities, and it is easy to see that the difference between this evaluation and the total letter of credit liability must be made up by the margin. For example, if the collateral evaluation is 75 percent, a 25 percent margin is required. But these evaluations — and their complementary margin requirements — are always mitigated by the resale status of the goods being purchased. This status can be divided into three categories:

- Back-to-back resale;
- Purchase order resale;
- Inventory purchase.

In the field of importing, particularly where the importer is a wholesale distributor of standard commodities which he or she does not process — but merely resells — the back-to-back letter of credit arrangement is frequently encountered. In this arrangement, the importer's customer actually opens a domestic bank letter of credit in favor of the importer who, in turn, puts this up with the bank which opens the foreign letter of credit. Although the total value of the two credits will differ (the one opened by the customer will be higher because the purchase will include the importer's markup) the basic stipulations of both L/Cs must coincide. It should therefore be obvious that back-to-back letter of credit applications will require no margin whatever, regardless of the underlying collateral.

Firm Purchase Orders

Margin requirements are also minimized, to a lesser extent, by the availability of firm purchase orders from creditworthy customers. Let us take, for example, sheet plywood in standard sizes, on which the commodity evaluation might be set at 75 percent. If the lender is presented with firm purchase orders from creditworthy customers covering the entire letter of credit risk, the lender will probably ask for only 10 percent margin. On the other hand, if the plywood falls into the third category of resale status — that is, ordered for inventory and future anticipated resale — the margin would certainly be 25 percent.

The margin may also be affected by the landing cost requirements. If the plywood has freight and duty cost of 15 percent, then a bank opening the credit would have to feel confident that the importer could come up promptly with these landing costs before opening a 10 percent margin letter of credit, even with the existence of bona fide customer purchase orders.

The Differences

Here is where the handling of letters of credit by specialized commercial finance companies may differ from the procedures followed by banks. Remember, first, that these differences apply primarily to the larger, continuing programs. The commercial finance company, which may come into the picture as volume increases, will set its margin requirements taking all costs into consideration. Banks generally tend to consider only the total L/C value in setting margins.

An importer of electronic items, for example, has a landed cost add-on of 30 percent, consisting of 17 percent duty, 1 percent customs and drayage, and 12 percent freight and insurance. The importer opens a letter of credit for $100,000 at its bank which, because the client is substantial and well known, requires only 10 percent margin. But the transaction is limited to the L/C financing only; therefore, the cash margin is $10,000. When the goods arrive at the U.S. port of entry, the importer is drafted by the bank for $90,000 ($100,000 L/C minus $10,000 margin already paid) and must also immediately pay out $30,000 in landing costs.

If handled by a commercial finance company specializing in international transactions, the purchase would be viewed in its entirety and the landed cost would be computed at $130,000. Ten percent margin would be $13,000, but the finance company would assume the responsibility for paying the customs, duty, freight and other landing costs. Usually, a letter of credit arrangement with a finance company is combined with an accounts receivable financing program plus the occasional further addition of an inventory financing line. Some commercial banks are now beginning to provide the full package. Therefore, if the borrower is able to provide the basic margin deposit, all other costs will be assumed by the lender and ultimate liquidation will come from receipt of payments from the importer's customers.

The package financing arrangements mentioned above make it possible for a going business to enter into direct importing without seriously dislocating its working capital to meet margin requirements. Take, for example, a wholesale housewares distributor who decides to add a line of Solingen cutlery imported from West Germany.

In order to obtain exclusive distribution of the line, the wholesaler must open a letter of credit for $100,000 on which his landing costs are another $35,000. A lender agrees to handle the arrangement on a 25 percent margin of landed cost, or about $34,000. Although he does not have this cash available, the wholesaler presently has a $70,000 inventory of domestic merchandise on which the lender agrees to make a 60 percent loan secured by an inventory lien. The wholesaler does not require all of this money but the liening of the inventory creates a fund availability of $42,000 (60 percent of $70,000 existing domestic inventory). The lender sets up this availability, then *freezes* $34,000 of this total to serve as margin. In other words, the wholesaler cannot draw these funds which have been made available through the liening of his inventory. But he does not have to pay interest for the use of this margin, as the lender has not advanced it in cash but has merely blocked it off in a bookkeeping transaction to serve as margin.

Pursuing this example, the letter of credit is opened for $100,000. Other than a small opening fee, the importer has no further cost until shipment is made from Germany and the shipper drafts payment. At that point, since the lender must advance cash, interest charges begin. When the goods arrive at the U.S. port of entry, the lender advances the various landing costs, and the entire international transaction is paid off by a 60 percent loan on the new imported goods as they go into inventory, ultimately to be resold and liquidated from the proceeds of accounts receivable financing.

Acceptances

Differing from the package financing arrangement described above, banks handle liquidation of some international financing transactions by using *acceptances*. The basic method of drafting payment of letters of credit is *at sight;* when shipment has been made and all stipulated documents are furnished to the foreign bank, cash is immediately disbursed to the exporter. But in continuing trade relationships it is recognized that the customer may function better — and order even more goods — if he or she is not limited to the amount of cash offered at time of draft. There is also recognition that a customer frequently cannot turn purchases into immediate sales. To accommodate such conditions, *acceptances* are created.

An acceptance documents the fact that the payment of a letter of credit is being deferred for a reasonably short period of time. Most acceptances run for 90 or 120 days. Here is how it usually works, using the example of a shipper in Japan who sells to an importer in California. By pre-arrangement, shipper and importer agree on 90-day terms as reflected in the letter of credit. When the shipper presents his documents and proof of shipment to the Japanese bank, the Japanese bank forwards a draft to the California bank. The bank in California stamps "accepted" on the face of the draft, makes a notation of the maturity date — for example, 90 days after the date shipment was made — then returns this "acceptance" to the Japanese bank. The shipper can then borrow against this acceptance from the bank in Japan. Since this *banker's acceptance* is actually an irrevocable promise to pay on the part of the California bank, the shipper has no problem borrowing up to 100 percent and at low interest rates.

Another Arrangement

Acceptances are also created in another way, involving only the importer and his bank. Taking the same example used above, the same basic letter of credit is opened, this time, however, calling for sight payment. The shipper presents his documents to the Japanese bank which immediately advances full cash payment. The Japanese bank calls for payment, and receives it, from the California bank. The bank in California forwards a draft to its customer, the importer, who accepts it on a 120-day maturity and returns it to the bank. The bank is secured under the letter of credit by a trust receipt, which remains the lien instrument for the acceptance. The importer may sell much of the goods prior to the maturity date of the acceptance and, being trustee under the trust receipt, must immediately pay the bank for the goods released from trust. These payments go into a *prepaid acceptance account* at the bank, to be disbursed for liquidation of the acceptance at maturity date. Interest is charged the importer for the term of the acceptance. Since banks sell these acceptances on the open market to raise funds, the interest is usually lower than normal bank interest.

When the terms have been agreed upon between importer and lender, several preparatory steps are taken. The importer signs an intention to engage in trust receipt financing or some other arrangement under the Uniform Commercial Code, which is recorded with the designated state office. Frequently, individual specific trust receipts in connection with each letter of credit transaction are also prepared in advance.

Prior to the opening of credits a customs broker must be designated. The selection of the proper broker is important. Not only should the broker be capable of handling the types of commodities in which the importer is dealing, but also — because the broker functions in a fiduciary position for the lender — the broker must be acceptable to the financing source. The use of a customs broker is practically a must. The broker's specialized knowledge, location at the port, and friendly contacts in the international commerce fraternity (including the customs inspectors) make it possible for the broker to do an amazing job of facilitating port clearance, insurance, payment of freight charges and duties — all at a remarkably low cost.

Requesting Credit

With the above preparation behind him, and having designated a customs broker who has probably also arranged for marine insurance, the importer requests his first credit. To insure proper structuring, a special application form should be obtained from a bank which has an international department.

The application form is given to the lender, along with the margin deposit, if required. Very soon thereafter, a bank letter of credit will be issued, with a copy supplied to the importer. The original goes to the foreign bank designated by the foreign supplier. If the supplier does not designate a bank, then the bank that opens the credit forwards it to a correspondent bank located in a city nearest to the shipper. Normally the credits are sent abroad via airmail; however, if there is need for rush, they may be transmitted by special cable codes, for which there is a slight additional charge.

The foreign supplier delivers his goods to the port, obtains on-board ocean bills of lading, and takes these, along with all other required documentation, to the foreign bank to which the L/C was forwarded. At this time, under most circumstances, he is paid cash in full. The foreign bank drafts against the U.S. bank that opened the credit which in turn calls for payment from its customer. This is usually the first notice the importer receives that the shipment will arrive imminently.

Shortly thereafter, the customs broker advises of arrival and requests instructions for drayage and delivery. If the importer has paid off the drafted L/C to the bank, the customs broker becomes solely responsible to the importer. If the lender remains in the picture, the customs broker also notifies the lender and calls for landing and clearance costs to be advanced.

The customs broker is instructed by the lender to clear customs in the name of the importer (to protect against the possibility that the lender will be called upon to pay for a later assessment by the customs office), but subject to receipt of a *delivery order* from the lender.

The lender has probably given this delivery order to the customs broker in advance, so there is little delay, although such an order may require a telephonic release from the lender after clearance through customs. At this point the goods are delivered to the importer, or transshipped according to his requests.

A Significant Role

The role of the customs broker in a financed transaction is quite significant. As mentioned previously, a trust receipt (or security interest under the Uniform Commercial Code) relationship is established with most letter of credit purchases.

The trust receipt validity arises from a true "three-cornered" transaction, involving the foreign supplier, the importer, and the lender, all of whom come together (transaction-wise) at the time the goods first enter the borrower's (importer's) ownership. The letter of credit will usually specify the customs broker as the agent "to notify," and he will be entrusted with the physical handling of the goods, protecting the lender's interest until the importer becomes trustee by virtue of the goods arriving at his premises as inventory.

Export Financing

While import financing is relatively well developed and accepted in the U.S., export financing has, until fairly recently, lagged behind. It is a sad fact that our country was a very slow starter in recognizing the financing needs intrinsic to competition for world markets. Even today, although some encouraging breakthroughs have been made, export financing availability in the U.S. is just approaching what it should be.

Yet this is a problem with which we certainly must reckon. To balance our imports we must build up our exports; otherwise we will have a continuation of balance of payments deficits, which the last several administrations in Washington have recognized and deplored. But in order to make the biggest export showing, we must compete strongly with other countries that, in the past, have effectively used a very important tool against us — better export financing.

A Financial Necessity

Most of the countries to which U.S. businesses sell their products were short of dollars and other hard currency. They had to rely on credit to make purchases which, in turn, abetted the growth of their internal economies so that they could become even better customers in the future.

To the American businessman, this situation was not only a national concern; it related also to the broadening of markets essential to individual business success.

Our business and financial communities were guilty in the past of not accepting the challenge of the problems — and there are indeed problems of risk — connected with export credit. European countries, particularly West Germany, stepped out briskly to beat us in selling competitive items to foreign customers by extending better terms. England, dependent on exporting to save its domestic economy, launched several well-publicized programs. The B.E.E.O.C. — a consortium of banks and private financial institutions — opened purchase credits with many foreign purchasers on extended open-account terms.

Lagging behind, the U.S. has finally taken remedial steps, the most notable being the formation of the Foreign Credit Insurance Administration and the subsequent involvement of the Export-Import Bank of the United State.

Prior to our realization that the problem deserved national recognition, American business had certain alternative terms to use in exporting which limited its sales potential. In earlier days, when competition was not serious, the exporter could insist on a bank letter of credit from foreign customers, guaranteeing payment in dollars. As a method of financing, of course, this is still most preferable. As an exporter you can draft against a good foreign letter of credit as soon as you have made shipment and presented the necessary documents to your bank. If you need some production money, and the bank has faith in your ability to perform, you can probably borrow against the letter of credit prior to making shipment. Unfortunately, although the purchase backed by a letter of credit is still widely used, it is becoming an increasingly smaller part of the financing and terms required for our total export volume.

Customers in some of the weaker countries are not in position to provide letters of credit. Customers in stronger countries take the position that they are stable enough not to have to put up letters of credit and that, if you insist, your competition will agree to dispense with such a requirement.

Cash Against Documents

Faced with such a problem, many U.S. firms began to ship on the basis of *Cash Against Documents (C.A.D.)*. This is a widely used procedure, particularly with manufacturers of repeat items, canned goods, and staples such as chemicals. In selling such items to their overseas distributors who maintain a continual buying relationship, sales on terms of cash against documents were found to be quite satisfactory. The goods are shipped to the foreign port, where they are held until released by an order from a bank in the same locality. The documents, including an *order bill of lading* which arranges the release of the goods, are forwarded to the foreign bank which calls upon its customer (the purchaser of the goods) to make the cash payment required. When this money is paid to the bank it releases the documents (which release the goods) and forwards the money through banking channels to the exporter.

When this arrangement is used, it is obvious that the foreign customer cannot obtain possession of the goods until he has paid for them. Many European banks established C.A.D. lines of credit for their clients, advancing the funds on a loan basis to release the documents and goods. But these lines have limits and therefore it is occasionally possible that the customer will be unable to pick up the order after it arrives. The U.S. exporter has not surrendered possession in such cases, but still faces the problem of disposal in a distant location.

Once again, we see also that competition is creating a reluctance to use certain terms, as pressure to get away from C.A.D. begins to increase. For one thing, the procedure is fairly cumbersome; it can frequently involve much running back and forth between the purchaser's place of business, the bank, and the port. Papers get lost in banking channels more frequently than you would expect; they sometimes arrive after the goods reach the port of entry, and the purchaser must then bear the cost of demurrage.

Drafts

The next easing step is the use of drafts — *sight drafts* (payable upon presentation) or *maturity drafts* (payable in a specific number of days). In using drafts, the shipment is made without any restriction; it does not require a release and merely has to be brought through customs by the foreign purchaser and into his inventory. The draft is a legal form which the customer signs, agreeing to make payment on the due date stipulated. This draft is forwarded by your U.S. bank to a foreign bank (agreed upon between you and your customer) for collection. Most drafts used in international trade are *protest drafts* which call for a protest report if collection is not accomplished by maturity date. Although it is not always significant, protesting a draft can cause the purchaser concern for his or her local reputation and ability to obtain future international credit.

When a protest sight draft is forwarded to a foreign bank for collection, this draft is handled in a very specific way if not honored. Actually, the collecting bank has no obligation for payment and in all countries, including our own, it is possible that the customer will not pay for a draft on the due date. This is known as failure to *honor the draft*. When protest drafts are not honored, the draft is stamped with the protest and returned to the shipper (creditor). In some countries all protested drafts are published in the daily commercial papers — a definite deterrent to the customer who values reputation. If, despite this, the customer does not pay on time, the stamped protest draft is usually the legal requirement for initiating a lawsuit for collection in a foreign country.

It is important that the draft be drawn in the language of the buyer's country, to facilitate collection or legal action. A consulate or your own bank can help you to obtain the proper form.

Drafts should bear interest, at least after maturity date. Not only does this provide an incentive to pay quickly, but it also provides a more readily financeable instrument. One of the tricks which seems helpful is the inclusion of any foreign broker's or agent's commissions in the draft. These individuals who are on the scene will take strong steps to facilitate collection of a draft which includes their remuneration.

Export Credit Criteria

The ability to finance exports is dependent upon proper credit screening. Export drafts may be financed on a 100 percent non-recourse basis by some commercial finance companies, or may be financed simply by loans from banks or other institutions. In either case, the credit-worthiness of the customer is vital. In the field of exporting, this is no easy problem to solve. Not only are the credit sources unorganized, but also the volatile character of the buyer's country can add another risk dimension. In fact, it is this latter factor which demands that most foreign credit extensions be relatively short term.

The credit information should be obtained from as many sources as possible. Occasionally international Dun and Bradstreet reports may cover an application, but this is frequently not the case, and the report may not be sufficiently definitive in approving a credit or setting a limit. A balance sheet should always be requested. The form of reporting may not be completely reconcilable to our own format, but it will help establish the credit limit which may run from 10 percent to 25 percent of the true net worth. Bank references should always be obtained — and they will usually be readily given. Many European firms actually print their bank references on their stationery (including their account number). Most European bank references are dependable, which is not always the case with information obtained from banks in Latin America or other parts of the world. But at least these reports do contribute a part of the credit jigsaw you are trying to assemble from as many sources as possible.

If your prospective buyer also purchases from other U.S. firms, this can lead you to information couched in a familiar form, and you should always check for the existence of such an established relationship. Finally, one of the most important checks comes from reports of reputable people who are on the scene in the buyer's country. A bank with an international department will usually have a representative or agent whose information can be trusted. Certain commercial finance companies have foreign agents, and also send their American executives on frequent trips into foreign areas to gather information. Such companies can provide not only information preventing possible credit loss, but they may also be able to handle the financing and collection.

Finally, it is important to ascertain whether the buyer's country requires an *import license.* Not all countries require these, and they may be needed only for certain categories of items. But the lack of an import license where one is legally stipulated can cause serious problems of collection and financing. Therefore, not only should its possibility be checked, but, if a license is needed, the exporter should be sure to have it sent prior to shipment.

Export Guarantees

One of the best ways to facilitate the financing of export drafts is by obtaining a good guarantee. Most U.S. businesses, unaccustomed to this possibility at home, are surprised to learn that it is common practice in many foreign countries to obtain bank, or even government agency, guarantees of purchases. In Latin America, many substantial import orders are guaranteed by banks. Naturally this enhances the U.S. exporter's financing ability. But also to the surprise of many of our businesses, not all Latin American banks are sufficiently strong for their guarantees to be meaningful. The bank stability may be a combination of its own resources and of the volatility of the country it is in. Information relative to the true stature of these banks is available from international departments of U.S. banks or, sometimes even more realistically, from some of the specialized commercial finance companies that are in the day-to-day business of taking some non-recourse risks against foreign bank guarantees.

Some government agency guarantees can be quite good. For example, there is CORFU in Chile, and Nacional Financiera in Mexico. These agencies are somewhat similar to our own Reconstruction Finance Corporation which helped so many industries in the U.S. get back on their feet during the Depression. A guarantee from Nacional Financiera, for example, is fairly widely acceptable in financial circles, at least up to two-year credits. Incidentally, rates of interest in Latin America are higher than our prime rates. The prime first mortgage rate in Mexico is 12 percent per annum. Mexican government purchase orders may stipulate 6 percent interest limitations, but, through the guaranteeing mechanisms, levels of 12 percent or more are achieved, and this is certainly helpful in arranging financing as the cost of discounting export drafts may easily run that high.

Foreign Credit Insurance

One of the greatest boons to financing U.S. exports was the creation of the Foreign Credit Insurance Administration in October 1961. At that time a group of insurance industry members under the FCIA umbrella joined with the Export-Import Bank (EXIM) to offer several forms of export insurance and guarantees. In subsequent years the possibility of a conflict of interest developed because FCIA members were major private insurance firms that in some cases were in direct competition with EXIM in writing export insurance. Therefore, in 1992 the relationship terminated, and the two groups began to function independently of each other.

The FCIA is now part of a private sector insurance group which competes with other major insurance companies in the field such as AIG, Reliance, Continental, and Lloyd's of London. In general these insurance companies offer credit insurance, domestic and international, as an option to a package of general casuality insurance for commercial customers. Rates and terms can be obtained through insurance brokers representing those firms.

Meanwhile, EXIM has emerged as a specially focused resource to encourage export activities for large and small firms. In so doing, EXIM plays an important role in facilitating the financing of export transactions. As of 1995

EXIM offered the following export finance assistance programs:

- *Working Capital Guarantees.* Up to 100 percent of the principal and interest on commercial loans to credit worthy, small- and medium-size businesses, for the purpose of financing the production or marketing of U.S. goods or services for export, will be guaranteed by EXIM. EXIM will issue a *Preliminary Commitment* (PC) delineating the conditions under which it will issue such a guarantee that can be presented to a bank which, relying on the guarantee, will extend favorable financing terms. As this program delegates more authority to commercial lenders, they will be asked to assume nominal risks in return.

- *Guarantees and Loans to Foreign Buyers of U.S. Goods and Services.* Medium-term (and even long-term for major projects) guarantees of commercial loans may be provided by EXIM to banks which lend funds to foreign buyers of U.S. goods and services. There is also a program for EXIM to guarantee fixed-rate loans to buyers who are required to put up a 15 percent cash deposit. In order to assist the U.S. business firm in competing for foreign purchase orders, EXIM will give it a bank *Letter of Interest* (LI) to indicate EXIM's willingness to consider a financing offer if the sale is completed.

The most significant differences are to be found in the varying terms which can be insured; therefore our discussion will treat the comprehensive and political categories as one and the same.

The *short-term policy* covers exporters selling on credit terms up to 180 days. The policy insures up to 95 percent of the credit risk and 100 percent of the political risk, leaving the exporter with a very nominal coinsurance obligation. Except for certain excluded buyers or countries, the exporter is expected to insure all of his exports in order to obtain equitable distribution of the insurance risk. But cash transactions and shipments to Canada may be excluded.

The policy may be written in any amount up to $500,000 (higher for major projects) and this is applicable to all buyers. In order to qualify the buyer, the exporter must *obtain and maintain possession* of two credit reports, one of which should be a bank reference. For amounts over

$100,000 the financial statement of the buyer must also be obtained

The *medium-term policy* covers terms in excess of 180 days up to five years (exceptionally up to seven years.) The policy is designed to provide coverage for capital goods, machinery and equipment. The length of the credit terms will be influenced by the nature of the product and its estimated life in relation to the period of credit. A product with a life expectancy of three years will not be insured for payment terms of five years. When long-term payments are involved, a down payment should be obtained, preferably as much as 20 percent. Payments may be made monthly, quarterly or semiannually. In addition, the exporter can charge interest on the sales contract that will be covered by the insurance policy. Unlike the short-term policy, medium-term coverage is arranged on a sale-by-sale basis by submitting individual transactions to the EXIM. Rates are again based on the country of the buyer and the credit terms.

EXIM insurance is designed to cover almost all foreign sales of an exporter so that the risk is spread over a number of customers (the *multi-buyer policy*). For that type of coverage there is a low annual deposit premium, usually about $500, after which the insured pays premiums based on actual shipments. If the exporter does indeed wish to cover only a single buyer, the minimum premiums are higher and can rise from $2,500 to $10,000 depending on the risk.

When single-buyer sales are substantial, the minimum premium will not amount to a large percentage cost, but it would obviously be prohibitive for a small single-buyer transaction. Fortunately, there is one exception; exporters meeting the U.S. SBA criteria for small business are charged a lower minimum premium of $1,000 regardless of risk type.

Rating and Cost of Export Insurance

The insurance policies written by EXIM are rated on the basis of several criteria. The most important differential is established by the country in which the buyer is located. These countries are rated from "A" to "D." A country rated "D," such as Egypt, requires an insurance rate over four times that of "A" countries such as England and France. Of course, ratings can change, depending on political conditions.

Length of payment terms also affects the rate. A class "B" country such as Mexico may call for a rate of $0.69 per $100 for one year, $0.54 per $100 for six months, $1.61 per $100 for three years, and $2.52 per $100 for five years.

The rate, determined by country and by length of terms, is also affected by the type of transaction. The above examples were based on open account or sight draft. On a Cash Against Document basis, the rate drops about 50 percent; where there is a letter of credit involved, drop is even greater, even if 90 day payment is allowed.

Without even considering the fact that the cost of the insurance could be loaded onto the price to the buyer, who is accustomed to paying far more for long-term payments, the insurance cost is very low, ranging from less than 1/2 of 1 percent to 2 percent or 3 percent on most of the five-year open-account transactions. Also — most important to our subject — the proceeds of EXIM policies are, by federal law assignable to banks and institutions to facilitate export financing.

Chapter 10
Acquisition Financing, LBOs

In the field of finance there is probably no activity which fires the imagination more than the financing of acquisitions or buyouts. For one thing, the very transaction itself — acquisition — represents a dynamic and relatively recent trend in our economy. As an adjunct to progress through orderly growth, a giant leap ahead is obtained by purchase of another operating company. The resultant news releases can frequently impart glamour to the acquirer, particularly if it is a public company.

But the financing techniques used in acquisitions have, until recently, been quite esoteric. As a result, they became potent tools in the hands of those versed in their use. More than a few deals were made possible through ingenious combinations of legal, financial, and tax know-how, sometimes resulting in leverages which, even in very substantial situations, called for little equity contribution by the purchaser. This possibility is being modified somewhat as financial institutions learn more about the pitfalls of improperly planned acquisition programs. Nevertheless, there is still broad financial availability for this purpose and each individual situation can present its own specific opportunities for the takeover of substantial assets with the use of relatively little equity capital. Such acquisitions are called *leveraged buyouts* or, more popularly, *LBOs*.

General Acquisition Purposes

It should be unnecessary to go into detail about basic motivations for making acquisitions. The reasons are well known: diversification, increase in asset strength and profit potential, better market coverages, and, in general, an acceleration in the progress of the acquirer. For public companies there is also frequently a psychological impact on the stock market, resulting in a higher multiple being placed on the company stock so that it reflects more than the mere addition of the profits of the acquired company.

Ideally, an acquisition should result in "one plus one equals three"; in other words, the resultant combination should yield more than the sum of the two parts. Frequently this does happen. Two companies each earning $100,000, for example, could merge and yield a profit of $250,000 — the additional earnings resulting from savings in a single overhead which eliminates duplication of cost.

Purely from a financial point of view, acquisitions can be constructive by supplying elements which will enhance and round out the balance sheet and earnings picture. A fast-growing company with good profits, yet with working capital needs high in ratio to its net worth, can benefit by merging with a company having substantial asset value. Conversely, a company with substantial assets but with slower growth in profits, which requires continuing investment in fixed assets, may benefit by acquiring a high-earning low-worth company to provide better cash flow needed to justify additional growth capital financing.

Why Acquisitions Are Available

Since most of the benefits described above accrue to the surviving company (the buyer), many people wonder why there are any sellers.

Most assuredly there are. The reasons for selling are always interesting to an acquisition financier as they should be to a potential buyer — at least to the extent that it can be determined that the seller is not attempting to unload a deteriorating situation. If this is not the case, the reasons for selling are usually the following:

- *Retirement of principals.* The sellers may not immediately intend to retire (sometimes they do wish to do so) but they are thinking of consolidating their gains, putting their individual finances in order, and diversifying their investments.

- *Taxes.* While operating a business, the principals usually earn only on a basis subject to ordinary income taxes. In making a sale, they may seek to capitalize the potential earnings of a going business so as to have the possibility of capital gains, or even deferred taxes (see below).

- *Lack of sophistication.* This is indeed a strange reason, but it does occur with surprising frequency. Many sellers, unfamiliar with acquisition techniques, do not realize they could just as easily be the buyers. When this happens, we see the "mouse swallow the elephant." Small companies, which logically could have been acquired, emerge as the buyer in a merger with much larger firms.

The first two of these incentives may induce the principals of a potentially good acquisition to agree to sell. As to the third condition, if it exists when the buyer makes the approach, thereafter the less said the better.

Acquisition Financing

In Chapter 3, we discussed methods of evaluating equities. These same principles apply in determining the price of an acquisition where seller's equities are being purchased. Of course, there are some cases where only specific assets are being purchased at their cost or market value; such evaluations are simple, but they are not always encountered. Just as frequently, a going business as an entity — or the stock of a corporate business — must be bought. As has been mentioned, the evaluation of a going business can be book value or an earnings-multiple, but not both.

Book value is obtained simply from the net worth on the balance sheet. It may frequently be readjusted upward if rapid depreciation has caused certain physical assets to be reflected at less than their fair market value. Book value may also be lowered to correct for obsolete tooling, dead inventory, and the like.

Much more frequent in today's acquisition picture is evaluation of a going business by an earnings-multiple. In other words, a business is evaluated by a total price representing a certain number of years times the *present* level of profits. If a firm is evaluated at five years' earnings and it is presently earning $100,000, the price would be $500,000, or a "five times multiple." Remember, the profit is always *after taxes*. If the seller is a corporation, the after-tax figure will be available from the corporate earnings statement. If the seller is a proprietor or a partnership, the profits will have to be translated into a pro forma corporate after-tax figure. The pro forma tax is usually figured at 40 percent to 50 percent, so a partnership which reported $100,000 profit would actually have a pro forma corporate after-tax profit of $50,000 to $60,000, to which the multiplier would be applied. Also, in non-corporate entities like partnerships, there are no principals' salaries, so these must be deducted from the pro forma to get true profits.[1]

Any financing source involved in an acquisition will want to see that the price paid by the buyer is proper. Early guidelines began to appear as a result of the increasing tempo of acquisition activity in the 1950s. The multiple, which is frequently referred to as the *price-earnings ratio,* was charted as follows:[2]

		P-E Ratio
1.	Business with long existence and established good will among many customers — for example, a milk business with established routes	10
2.	Businesses established for some time with proven ability to survive or manufacturing companies with large capital investments	8-7
3.	A business established less than ten years or grown up around a single personality	6
4.	Industrial corporations requiring management skill but not unusually rare special knowledge, without particular patent or trademark protection where capital requirements are not great	5
5.	Small special character businesses such as local shoe shops or bakeries	4
6.	Highly specialized businesses dependent on the skill of a small group, or seasonal, or dependent on weather	2-1
7.	Businesses of a personal service character or dependent on the skill of a single person such as an author's agency or an animal hospital	1

The earnings multiple will usually prevail over the book value. In a well-balanced business, the price based on the multiple will exceed the book value, so the higher evalua-

---

[1]But the deduction will be only about half the postulated amount, because corporate salaries are pretax expenses and are tax deductible.

[2]Dewing, *The Financial Policy of Corporations,* New York, The Ronald Press, 1953.

tion is used. Occasionally the book value is slightly higher than the multiple and, if the difference is not significant and the assets can serve as financing collateral, the purchase may be made on the book value basis.[3]

Removal of Nonoperating Assets

In some cases legitimate book values are simply too high for the earning power of the business. Occasionally this results from outside activities of the seller which have been thrown into the business for convenience, even though they had no connection whatever with the business. A large trucking company, for example, used surplus funds to buy land which, though valuable, created no income for the company.

There is a simple solution to such conditions: Ask the seller to buy back (or deduct from the selling price) such assets at book value. In the alternative, if the seller refuses, include these assets in the purchase if you know you can spin off the assets by selling them quickly in the open market for the book value paid for them. Frequently spinoffs can be made at good profits.

Another very common situation is where the selling company owns its own plant or premises. If there is a big equity in the property relative to the total value of the business, this can cause a pricing problem. The property may be a good real estate investment but real estate investment returns are lower than returns on equities in operating businesses. For example, one of my clients was interested in acquiring a company earning $100,000 after taxes, but with a book value of $1 million, of which $600,000 was an equity in the plant building. An eight times multiple was as high as the buyer would go, but the seller would not accept $800,000 on his $1 million net worth. The deadlock was solved by removing the building from the deal. The buyer agreed to pay $50,000 a year rent as a tenant of the building. This made a pro forma $50,000 increase in rent expense (none had been paid by the seller since he owned the building) but there was a decrease in depreciation of $20,000 (since the buyer would not own the building) — which netted out to $30,000 more expense before taxes, or $15,000 less profit after taxes. The seller's profit figure was therefore adjusted from $100,000 to $85,000 and the

---

[3]More sophisticated acquisition evaluations are described in Chapter 13.

buyer paid eight times, or $680,000, for the business excluding ownership of the building. The seller agreed because in his mind he was receiving $1,280,000 (his $600,000 building plus $680,000 cash from the seller).

Use of Securities for Payment

After the evaluation of a proposed acquisition has been made, the next step is to determine the method of payment. Obviously an all-cash purchase is the simplest approach, but this may not be possible or desirable, for the following reasons:

- Tax considerations of the seller (see below).

- Buyer's lack of sufficient cash.

- A recognition of the need to tie in the sellers by means of stock ownership after the acquisition. Frequently the sellers may agree to a merger in order to pocket some personal gain, but with an announced intention of remaining with the company. If such sellers are vital to continuing progress after acquisition, they can be given stock holdings in the resultant entity as incentive for continuing affiliation and effort.

The securities which may be used in connection with acquisition include common and preferred stock, debentures, notes — indeed the entire gamut of securities found in corporate structures. If common stock is used, there is greater *dilution* of the resultant entity's earnings, and therefore the buyers will sometimes attempt to limit the amount of common stock used for this purpose. In fact, where the buyer is a profitable company with ample funds, it will prefer to make cash purchases and avoid any earnings dilution whatsoever. Conversely, the sellers may not want to take their chances on future appreciation of the buyer's stock and may insist on the greater safety of a senior security, such as preferred stock or debentures. Between these two extremes there can be mixtures of common stock and senior securities, debentures convertible into common stock, notes with stock purchase warrants — or a mixture of these with some cash. The form of payment used is most frequently set to satisfy the sellers' wishes in a desirable acquisition as follows:

- If the seller merely wants to sell out — and get out — he will want all cash or a substantial cash down payment with subsequent installment cash payments evidenced by notes.

- If the seller desires safety but wants a "kicker" to sweeten the deal, it may be necessary to issue debentures which are convertible into some stock, or which have some stock purchase warrants attached. If the seller is predominantly interested in obtaining a strong equity position in the resultant entity and is bullish about future stock prospects, he or she will want either very heavy conversion rights or all common stock.

- If the seller has strong aspirations for common stock but holds assets such as buildings or nonoperating assets, senior securities (notes or preferred stock) may be granted for such assets, with the purchase being rounded off by common stock on an earnings multiple basis.

The buyer will be influenced in choosing a method of payment by a somewhat different set of criteria as follows:

- If the buyer wants to build up equities so that the resultant entity represents the combined worth of the two companies, he will use as much common stock as possible.

- If the buyer desires to acquire assets but needs time to pay for them, he will issue debentures or notes to the greatest possible extent.

- If the buyer wants to lock in some key principals of the seller, he will issue warrants or conversion rights in connection with the senior securities used for payment.

- If the buyer has ample funds and wants to enhance his own profit picture without dilution of his stock, he will try to make the purchase for cash.

Each situation differs, not only with respect to the seller's desires, but also in regard to the aims of the buyer. Later in this chapter we cite some actual examples to illustrate mixes of purchase methods.

Forms of Acquisitions

Before examining the tax aspects which will frequently influence the method of payment, it is necessary that we understand the difference between the basic types of merger or acquisition. These procedures create differing tax situations. They are:

- *Asset Purchase.* The assets of the seller are purchased as individual items. No liabilities are
  assumed. Usually the company cash is retained by
  the seller, who sometimes also retains the accounts
  receivable so as to reduce the cash that the buyer
  must invest. The going business, as a single entity, is
  not purchased (although good will may be paid by the
  buyer); the individual assets are bought.

- *Statutory Merger.* Two corporations are consolidated
  in accordance with the laws of the state in which they
  are located. Usually these laws require approval by
  the stockholders of *both* the buying and the selling
  corporations. The statutes vary; some states, for
  example, demand approval by two-thirds of the
  stockholders. In a statutory merger the acquirer is
  called the surviving company.

- *Acquisition of Stock.* The purchase of the controlling
  stock of one company by another. This differs from
  the statutory merger in that approval does not have
  to be obtained from the stockholders of the buyer;
  board of directors approval is sufficient. The shareholders of the selling corporation show their individual approvals by accepting the tender (offer to buy) of
  the buyer.

Other than the differing tax considerations which we will
presently discuss, there are obvious advantages to each
method. While the stock acquisition involves a broadbrush purchase of a complete going corporation, it is
sometimes not as simple to implement as a merger. The
merger, on the other hand, requires the most stockholder
approvals, which may be cumbersome to obtain, particularly if the buyer's stock is widely held. The asset purchase is loose and requires more definitive legal work in
the purchase documents, but it is sometimes used where
the buyer is concerned about being subject to some
unknown liabilities of the seller. Also, as we will point out,
some financing problems in corporate acquisitions can be
solved through an asset purchase.

Tax Aims of the Seller

A great number of acquisitions involve sellers who wish to
make a complete sale and step out of the picture entirely.
Such sellers know they are faced with a gain which is taxable immediately upon receiving payment and they are
prepared to pay the full tax at the same time. No tax angles

will appeal to them, and the buyer who is prepared to make full payment need not contend with any further tax considerations.

Installment Purchases

Another type of seller, seeking to sell out completely, may not need cash immediately and may choose instead to defer some taxes. This is particularly true if the seller does not anticipate a high taxable income after the sale of the business. Under tax law, if the seller receives less than 30 percent of the total price during the calendar year in which he sells, he will only have to pay taxes computed on the money received that year, and similarly computed only on the installments received in each subsequent year. This is the 29 percent installment purchase plan, so named because it is the maximum below the 30 percent level at which this tax treatment becomes unavailable. This tax ruling is helpful in persuading certain sellers to accept partial payments. Further, it establishes a relatively reasonable down payment — 29 percent — as the maximum which can be paid to qualify for the special tax treatment. In subsequent years, the balance can be paid off in any agreed amounts, with payments spread over any number of years. For example, if the purchase price is $100,000, a down payment of $29,000 might be made with five subsequent annual payments of $14,200 each.

Installment payments are a very useful tool in the financing of acquisitions because, in a sense, the seller helps finance the acquisition of his own business. Often there are definite profit advantages, based on the return the buyer earns on invested capital. Let us say that a buyer has $200,000 invested in a business earning $40,000 per annum. The return on capital is 20 percent. Therefore, any capital the buyer can retain (particularly if he needs all the capital at his disposal) can earn 20 percent. Using the above example of a $100,000 acquisition, the buyer would have the use of $71,000 of the seller's money (after the down payment of $29,000) for five years. Actually, since there are annual repayments of $14,200 required, the buyer does not have use of the full $71,000 for five years, but rather the average of $35,500 (the average between $71,000 at the time of purchase and zero at the time of complete payout). The buyer earns 20 percent return on available capital, but must pay 6 percent per annum interest to the seller on the unpaid portion of the purchase price. But this still leaves the buyer with a 14 percent advantage (20 percent minus 6 percent) accruing from the use of the seller's money. On $35,500 this 14 percent advantage amounts to $4,970 per year, or a total of $24,850 for the five-year payout. Therefore, if the negotiating for acquisition becomes tough over the question of selling price — or over the possibility of an installment purchase — the buyer has nearly $25,000 leeway to increase his purchase offer if he can obtain an installment payout.

Tax Free Exchange

One of the most powerful incentives for sellers to accept corporate securities (and thereby help finance the acquisition of their own companies) in payment for the equities they are selling is the possibility of accomplishing a tax-free exchange. Transactions which qualify for this type of treatment result in no taxes having to be paid on sales negotiated with securities rather than cash — at least not until some later time when the securities received might be sold for cash. A seller might own stock in a company which originally cost $5,000. After building his profits he sells his stock to a public company in return for $500,000 worth of its stock at true market value. Despite this tremendous gain, the seller has to pay no taxes. At a later date, if he finally does sell the acquirer's stock, he will then be taxed on the basis of what he receives in cash from such a sale versus his original cost basis of $5,000. Obviously, the tax-free exchange offers a fine opportunity to build up equities — or to capitalize earnings of a business being sold — without paying taxes. There is a further advantage related to the creation of an estate for heirs. Without going into detail beyond the purview of this book, it can be simply said that the tax-free exchange allows a stepped-up basis of cost which provides substantial inheritance tax benefits.

The sale of the assets of a business for securities of the buyer qualifies as a tax-free exchange, as to that part of the purchase price which is not in cash — provided at least 90 percent of the purchase is in stock.

The sale of the stock of a corporation in an acquisition, in return for stock of the buyer, is much more restricted. In order to qualify for tax-free exchange treatment, at least 90 percent of the seller's stock must be acquired and the payment must be made solely in common stock.

Tax-free exchange in statutory mergers is much less restricted. Whereas acquisition of one corporation by another, using the acquirer's stock for payment, requires that only common stock can be used to qualify for tax free treatment, any form of security — common or preferred stock, debentures or notes — can be used in a statutory merger while still qualifying as a tax-free exchange. Moreover, a nominal amount of cash or property can be made part of the payment without disturbing the tax status of a statutory merger. From a financing point of view, therefore, the merger can present the greatest variety of possibilities in using the "paper" of the acquirer to constitute payment of the purchase price.

The buyer is usually not in conflict with the tax aims of the seller. In fact, the buyer will frequently stress tax advantages in an effort to accomplish an installment purchase or to persuade the seller to accept some of the buyer's securities in lieu of cash. The only place where the tax considerations of the buyer and seller may not coincide is in the *allocation of value* to the assets. The seller wishes to value inventory at a lower price because higher evaluations of this stock-in-trade can create gain taxable on an ordinary income basis. The seller may want to allocate a larger portion of the price to good will, which the buyer cannot later depreciate as a pre-tax deduction. The buyer will prefer to place higher values on assets like machinery and equipment, which give a higher basis for depreciation and subsequent tax savings.

Bear in mind that these problems arise from allocation of values within the structure of the agreed purchase price, and do not change the price itself. From a financing point of view, the higher evaluation of depreciable assets is beneficial because it allows for higher cash flow (through reduction of taxes after the acquisition), available for amortizing the debt which might have been created specifically to finance the acquisition.

Buying a Business with Its Own Assets (LBOs)

Occasionally mergers involve the combination of two business entities on an exchange of stock basis with the sole purpose of achieving a resultant company which benefits all stockholders for the reasons enumerated in the early part of this chapter. Such mergers take no money out of the business, and the possibilities of getting together depend primarily on negotiating an agreement between the two original companies as to the evaluation of the stock of each in the reorganization which creates a single entity. More frequently, however, one company acquires another in a transaction requiring at least some cash payout to the selling shareholders. This is true whether the route of statutory merger or stock acquisition is followed. In such cases the role of acquisition financing becomes vital.

The acquiring company will easily know what financing is available to it on its own resources. More often than not, the buyer will be fairly close to full utilization of its own borrowing ability. In fact, strange as it seems, the company being acquired often has more potential financing leeway than the buyer, but has not used it either because of lack of sophistication or simply because it has had no need of additional funds. In the buyer's eyes, however, the sellers' assets are a possible source of additional capital; therefore, they will be examined very carefully to see what they can produce. In other words, an acquirer can use money borrowed on the seller's assets (subject to some restrictions mentioned below) to provide part of the cash purchase price payable to the seller.

Evaluating Financing Possibilities

The financial statement of the selling company must be examined very carefully to determine the financing possibilities. The key, of course, is the balance sheet, because it reflects all of the major asset categories as well as the encumbering liabilities. From an overall point of view there may be unused unsecured borrowing potential. For example, a seller may be borrowing only $75,000 from its bank for working capital, yet may have a net current asset position of $300,000. The buyer has an unsecured bank line equivalent to 50 percent of net current assets; therefore, the buyer can obtain $75,000 cash for payout by bank borrowings on the additional net current assets created by the acquisition.

Another simple blanket form of financing is through the pledge of the seller's stock by the buyer to an outside source of funds. Certain financial institutions make term loans against stock, particularly if they are given a modest "kicker" in the form of options on a few percent of the stock. It must be noted, however, that lending on pledges is usually limited to the stock of public companies, or to the stock of well-established privately held companies with proven profit stability. The acquisitions of small banks or savings and loan companies frequently utilize borrowings secured from large banks or other financial institutions on a pledge of stock.

If neither of the above approaches will yield sufficient cash to complete the acquisition, the buyer must look to the assets of the seller, usually in the following sequence:

- *Real Estate.* Real property owned by the seller has usually been in its possession for some time prior to the acquisition. Normally there is a mortgage on the property; however, there is also an excellent possibility that the equity in the property has increased since the time it was mortgaged as a result of amortization payments and property appreciation. The buyer should consult a real estate lending institution to see how much money may be obtained by increasing the mortgage based on current valuation. The buyer may allow the existing mortgage to stand, but on the basis of being able to demonstrate the possibility of a higher mortgage loan, may obtain a second mortgage loan from a commercial finance company in a package financing deal including other assets. In other words, if the existing mortgage is $100,000 — but could be increased to a new first mortgage of $150,000 — a commercial finance company should increase its package loan on other assets $50,000 on the basis of a second mortgage.

- *Machinery, Equipment and Fixtures.* This category of assets presents ideal collateral for a medium-term loan. The net depreciated value of fixed assets on the balance sheet will give an approximate basis for loan values (see Chapter 6), but it is very important to get an accurate and realistic appraisal because some significant borrowing potential may otherwise be overlooked. A successful selling company may have followed accelerated depreciation and expensing procedures which have resulted in a material understatement of its fixed assets. I have previously cited the example of an acquisition where the net depreciated book value of the fixed assets was $196,000, yet the auction value appraisal was $375,000 (on which the buyer obtained a loan of $450,000). While the seller could not increase the value of the equipment on the books, the buyer was able to obtain over $250,000 cash acquisition financing on it, over and above its reflected value. With good cash flow the buyer might have obtained an even higher price on a sale-leaseback.

- *Accounts Receivable.* The receivables should be checked to see if they are encumbered. If unsecured bank borrowing is used — even in addition to some chattel borrowing—there should be some leeway for additional financing. Assume 10 percent of the gross receivables reflected to be ineligible for one reason or another, then postulate an 80 percent receivables financing program on the balance. Later in the negotiations, review carefully the accounts receivable detail aging, to arrive at a more specific availability.

- *Inventory.* Although low on the scale as collateral for borrowing, substantial inventories are frequently free of lien and can therefore contribute to the total package of available financing. The buyer should analyze the inventory into raw materials, work-in-process, and finished goods (see Chapter 5) in order to determine potential borrowings.

As a result of analyzing the assets, the buyer should be able to determine how much may be obtained through borrowing on the seller's own assets. The only limiting factor may be the ability to demonstrate sufficient cash flow to meet the repayment schedule required by the lender. Of course, this is a criterion of all term lending; moreover, the resultant entity will have the benefit of both the buyer's and seller's cash flow combined.

Let us analyze an example of acquisition financing availability by referring to the following hypothetical balance sheet of the seller:

Assets

Cash	$ 50,000	
Accounts receivable	250,000	
Inventory	300,000	
Total current assets		$600,000
Fixed assets	$400,000	
Less depreciation	250,000	
Net fixed assets		$150,000
Real estate, net		125,000
Prepaid and other items		100,000
Total assets		$975,000

Liabilities

Accounts payable	$200,000	
Bank loans payable	150,000	
Taxes and accruals	75,000	
Current portion long-term debt	50,000	
Total current liabilities		$475,000
Advances from stockholders	$100,000	
Chattel mortgage loan	40,000	
Real estate mortgage	60,000	
	$200,000	
Less current portion above	50,000	
Total long-term liabilities		150,000
Total liabilities		$625,000
Capital stock		50,000
Earned surplus		300,000
Total liabilities & net worth		$975,000

In this example about $180,000 should be realized from accounts receivable financing (80 percent of the 90 percent eligible for advance). The raw material inventory is found to be $150,000 which is placed in a field warehouse for a 70 percent loan of $105,000. The balance of the inventory ($150,000) is subject to an inventory lien on which another $50,000 is loaned. An appraisal is obtained on the machinery and equipment which reveals an auction value of $200,000 — against this a chattel mortgage loan of $250,000 is obtained. A mortgage banker currently appraises the real estate at $150,000 on which the banker can arrange a 60 percent first mortgage loan of $105,000. But the buyer decides to retain the existing first 6 percent mortgage and, instead, arranges for a commercial finance company to advance the $45,000 excess loan availability against a second mortgage as part of the entire package. The buyer then totals all these availabilities, less the present encumbrances to be paid off, as follows:

Receivables financing	$180,000
Warehouse loan	105,000
Inventory lien	50,000
Equipment chattel	250,000
Real estate 2nd mortgage	45,000
Total availability	$630,000

Less: Bank loan payable	$150,000	
Existing chattel mortgage	40,000	190,000
Available for acquisition financing		$440,000

Obviously a nice leverage can be developed in a situation such as this! The selling corporation earns a profit of $120,000 net after taxes and is willing to sell for $700,000 (which you will note is nearly double the seller's net worth, the price having been determined on an earnings multiple basis). The seller agrees to take $500,000 in cash and a ten-year note for $200,000 at $20,000 per year. Therefore, the buyer needs only $60,000 to complete the transaction, the balance of which will pay itself out from its own earnings.

But the lender insists that the buyer come up with at least $100,000 personally as a minimum equity. This the buyer does willingly and, along with the $50,000 cash the seller shows on the balance sheet, is assured of adequate working capital for the future.

This deal, almost identical to an acquisition I recently financed for a client, made it possible for the buyer to acquire for only $100,000 of his own another company making $100,000 profit after taxes annually! The additional interest is tax deductible, and profits plus depreciation create a cash flow sufficient to service the debt handily.

Route Problems

In many cases a corporate purchase is the most highly desirable form of acquisition, the business being acquired by a purchase of 100 percent of its common stock. But even when all the financing is available as we have illustrated, there can be one serious obstacle: *how to get the money out of the corporation and into the hands of the sellers.*

Corporations are subject to laws governing the removal of their assets, including cash. Cash may be used to pay corporate obligations, but it is not a corporate obligation to pay for stock a shareholder sells to an outside buyer. The only other way money can be taken out of a corporation (which is to continue in business and not be liquidated) is by declaring dividends. But here we have another restriction: Dividends may be paid only out of earned surplus. Therefore, the amount of earned surplus will limit the

amount paid out of the corporation to its selling shareholders, regardless of how much can be borrowed on the
corporate assets. After all, the money borrowed on the
corporate assets must go into the corporation bank
account. The corporation is the borrower, not the
stockholders.

An Exception

There is one important exception to the earned surplus
limitation. As we have previously explained, private corporations are sometimes initially capitalized on a "thin"
basis; that is, part of the original investment is made in
return for common stock, and the balance is loaned to the
corporation by the principals (who can receive this
amount later as a tax-free return of capital). On the balance sheet such investments are reflected as "officers' (or
principals') advances to the corporation." These are *obligations* of the corporation (even though they constituted
part of the original investment), so they can be repaid with
cash any time the money is available.

Now look at the balance sheet we have used as an illustration for analyzing the acquisition financing possibilities.
You will recall the following:

- The seller requires $500,000 cash down payment.

- The buyer is coming up with $100,000 cash of his
  own.

- There is $440,000 available on the corporation's
  own assets for acquisition purposes.

Referring to the balance sheet, notice the $300,000
earned surplus; this is the limit beyond which a dividend
cannot be paid. But notice also the corporate obligation of
$100,000 to the officers, who are the selling shareholders.
And finally, our buyer has $100,000 cash which he is free
to use as he pleases. Even if the buyer is a corporation
(which is usually the case) its own cash may be used for
any purchase for which value is received.

Therefore, follow the steps which make this acquisition
legally possible:

- Selling shareholders and buyer execute the purchase agreement. This agreement creates a liability
  on the books of the buying corporation to pay
  $500,000 cash to the sellers. The agreement is

joined into by the financing source (lender) to create a *turnaround.*

- The turnaround calls for the sellers to deliver their corporate stock to the buyers who simultaneously pledge the stock to the lender as the lender's funds are advanced to the corporation being acquired.

- The buyers have agreed to vote the stock of the corporation to authorize the pledge of the various assets to the lender which are required as security for the acquisition financing. As soon as the stock is delivered by the buyers, they do so, and the lender substitutes liens on the assets for the pledge of stock — thereby completing the turnaround.

- The buyers have paid their own cash contribution of $100,000 directly to the sellers. In other words, this payment was not made through the corporation being purchased, but outside of it. This leaves $400,000 still owing on the cash down payment requirement.

- The lenders have advanced $440,000 into the selling corporation on its assets. Of this, $100,000 is used to liquidate the advances from shareholders. Since this is a corporate obligation, this may legally be done. This now leaves $300,000 cash owing on the down payment.

- All of the stock of the selling corporation is now owned by the acquiring corporation which, through its appointed directors, declares an "upstream" dividend from the new subsidiary to the parent (the buyer). This dividend of $300,000, which is the total earned surplus, is paid in cash to the parent corporation (the buyer) on a virtually tax-free basis because the acquisition is reported on a consolidated tax-return basis. (Your accountant can give you more information about these matters, whose details need not concern us here.)

- The parent corporation (the buyer) has already incurred a liability for payment to the sellers of the purchase price for the acquisition. It is therefore legally empowered to use the $300,000 cash dividend it has just received to pay off this corporate obligation — thereby completing the $500,000 cash payment required by the sellers. To recapitulate, the sellers received their cash down payment from the following:

Paid by the buyer outside the selling corporation	$100,000
Repayment of the selling corporation's indebtedness to its shareholders	100,000
Payment of the buyer's obligation to the sellers for their stock — using funds received as dividend from the acquired corporation	300,000
Total cash payment	$500,000

The parent corporation, which has been the buyer in this acquisition, will be responsible for payment to the sellers of $20,000 every year to liquidate the $200,000 deferred payment. This can easily be accomplished with funds received as subsequent dividends from the profitable subsidiary which has been acquired.

Asset Purchases

From the foregoing description it is obvious that there will occasionally be acquisitions which cannot be accomplished as a purchase of corporate stock. This is true where the total cash down payment required exceeds the total of 1) earned surplus of the corporation to be acquired, 2) the cash the buyer has available to pay to the selling shareholders outside the corporation, 3) the amount owed by the selling corporation to its principals. In such cases an asset purchase is usually resorted to. As explained earlier, this is merely an acquisition of the individual assets of a corporation, free of all liabilities, and having no claim on the stock of the corporation. Even a complete going corporate business can be sold this way, with good will paid as part of the purchase, leaving the seller with an empty corporate shell which he may collapse or retain on an inactive status until he finds another use for it.

Of course the acquisition of a partnership or proprietorship does not become involved in corporate route problems because the buyer is then not confronted with a corporation in the first place. Such acquisitions are, by their very nature, asset purchases. Where a corporation does exist which cannot legally be used to meet the cash payment desires of the sellers, and an asset purchase is not desired — either by the buyer or the seller, for various reasons — the whole problem may be resolved by resorting to a statutory merger.

Under the merger route, the surviving corporation will represent a pooling of the assets and liabilities of both of the original corporations. Therefore, funds borrowed on the assets of the total complex should be available to liquidate the purchase obligation of the acquirer as it becomes an indebtedness of the surviving entity. In some cases this may be the only solution, but it does present hurdles of its own. As explained previously, the statutory merger requires greater stipulated approvals from the stockholders on both sides of the transaction. Further, the merger must usually be completed before payouts can be made to the sellers, and there are many sellers who will not go along with this type of arrangement. As you will recall, in a straight corporate acquisition the sellers can be paid simultaneously with the release of their stock which they have delivered into the purchase escrow. This usually cannot be done if substantial outside financing is required for a consolidation accomplished through the statutory merger process.

Combining Techniques

While many acquisitions simply follow one of the procedures previously described, there are also numerous cases where all the available techniques must be sifted in an effort to find a combination satisfactory to the buyer and the seller. Regardless of the legal route followed, it may still be necessary to mix cash with various types of securities — stock and corporate obligations. Most of the usual tools have already been discussed which, because of their variety, cannot be shown in all their possible combinations. But a few examples should illustrate how these tools can be mixed to achieve the desired result:

Case #1: A very simple example of asset purchase. Seller has a small profitable business, distributing material handling equipment, and he wishes to retire. He sets a price of $75,000 on all his assets, including the good will of the going business. The buyer agrees to assume current trade obligations of $16,000 (which, although he will pay off when due, will be replaced by other newly incurred accounts payable. Remember, as we have pointed out, that accounts payable provide an increment of working capital). Buyer agrees to pay off a bank loan of $20,000 secured by a chattel mortgage. The seller already has receivables financing, so no extra funds are picked up from this asset. But a combination of inventory lien and a new chattel provide $50,000. The buyer has only $5,000 of his own cash, but he owns an apartment on which he persuades the package lender to advance him $15,000 (secured by a third mortgage which, although in this case the owner's equity is good, would not ordinarily be financeable except as part of an acquisition package loan). There is sufficient working capital in the business residual in the small cash bank balance and receivables financing. Therefore, the transaction initially shapes up like this:

Cash from buyer	$ 5,000	
Chattel and inventory lien	50,000	
Apartment equity loan	15,000	
Total borrowing availability		$ 70,000
Less payoff existing bank chattel		20,000
Available to pay seller		$ 50,000

Actually, for tax reasons the seller wishes 29 percent down ($21,750) the first calendar year. Since the sale takes place in November, the buyer has to provide immediately for the second year. The buyer gives a note for payoff of the balance of the purchase price in three subsequent equal yearly installments of $17,750 each. As you can see from the above table, the down payment and first subsequent installment payment are easily covered by the $50,000 availability. The later installments will be provided for as the result of the ensuing three years' profits.

Case #2: A more advanced asset purchase. The seller owns a machine tool manufacturing company with excellent profits over $140,000 per year, but he has taken accelerated depreciation to such a great extent that he has backed himself into a tax corner. He is using receivables financing because he has withdrawn $200,000 cash from the company bank account to make an outside investment.

An agreement is made to sell the company assets for $700,000, for which the buyer will receive all machinery and equipment, inventories, and the going business. The seller is to keep the cash which is in the company bank account at the time of sale. A purchase escrow is to be opened by buyer and seller on May 1 with a deposit of $150,000, the total cash outlay by the buyer in making this acquisition. On June 1 the sale will be completed and all accounts payable and accounts receivable created in the normal course of the business from May 1 will be assumed by the buyer. (Since the business is doing a sales volume of $100,000 per month, and material purchases represent 60 percent of sales, it is assumed that the receivable asset will be $40,000 higher than the accounts payable liability the buyer will have to assume.) The generation of new receivables will therefore provide some of the going-forward working capital. The heavily depreciated equipment is found to have an auction appraisal of $375,000 and, with an equipment chattel and inventory lien, $400,000 is committed by a lender who also agrees to finance the receivables of the new owners. The assets mentioned above are acquired by the buyer and placed in a new corporation. The stock of the new corporation is to be 100 percent owned by the buyer's presently existing corporation, which, therefore, becomes the parent of the newly formed subsidiary. The subsidiary is set up to reflect a $500,000 liability to the seller for the cash down payment increment of the $700,000 total purchase price for the assets; this liability is paid off by using the $400,000 advanced by the lender plus part of the $150,000 cash put up by the buyers. The parent corporation then issues a debenture for the remaining $200,000 due to the seller. This debenture calls for repayment of $20,000 per year for ten years and is secured by a mortgage on some real estate owned by the parent.

It is interesting to note that the seller has no further direct claim against the profitable business he has sold; it is a wholly owned subsidiary of the parent corporation which will be able to derive about $100,000 in annual upstream dividends from this subsidiary, out of which it will easily meet the $20,000 yearly debenture amortization. Another significance of the debenture being issued by the parent corporation is that the lender would probably insist that it be subordinated if it were an obligation of the subsidiary to which the lender is advancing funds. Since many sellers balk when asked to subordinate their securities to loans made on their own assets, the proceeds of which are used to pay them out, the arrangement described above nicely skirts this problem. Summarizing this example, the buyer has purchased a business making $100,000 net profits after taxes for a total price of

ACQUISITION FINANCING — CASE # 2

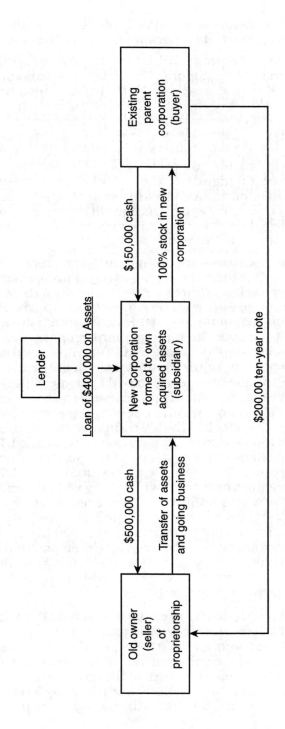

Lender

Loan of $400,000 on Assets

Existing parent corporation (buyer)

$150,000 cash

100% stock in new corporation

New Corporation formed to own acquired assets (subsidiary)

$200,00 ten-year note

$500,000 cash

Transfer of assets and going business

Old owner (seller) of proprietorship

$700,000, while using only $150,000 of his own money. The accompanying diagram charts the transaction.

Case #3: A more substantial true acquisition of all the common stock of a company. The seller is a well-established chain of retail stores in which there is a longstanding feud between management and some substantial inactive stockholders. From an initial capitalization of $100,000, the corporation has grown over the years to a point where it has earned surplus of $2.2 million and no debt. Management has held on to every penny earned and has neither paid dividends to the stockholders nor made any effort to expand. As a result, many opportunities have been missed. Instead of the liquidity having been used for sound growth, it has become merely a ripe fruit ready for an acquisition harvest.

Certain pressures are brought to bear on management by the inactive stockholders so that management finally agrees to sell its shares for $1.7 million cash. Meanwhile the inactive stockholders have been approached by a small outside company in the same industry who are willing to take over the management responsibilities after acquisition and to offer $250,000 cash; in return they ask for 50 percent of the common stock of the acquisition. These outside buyers are joined by some of the dissident inactive investors in the purchase of the company. These former shareholders of the selling company agree to surrender their stock in the old company in return for 50 percent of a new parent corporation to be formed. Their old stock represents one-third of the sellers' stock. Since management's two-thirds was evaluated at $1.7 million, the investors one-third which they will surrender to the buyer is worth $850,000. They are therefore making a much larger contribution to the buyer's equity than the outsiders who are putting up $250,000 in cash. But the investors are anxious to terminate their position of having been locked in for years without receiving any dividends, and they do not have the cash which any lender would insist be put up by new buyers.

The above disparity is easily corrected. The new parent corporation is formed, its capital reflecting that 50 percent of the common stock is given to the outsiders, who are coming in as new management, in return for $250,000 cash. The other 50 percent of the common stock — plus a corporate note for $600,000 from the new parent corporation to make up for the disparity in contributions

($850,000 value of one-third selling stock minus $250,000 equals $600,000) — is given to the former inactive investors in return for selling to the new parent corporation their one-third stock in the old company being acquired. The new parent corporation then incurs a liability to pay to the selling management $1.7 million cash for its two-thirds stock in the old company. In this way it has contracted to purchase 100 percent of the old company.

The old corporation, as we have mentioned before, has no debt and is very easy to finance. On its real estate alone, $950,000 is borrowed on a first mortgage. The consumer accounts receivable qualify for a bulk commitment of $250,000 more, and a chattel mortgage on the store fixtures creates $450,000 more availability. The total acquisition financing potential shapes up as follows:

Cash from outside new management	$ 250,000
Real estate mortgages	950,000
Store fixture chattel mortgage	450,000
Bulk receivables financing	250,000
Total potential financing	$1,900,000

Obviously the purchase price is available. The corporation has over $200,000 cash in the bank when purchased, which provides good working capital. In addition there is a small building which is not mortgaged and since it is no longer essential to the operation, it is sold for an additional $125,000 working capital.

In broad strokes, this case describes an actual acquisition in which I was involved and it illustrates how new management, with a relatively small investment, obtained a dominant position in a substantial established company. The "turnaround" method described earlier was used, with a commercial finance company advancing $1.7 million into the purchase escrow in return for a pledge of the stock of the corporation being acquired. This money was paid to the old management for their two-thirds stock holding. Using the voting powers of this stock, the new owners voted to create the real estate mortgages, chattel and receivable liens. Against these liens the finance company advanced $1.7 million in a secured financing transaction. In an exchange of checks, the acquired subsidiary accepted the loans, then declared a $1.7 million dividend to the new parent company (remem-

AQUISITION FINANCING — CASE # 3

ber, the old company which was acquired as a subsidiary had earned surplus reflected as $2.2 million so this dividend was quite proper) which in turn issued its check for $1.7 million to the finance company to pay off its loan in that amount against the pledge of stock of the old company. The finance company ended the turnaround by having a single $1.7 million loan secured by real estate mortgage, receivables lien and store fixture chattel. This loan was quickly reduced to $1.3 million because of the extra cash in the corporation coming from the sale of the nonessential building and from the corporate bank account. Further, the lender gave its clients the right to substitute the real estate mortgages with longer-term lower-cost institutional loans after one year. The accompanying diagram charts the transaction.

The foregoing case histories have dealt primarily with acquisitions where outside financing from a lender was required because the major part of the consideration paid to the seller had to be in cash. These same techniques can be mixed with securities, particularly where it is desirable to remove an overhanging obligation for making unusually heavy installment payouts after the purchase. When a seller originally insists on receiving only cash plus notes for subsequent cash payments, it is sometimes helpful to make these notes convertible into some of the buyer's stock, particularly in public corporations. The conversion price is set above the market price of the buyer's stock at the time of acquisition. If, as a result of the acquisition, the buyer's stock rises, the seller will have an incentive to convert his remaining unpaid notes to stock, particularly if its market price goes above the conversion level of the notes. In this way, even though the seller originally refuses to accept stock as part payment for his company, he may eventually wind up by owning the stock through conversion.

CHAPTER 11
PRIVATE PLACEMENTS

Earlier this book mentioned that there are certain forms of borrowing which, because of their special characteristics, serve many of the practical requirements of equity capital. *Private placements* occasionally do just that. Either through original design, later conversion, or practical effect, the obtaining of private placement financing can frequently be equated against equity benefits.

A private placement is a financing which consists of the securing of funds — in a relatively substantial amount as far as the recipient is concerned — from a few sources (as opposed to a public issue which involves many investors and underwriters). Certain types of institutions, described later in this chapter, provide private placement funds. The arrangements are longer-term than those provided by most growth and working capital programs. Therefore, there is somewhat the same sustained usage of funds which only equity can otherwise provide. In addition, the drain of cash flow resulting from modest amortization and interest requirements can be less than the participation (through salaries, expenses, or sharing of profit) which an individual equity investor might demand.

Private placements almost always provide additional financing leverage because, to a current lender such as a bank, they constitute equities which are subordinate to short-term loans. Many private placements actually contain specific subordinations to banks and other financial institutions. Even if such subordinations are lacking, the stretched-out term of amortization of the private placement will have the same practical effect of retaining funds in the company far beyond the maturity dates of any short-term financing.

Types of Placements

Although private placements of common stock are occasionally made, the greatest majority of such transactions involve some form of senior security. This is because the recipient is usually in a middle stage of growth where it is desirable to use borrowed money before diluting owner equities. Also, because the borrower is in an intermediate growth stage, the fund source will want to have the liquidation preference on assets that a senior security enjoys. The types of senior securities most commonly used are *mortgage bonds, debentures, convertibles, notes* and *preferred stock.*

Mortgage Bonds

Although the most venerable, this form of security has in recent years given way in popularity to other forms of placement securities, particularly where young growing firms are involved. Yet stemming from this classic form are most of the standard provisions which are otherwise stated in varying arrangements.

Early bonds — or those widely distributed to public investors — were *coupon bonds* payable to the bearer upon presentation of coupons which matured on specified dates. [1] In modern private placements, the coupon bond has been largely discarded in favor of a *registered bond.* The registered bonds are identified by number, and records of these numbers and the names of the legal owners are kept by trustees, transfer agents, and corporate treasurers. The institutions that buy bonds in exchange for private placement funds find it much easier to keep track of bonds under the registration arrangement. Registered bonds issued to a number of holders are frequently arranged and numbered according to maturity date, being known as *serial bonds.* All bonds of "series 1990" are, for example, due and payable in 1990. In private placements the final date for payment in full is often referred to on the financial statement of the recipient as "series." Therefore, the total indebtedness of a bond amortized in equal semiannual installments, but not due to be fully repaid until 1992, would appear on a corporate balance sheet as "mortgage bonds, series 1992."

Mortgage bonds usually involve first liens on property, real or personal, as security. They bear interest on the unpaid balance in a range of 4 percent to 9 percent per annum and, depending on the quality of the issuer, sometimes even higher. Corporate mortgage bonds are geared

---

[1]Many Eurodollar bonds are still issued in the coupon format.

to the useful life of the collateral and may extend in term from ten to 40 years. Because of their long terms, certain standard protective provisions have been developed. A list of restrictive provisions is agreed upon and this list is formally set forth in what is known as the indenture. Simply stated, the bond itself is the security that is issued, and the indenture gives the terms of the issue. Most of the indenture, which can be quite lengthy, is devoted to a standard recitation of legal "boilerplate" to give the arm's-length long-term lender legal protection against the myriad of future pitfalls that could develop. These are interwoven with much more specific provisions, relating to the particular transaction, which do the following:

- Establish the basic security and collateral, describe it in detail, evaluate it, restrict its disposal without permission, and provide for maintaining its value.

- Stipulate certain standards of financial "health" on the part of the borrower, such as limiting maximum current borrowings, purchases of new equipment or investments in fixed assets. Working capital may be required to be kept above a certain minimum — and debt-to-worth ratio below a certain maximum. Cash dividends may be allowed only upon achievement of stipulated profits.

- Provide for acquisitions, mergers or future stock issues.

- Establish remedies or courses of action in event of default or failure to meet with other indenture provisions.

The term, interest, and repayment of principal are stated on the bond, but are usually repeated in the indenture. Since the indenture contains many provisions to be "policed," the services of a *trustee* are frequently used. This is particularly true where bonds are held by many individuals or entities, in whose interest the trustee is charged to act. Such trustees are usually corporations whose qualifications and procedures are regulated by the Trust Indenture Act of 1939 under the administration of the Securities and Exchange Commission.

Remember, also, that there will be mortgages involved with bonds as we have discussed them, and that there may be significant limiting factors regarding them in the indentures. Some indentures prevent mortgaging additional fixed assets purchased in subsequent years. Others extend the lien of the bond holders to all *after-acquired assets.* Inclusion of such restrictions must be weighed carefully in light of future growth financing aspirations.

Sinking Fund

After the type of amortization is agreed upon for a private placement, certain requirements are set up in connection with these repayment provisions. Nowadays the making of a private placement with a single institution has brought about simplification. As originally established, the *sinking fund* was created by a stipulated schedule of repurchases (or retirements) of bonds over the total term. Each year the borrower was required to purchase a roughly proportionate amount of the total indebtedness, usually so that at least 80 percent of the bonds were retired by the last year before maturity. For example, if $1 million in bonds were originally sold with a ten-year maturity, the borrower might be required to repurchase $80,000 worth of bonds each year. These repurchases would constitute the sinking fund.

In the place of a sinking fund, *serial repayments* are sometimes used. Under this arrangement, the borrower repurchases bonds bearing certain specified serial numbers each year. This repurchase is at a fixed price, and will be the method usually favored in placements of bonds with a single fund source. Whereas, under the sinking fund arrangement, the borrower, faced with a spread-out holding of bonds, might be able to buy some of his own bonds at a discount in a depressed market, no such possibility exists with a serial repayment to a single institution. But with the present custom of fixed amortization schedules well established, you may hear discussions of private placements with institutions which refer to the repayment scheduling as "sinking fund provisions."

Debentures

A *debenture* is a general claim on the assets of a business. Therefore, individual assets are not specifically pledged to the debenture holder. Debenture holders are senior in position — as to claims on assets — to the stockholders of a corporation. This position is established by law in the very definition of the word "debenture." Because a debenture is not directly geared to the value of specific underlying collateral — or to its expected useful life — the criteria on which debentures are placed with an institution rest heavily on the general financial soundness and future profit potential of the borrower. Of course, the indenture to a debenture may preserve a first position on specific assets by denying the right of the borrower to mortgage those assets. Therefore, even though there are no mortgages connected with a debenture issue, the debenture holders can prevent another secured lender from sliding in under them with regard to collateral.

Actually, the denial of future hypothecation of physical assets is frequently not rigidly set, once again because it might inhibit the healthy growth of the company on which the debenture placement has been postulated. It is true that, because the claim is general, and there are fewer standard legal protections to debentures than to mortgage bonds, the indenture to a debenture issue will tend to be even more lengthy and restrictive. On the other hand, these restrictions, which are applicable more to overall financial condition than to control of assets, may be much less limiting of the flexibility required for mergers and consolidations.

Unquestionably debentures are becoming more popular and widely acceptable to the financial community. As credit analysis has improved and the writing of indentures has become refined, the use of *subordinated debentures* has become more common. The institutional lender will in many cases insist on the presence of unsecured bank lines, to which his debenture will be subordinated. The theory here is that the debenture lender makes a long-term loan and is in no position to monitor the borrower frequently. Unsecured bank lines, however, are traditionally renewable every 90 days; the debenture holder hopes that, as some of these renewals are made, the bank will be reviewing the trend of the borrower and will alert the debenture holder to any adverse changes.

Most bond and debenture private placements are made *at par;* that is, the lender pays the full face value of the debentures. Occasionally, for various reasons, a debenture will be placed at a *discount,* particularly if low interest is to be charged. For example, most debentures are issued in $1,000 multiples. One thousand of these debentures (total face value of $1 million) might be sold for $998.75 each in order to obtain a 4¾ percent interest rate instead of a slightly higher cost which would hamper cash flow in the early years of the term.

It is also true that, in private placements, the face value of the bond or debenture represents the total amount to be repaid. But this amount — called the *redemption price* — must be clearly specified since the redemption price can be higher than the face amount, particularly in the event of prepayment of the principal amount.

Kickers

Many private placements create tremendous growth opportunities for a progressive business, yet because they are *funded debt* (long-term repayable financing) the lenders receive only interest return and do not ordinarily share in the profit potential they help to create. For this reason, a modest added incentive — a side bonus usually called a *kicker* — is sometimes made part of the deal with an institutional lender. The kicker can be in the form of *warrants,* which give the holder the right to buy a modest amount of common stock at an advantageous price within a certain period of time. Warrants should not be confused with rights. Rights are offered to existing stockholders, granting them a purchase advantage on new stock to be issued. Warrants are actually an option to make a purchase, with a time limit established within which the option must be exercised or dropped. For example, the common stock of a company might be evaluated at $20 per share at the time a private placement is made. The lender, who is purchasing $1 million in debentures, is given warrants to buy 2,000 shares at $25 per share within a five-year period. If the company prospers and its stock rises above $25, the lender will undoubtedly exercise this option and pick up some extra return.

Convertibles

As with the public market, *convertible debentures* have become increasingly popular with certain sources of private placement funds. Here again there is an option to make an advantageous stock purchase as a kicker to the lender; however, under the conversion arrangement no additional money is required for the common stock purchase. The lender originally purchases debentures which carry a conversion feature whereby the debentures can be exchanged for common stock. The conversion option can be for a fixed price throughout the possible conversion period, or it can be scaled upward through several price levels over a period of years. The escalation of the stock purchase price tends to serve as an incentive for conversion if the borrowing corporation is demonstrating the kind of progress showing a good possibility for future appreciation.

The convertible debenture presents an example of a financing which begins as a loan but can culminate as equity capital. If the lender elects to exercise the conversion option, the lender's money becomes a part of the permanent corporate capital represented by common stock. This arrangement is frequently advantageous to a privately held corporation, but it can present a unique problem when a public stock issue is contemplated. This is because an *overhanging convertibility* can affect the market price of a firm's common stock; analysts tend to compute per share earnings as if the conversion had already been made — penalizing the stock for potential dilution at the same time the corporation's earnings are being reduced by the payment of debenture interest. The solution of this problem can be anticipated by the establishment of a realistic *call price* for the debentures. If the call price is below the per share value of the shares of common stock to which a debenture can be converted, the debenture holder can be *forced to convert* because he or she can sell the common shares for more than the value of the debenture. If there were no call privilege on the part of the borrower, the forced conversion would have no teeth in it because the lender could delay in converting. But when the borrower can call debentures, the lender must either convert quickly (ten to 21 days is normal) or be paid off and lose a profitable conversion opportunity.

Private Placement Sources

Private placements are made with the following sources:

- Venture capital funds;
- Mezzanine capital funds;
- The Small Business Administration (SBA);
- Insurance companies and pension funds; and
- Private investment funds.

Venture capital funds are usually closed-end investment funds managed by some general partners with a number of limited-partner investors such as pension funds, retirement funds, and various family and corporate trusts. Management has a great deal of flexibility in the amount of money it can advance, ranging from several hundred thousand to several million dollars. Usually venture capital funds form a syndicate of similar investors so that, in the event that more than a few million dollars is required, each fund can participate up to the limit it deems feasible.

The original venture capital funds concentrated on first-stage high technology investments. Therefore, a great number of the investments made by those funds are in the fields of electronics, biotechnology, computer hardware and software, medical diagnostic equipment, etc. When these funds make an initial investment, they are usually prepared to join in second- and third-round financings before the company in which they have invested qualifies for other types of finance. In recent years some venture capital funds have widened their portfolios to include new ventures which are not quite as involved in advanced technology as has been the case in the past.

Mezzanine capital funds are also called late-state investment funds. These organizations step in after a company has demonstrated progress in the early stages but has an additional need for venture capital. Some of the larger venture capital funds have recently added an increment of mezzanine financing to their portfolios.

The usual form of investment of both types of venture capital funds is the purchase of preferred stock which is convertible on a one-for-one basis into common stock should the company succeed and be acquired or go public. The preferred stock does not pay a dividend but does have a liquidation preference. Because these funds invest at a time of great risk, they normally want anywhere from 30 percent to 50 percent of the total stock ownership of the company. But it should be noted that their investments are not in the form of debt, that there is no interest-payment burden involved, and that they usually allow some facilitating bank debt to be used as the company progresses. Occasionally, to help management over a rough period, these funds may make some interim advances which can be converted into stock during the next round of financing.

Private investment companies, while quite a factor a generation ago, have not proliferated in the same way as the venture capital funds. They range from loosely knit private syndicates to organizations which function on a continuous integrated program of making loan and stock investments. Frequently they make secured loans and ask for warrants to purchase stock in the future. Bankers and financial consultants are usually in contact with these sources in a particular local area. Some are fairly well known, such as Amsterdam Pacific in San Francisco, American Research and Development Corp. in Boston, and General Electric Corp. nationally.

The Small Business Administration

Many government agencies have been designed to assist small business, but, by directly attacking the financial problems of young growth companies, the Small Business Administration (SBA) has probably been the most effective. After World War II, as big companies grew ever bigger, dominating the American economy, legislators in Washington saw a need to give small business a boost. Congress set up the SBA in 1953 to succeed the Small Defense Plants Association, organized at the beginning of the Korean War. Prior to the formation of the SBA, lending functions of this type had been handled by the depression-born Reconstruction Finance Corporation; but while RFC loans were initially emergency or restorative measures, SBA loans were designed to be constructive and forward-going.

Many professionals in the financial field originally disputed the fact, but there is now almost universal acceptance of the need that the SBA was founded to meet: the inability of small businesses to obtain funded debt. Both with public issues and institutional private placements there is a prerequisite of relative bigness. A small business may be able to borrow short term — if at all — but has very few avenues of appeal for loans of more than a few years' duration.

Some of the early objections to the SBA were founded on the suspicion that this agency would put the government into direct competition with banks and other financing institutions. The act contains provisions which practically make such a claim invalid; moreover, after the first few years of its existence, the SBA showed that it was designed to reinforce, rather than compete with the financial industry.

Before examining the particular lending gap which SBA fills, the definition of a "small" business should be understood. According to the SBA, small business is defined as follows:

- *Manufacturing* concerns if they employ fewer than 250 persons — although a firm which employs not more than 1,000 persons can still be considered eligible depending on a set of employment size standards which SBA has developed for particular industries.

- *Wholesale* concerns if their annual sales volumes are $5 million or less, or if they employ fewer than 100 people.

- *Retail* businesses if annual sales do not exceed $1.5 million.

Obviously, when you have outgrown these limitations, you should be well qualified to satisfy your financing needs from one of the many other sources mentioned in this book. Realistic members of the financial fraternity had to admit, from the inception of the SBA program, that small businesses could not obtain loans which included stated terms of repayment that could reasonably be met. The solution supplied by the SBA was well tailored to fit the situation: While existing resources provide short-term loans, primarily unsecured, or secured by *current assets* such as accounts receivable, the SBA provides loans up to ten years, secured primarily by *fixed assets*. Here the contention is that, given the breathing time afforded by reasonable repayment requirements, a small business has a much better chance of reaching successful maturity.

The SBA provides a number of advisory and management information services. In this book, however, we are concerned only with the financing services it offers. The SBA makes and guarantees loans — very successful loans, if viewed by its historic records of loss. Yet many of these loans could not have been obtained elsewhere. Either because of form, term, or other criteria, no conventional lenders would have extended the credit on most of the loans which have performed so admirably.

It should be pointed out here that the SBA provides several kinds of loans:

- *Direct loans.* These loans are processed directly by the SBA and involve solely the use of SBA funds. The application (SBA Form 4) must state that the financing sought is otherwise unavailable, and this declaration must be supported by letters from one or more banks. Direct loans are limited to two groups: military service veterans and the handicapped.

- *Guaranteed loans.* The SBA will guarantee banks loans up to $500,000. The guarantee covers between 70 and 90 percent of the bank loan while the bank administers the loan.

The first step to initiate the procedure is to obtain from a commercial bank or from the SBA office nearest to you its regular application form.

This form contains a section in which a bank can indicate its desire to enter into a participation. Preparation of this form in proper and good order will provide a bank lending officer with the type of submission that deserves respect, if not credit approval.

If the credit is borderline, you still may be able to obtain the bank's participation. The reason is simple. Let us suppose you apply for a $40,000 loan for five years, primarily secured by equipment you own plus some special pieces you wish to acquire to handle your business. Most banks will not be enthusiastic about a fixed asset loan in this amount over such a long (for them) term. But when you point out that the SBA will take 90 percent of the loan, that the bank share will be a mere $4,000, the loan officer may see that, with this minor exposure, you may be able to use this more substantial financing to become a good future customer of the bank.

SBA Loan Characteristics

There is no minimum SBA-guaranteed loan, although most lenders do not lend amounts less than $50,000; the maximum is $500,000 to a single borrower. In recent years SBA-guaranteed loans have averaged $210,000. Proceeds from an SBA-guaranteed loan may go to a variety of business purposes, including working capital, inventory, machinery and equipment, leasehold improvements and the acquisition or construction of commercial business property.

Interest on SBA-guaranteed loans may not exceed New York prime plus 2¾ percent. Terms vary from five to seven years for working capital loans, ten years for loans on fixed assets, and 25 years for real estate acquisitions.

As compared to the fixed asset growth capital financing described in earlier chapters, the SBA takes a somewhat different approach to evaluation of collateral than that followed by institutional and commercial finance lenders. The SBA loan processors use market value appraisals in setting up loans secured by equipment; in fact, they are directed not even to refer to auction value in their processing. The usual range of advance against this value is 70 percent to 80 percent amortized over the life of the loan. Of course, other general credit criteria — for example, ability to repay — are considered by the processor.

While it is preferable that the cash flow needed for repayment of the loan be proven by past performance, the SBA recognizes that the funds it provides or guarantees can make the sole difference in making changes in a business which will create future cash flow to repay the placement. Therefore, a well-prepared cash flow projection may satisfy the loan processor in this regard. In fact, a projection is required with each SBA loan application, whether or not adequate cash flow has been proven by past experience. The accompanying table is a simple example of such a projection.

The SBA has two programs intended to encourage more modest applications. Under the small loan program loans in amounts up to $15,000 are made up to maximum terms of six years at 5½ percent simple interest. The processing is more streamlined on these loans, and, even though the collateral may be borderline in value, an applicant may obtain approval if the future appears bright and if the applicant's character and history are good.

Recently the SBA has added still another type of loan to its offerings, the very small business loan. Sometimes referred to as the six-for-six, this category covers loans not in excess of $6,000 over a maximum term of six years. Once again, the application procedure is very streamlined, bare minimum documentation is required, and even greater emphasis is placed on the individual character and reputation for integrity of the applicant.

Small Business Investment Companies

The Small Business Investment Companies (SBICs), which were set up by an act of Congress in 1958 under the jurisdiction of the Small Business Administration, may prove one of the most important sources of private placements and funded debt for small businesses. By this act, the government has encouraged the establishment of privately owned investment companies, which run their own

Proposed A.B.C. Corporation

PROJECTED STATEMENT OF INCOME AND CASH AVAILABLE
(cents omitted)

	July 1993 and prior	Aug. 1993	Sept. 1993	Oct. 1993	Nov. 1993	Dec. 1993	Jan. 1994	Total
SALES	$100,000	$200,000	$400,000	$500,000	$500,000	$200,000	$100,000	$2,000,000
COST OF GOODS SOLD								
Beginning inventory	$ 0	$190,000	$380,000	$475,000	$395,000	$207,500	$132,500	$ 0
Labor	56,876	66,252	61,252	26,876	0	0	0	211,256
Material and other	170,624	198,748	183,748	80,624	0	0	0	633,744
Total	$227,500	$455,000	$625,000	$582,500	$395,000	$207,500	$132,500	$ 845,000
Ending inventory	190,000	380,000	475,000	395,000	207,500	132,500	95,000	95,000
COST OF GOODS SOLD	$ 37,500	$ 75,000	$150,000	$187,500	$187,500	$ 75,000	$ 37,500	$ 750,000
GROSS PROFIT	$ 62,500	$125,000	$250,000	$312,500	$312,500	$125,000	$ 62,500	$1,250,000
SELLING AND ADMINISTRATIVE EXPENSES	33,000	66,000	132,000	165,000	165,000	66,000	33,000	660,000
(Before income taxes) NET INCOME	$ 29,500	$ 59,000	$118,000	$147,500	$147,500	$ 59,000	$ 29,500	$ 590,000
CASH ADJUSTMENTS								
Add: Accounts receivable at beginning of month	0	100,000	200,000	400,000	500,000	500,000	200,000	0
Accounts payable at end of month	170,624	198,748	183,748	80,624	0	0	0	0
Less: Accounts receivable at end of month	100,000	200,000	400,000	500,000	500,000	200,000	100,000	100,000
Accounts payable at beginning of month	0	170,624	198,748	183,748	80,624	200,000	100,000	0
CASH AVAILABLE OR (SHORT)	$100,124	$ (12,876)	$ (97,000)	$ (55,624)	$ 66,876	$359,000	$129,500	$ 490,000

1: No provision has been made in this projection for federal income taxes.

2: The operating cash requirements peak to $65,376 at the end of October, 1993.

the government has encouraged the establishment of privately owned investment companies, which run their own businesses and make their own credit decisions, to provide funded debt to American small businesses ("small" within the framework of the definitions given earlier).

Once again, this offshoot of the SBA is attempting to provide the type of needed business capital which is not generally available to growth companies — namely, long-term capital. While the SBA lends only to going businesses, SBIC's may also fund start-ups. SBIC funds may be provided on a secured basis as a loan against collateral, as unsecured general obligations partially convertible into stock, as loan and stock combinations, or as straight stock equity placements. To provide the profit needed in private enterprise, the SBICs are allowed to charge higher fees than the SBA. Interest may be fairly low where warrants or other kickers are present — such as the case with convertible debentures — or it may be 10 percent per annum or higher (SBICs are limited to a maximum of 15 percent *cost of money*, which must include all service or administrative fees as well as interest). But the SBA officials connected with the SBIC program point out that small business is not hurt by interest but by term. I completely agree. The cost of money should always yield sufficient profit to make the acceptance of capital worthwhile; only the need of unrealistically accelerated loan repayments can hurt a business which is making profits as the result of a particular financing.

SBIC loans must be for at least five years, and the terms can extend as long as 20. These funds therefore create growth and profit potentials which would otherwise be unattainable for many small businesses. To make this possible, the SBA helps to provide capital to the SBICs in a special way prescribed by the act itself.

SBICs have already advanced more than $500 million to about 10,000 small businesses. An SBIC can invest up to $500,000 — or not to exceed 20 percent of its capital, whichever is less — in the business of a single client. Although convertibles and various types of equity are purchased by the SBICs, they are prevented by law from acquiring more than 49 percent of a company. An SBIC, by this simple restriction, is obviously expected to be an investor, a lender, or both — but not to emerge as the owner and operator of a business by virtue of having achieved controlling interest.

As mentioned above, the SBA helps provide some of the funds which SBICs, in turn, place with their clients. This is done by the purchase of an SBIC debenture by the SBA. The SBA can purchase debentures equal to the entire capital of an SBIC, therefore matching the investment, up to a maximum of $700,000. In other words, if an SBIC has its own capital of $700,000, the SBIC can place another $700,000 debenture with the SBA. This debenture is subordinated and therefore would provide a total of $1.4 million subordinated worth to another lender, such as a bank.

In fact, the SBA can also lend or guarantee up to 50 percent of the worth (including the subordinated SBA debenture) to an SBIC. Both the debentures and the loans can have maturities as long as twenty years, and bear interest of 5 percent.

With its fairly high capital cost, it is obvious that an SBIC would find it difficult to make much of a profit simply on the differential between loan cost and loan return. This is quite proper because the whole concept of an SBIC is to establish capital gains by investing in companies with good growth potential.

Many members of the financial fraternity have felt that, because the really lucrative capital gain SBIC investments have been relatively few, the SBICs would move closer to routine loans and away from the semi-equity investments they were meant to provide. Actually this has not been the case. The recipients of SBIC funds cover almost the entire spectrum of American industry.

A list of SBIC companies in any area can be obtained from the nearest SBA office. While coming under the licensing jurisdiction of the SBA, the SBICs have far greater latitude in their autonomous granting of credit. For this reason, the SBIC should be considered when flexibility and non-stereotype applications are desired. An SBIC can — and frequently does — subordinate its loan position; SBA loans may not be subordinated. All SBA loans can be prepaid without penalty. This is a matter of individual negotiation with the SBICs.

We have already mentioned that SBIC loans can have longer terms than those allowable to the SBA. But the most important single difference — and that element which is most definitive about the uniqueness of the SBIC practices — is the fact that, either by use of an original security, or by later conversion into such a security, SBICs do take equity positions.

Institutional Placements

Most of the modern private placements with institutions such as insurance companies and pension funds utilize debentures or senior notes. Almost invariably such financing can only be obtained if the applicant has — or will have as a result of the placement — an unsecured bank line of credit. This introduces into the picture a current lender who will be watching the financial condition of the borrower on a 90-day basis, and this provides some protection to the long-term lender who provides the private placement funds. For this reason the institutional lender may sometimes provide a subordination of its funds to banks and financial institutions who extend short-term current financing programs.

It is true that private placements vary in term very widely, but there is a strong trend for institutions to make their growth capital available largely on terms of twelve to fifteen years. The notes or debentures which run such a term usually do not require a sinking fund in the classic sense. Instead, since the financing is based on the general soundness and growth potential of the borrower, it is assumed that future profits will provide the necessary cash flow to meet debt repayment schedules. To assure the generation of the cash flow required, the modern private placement will usually defer all principal repayments beyond the first two or three years of the total term. As the institutions view it, this deferment actually creates a sinking fund of sorts.

For example, take a private placement made by an insurance company in the amount of $1 million with a term of twelve years. During the first two years of the loan the recipient would pay interest only, making no principal reductions whatever. Beginning with the third year, however, the recipient would be required to make payments of $100,000 plus interest on the unpaid balance. After making such payments for ten years — which would be twelve years from the time the loan had been first extended — the placement is paid off in full.

Typical institutional private placements as described above are limited in amount according to the *bottom line capital* of the applicant. The bottom line consists primarily of the common stock and surplus found in the capital section of the balance sheet. If there is preferred stock in the corporate picture, and if this is clearly subordinate to the placement, the paid-in value of the preferred stock will also be considered as part of bottom line equity (the institution can always place in its indenture a restriction against calling the preferred before the private placement is repaid).

Relatively young growth companies, particularly those applying for their first private placement, will find that they will be limited to a senior subordinated placement not in excess of 50 percent of their bottom line equities. Further, depending on their net current asset position, such companies will be able to obtain bank lines equal to, or somewhat greater than, the private placement amount. Therefore, a corporation with $2 million bottom line equity and net current asset position of $2.5 million might have a capital availability picture as follows:

Unsecured bank line	$1,250,000
Debenture placement	1,000,000
Capital and surplus	2,000,000
Total capital availability	$4,250,000

Pre-Placement Preparations

Before seeking a private placement you should be well prepared along specific lines. The preparation is similar to that earlier described for term loans, but more refined. Once again, do not underestimate the importance of submitting a well-prepared proposal to the fund source. Depending on the size of the credit being sought, the financial information should be as full as possible.

The lender will want to analyze your picture in two directions—backward and forward. The lender will want to see your financial statements, both balance sheet and profit and loss, for the previous three to five years, along with a projection of your future operations with emphasis on two factors: 1) your *cash need* projection, which is the demonstration of your requirement for the funds being sought, and 2) your *cash flow* projection, which illustrates how the funds will be created to repay the loan.

A.B.C. Company
FINANCIAL STATISTICS AND FIVE-YEAR FORECAST
(thousands omitted)

	Actual					Projected		
	Yr. End Dec. 90	Yr. End Dec. 91	Yr. End Dec. 92	Yr. End Dec. 93	Yr. End Dec. 94	Yr. End Dec. 95	Yr. End Dec. 96	Yr. End Dec. 97
Net sales	$ 146	$ 490	$ 906	$ 1,600	$ 2,500	$ 3,500	$ 5,000	$ 6,000
Cost of sales	106	345	824	1,137	1,750	2,450	3,500	4,200
Gross Profit	40	144	82	462	750	1,050	1,500	1,800
Sales expense	24	99	200	223	325	455	650	780
General and administrative	21	38	50	111	175	245	350	420
Operating profit (loss)	(5)	7	(168)	128	250	350	500	600
Other expenses	(1)	6	4	22	32	45	50	50
NET PROFIT (LOSS)	(4)	1	172	106	218	305	450	500
Federal Income Taxes	0	0	0	0	72	152	230	280
ASSETS:								
Cash	$ 14	$ 40	$ 17	$ 10	$ 20	$ 30	$ 50	$ 70
Receivables	60	71	146	255	380	550	700	850
Inventories	56	124	151	200	500	700	900	1,200
Prepaids, etc.	8	19	19	12	20	30	50	80
Total current assets	138	254	333	477	920	1,310	1,700	2,200
Fixed assets	37	93	162	260	400	550	800	1,000
Less depreciation	(2)	(14)	(33)	(101)	(200)	(350)	(500)	(700)
Other	28	22	63	5	10	20	30	50
TOTAL ASSETS	$ 201	$ 355	$ 526	$ 641	$ 1,130	$ 1,530	$ 2,030	$ 2,550
LIABILITIES:								
Trade Payables	55	31	118	103	150	200	250	300
Accruals	6	16	38	38	60	80	100	150
Total current commitments	61	47	156	141	210	280	350	450
Debt—Bank loan	0	0	140	160	300	440	560	680
Debt—Other	34	10	25	19		0	0	0
Capital—stock	110	110	119	120	145	145	145	145
Capital—Surplus	0	192	261	270	270	270	270	270
Earned Surplus	(4)	(3)	(175)	(69)	77	230	450	720
Total stockholders' equity	$ 106	$ 299	$ 205	$ 321	$ 492	$ 645	$ 865	$ 1,135
Capital needed	0	0	0	0	$ 128	$ 165	$ 255	$ 285

The accompanying table is an example of how one company tackled this problem. The illustration is unique in that the applicant included some of his historic figures alongside his projection. Actually, he had also provided regulation financial statements for three years of operations prior to the forecast. But he repeated these in a summarized form to illustrate the continuity of the trend into the forecast portion. You will also note that the illustration includes both profit and loss and balance sheet information. All this is correlated to create the cash need requirement developed along the bottom line of the report. Properly done, the illustration should have been carried out for several years more, to show how the cash flow profits at the $6 million sales figure postulated to stabilize at the end of 1994 would create the funds required to repay the $285,000 capital being sought to satisfy the capital need.

While cash need and cash flow projections can be prepared fairly simply for smaller placement applications, the firm's accountants should be given this task where more substantial financings are being sought. Also, if the amount of capital sought is in the range of institutional placements (from $250,000 up) it is advisable to use a financial consultant or investment banker for this purpose. As is mentioned in connection with several other types of financing covered in this book, these professionals are experienced and well qualified in the eyes of the lenders who give serious consideration to their recommendations. The business owner who is not familiar with these channels can make a few false starts and, when this is done, the word somehow drifts through the financial community that the deal is being "shopped around" — a phrase which almost always dashes all hope for a private placement. In one case I know of, the president of a privately owned steel company, whose statement and earnings history undoubtedly deserved a private placement from any first-rate institutional lender in the country, made up 20 presentation packages for a million-dollar debenture and mailed them to an equal number of investment bankers and life insurance companies. Not realizing this, one of the investment bankers called on an insurance company that had received one of the presentation packages and was dismayed when the insurance company loan officer said he had already heard of the deal. As a result, both the loan officer and the investment banker decided the deal was being shopped around. The word spread through the financial community, and the steel company lost all chance for the placement it sought. The cost of professional handling is only a small percent of the total placement but, once mishandled as in this case, no professional will accept the assignment regardless of the fee. The brokerage charges for a $1 million placement, for example, will range from 1½ percent to 2½ percent, with the percentage varying in proportion to larger or smaller fund requests.

Real Estate Investment Trusts (REITs)

Real estate investment trusts (REITs) were created by federal legislation in the 1960s. Congress wished to establish a corporate format which would enable many small investors to have, in effect, direct real estate investments. By providing the ability to own a small piece of larger properties, Congress hoped to give the small investor access to high quality, low risk real estate investments. In an effort to insure that the trust would not be dominated by major players, the legislation stipulated that, in effect, no single investor or affiliated group could own more than 5 percent of the trust.

Other provisions were also expected to benefit the small investor, including an exemption from corporate taxes. The REIT was required to distribute to shareholders 95 percent of its annual income, and the shareholder paid personal taxes on the income received. In some cases that income would be partially designated as capital gain or return of capital — resulting in a lower overall tax obligation to the investor, who also avoided the usual double taxation on stock dividends from an ordinary corporation.

As has frequently been the case with well-intended legislation, the first decade of REIT operations was full of abuses and poor management. One of the outstanding failures was sponsored by Chase Manhattan Bank in New York. The primary cause of the failure was poor investment judgment — financing speculation in raw land and investing in poorly researched development properties. Fortunately REITs learned a lesson, and today they form a good pool of funding for worthwhile projects and business operations.

In forming REITs, the promoters usually arrange for the purchase of a group of income producing properties to be financed by a public offering of stock. As the REIT grows, more funding can be obtained through bank lines, institutional debt placements and subsequent equity and debt underwritings. Investors are interested in buying the securities because they offer above-average income. Dividends of REIT common stocks generally range from 6½ percent to 11⅕ percent with some tax benefits to the investor.

As a source of business finance REITs tend to provide long term funding based on sale and leaseback of real estate or on long term mortgage loans. The characteristics of REIT financing are as follows:

- Real property, including land and buildings, is either sold to the REIT or subjected to a long term first mortgage.

- The REIT is not permitted to purchase or lend against other types of assets such as equipment.

- REITs are prohibited from operating any business to which they have advanced funds; however, they have the right to demand regular reports of operating results from the clients, usually on a quarterly basis.

- Whether the funding is accomplished by sale and leaseback or by first mortgage notes, there is a provision for the REIT to share a small part of the growth of the client and, coincidentally, to protect itself against inflation. This is accomplished by giving the REIT an annual payment of about 5 percent of the *increase* in net revenues (not total net revenues, but only the increase).

- Mortgages are usually long term, with maturities going out 15 or 20 years. Sale-leasebacks may have an initial leased term of ten years or more and usually give the client the option to renew the lease for several five-year terms at agreed-upon rentals.

- Since the REIT bases the amount of funding on a property on its income generating capability (economic appraisal), REIT financing can provide considerably higher advances on properties than traditional institutional mortgage lenders.

- The cost of funding from REITs, whether in the form of loan interest or lease payments, is usually quite competitive. REITs are players in the competitive financial market field, so their rates are set by the condition of the money market at the time a deal is made with a client. Rates are usually set at 150 to 300 *basis points* — that is, 1½ percent to 3 percent — above the ten year U.S. Treasury bond rate. For example, if Treasury bonds are yielding 6 percent interest, REIT rates would range from 7½ percent to 9 percent per annum.

For the business which can benefit from allocating most of its financial resources to its operational needs to support growth, the ability to release funds tied up in relatively nonproductive plant or real estate investment can be beneficial.

There is also a more advanced use of REITs in larger situations — the spinoff of a substantial group of properties by a large public company. I have been involved with a $500 million spinoff which gave the corporation a lower leasing cost than the depreciation which had previously reduced reportable bottom line and per share earnings. Such a situation develops when the spun-off properties have been owned for some years and, although the book value has been decreased by depreciation, the annual depreciation charge has remained the same as it was when the property was first acquired. In fact, if the property has been greatly depreciated but well maintained, it can be sold to a REIT at a reportable profit above book value while not increasing the annual fixed charges. A number of public companies have actually packaged large groups of spinoffs to form a standalone REIT, take it public, and use the cash proceeds of the public offering to pay the corporation for the spinoffs. In the right situation this strategy can be quite beneficial.

CHAPTER 12
PUBLIC STOCK ISSUES

Companies that have progressed through various stages of financial growth achieve the ultimate by *going public*. Almost every discussion about public stock issues goes into a standard lineup of pros and cons. Yet here I disagree with many of my colleagues in the financial fraternity; it is my opinion that all discussion on this subject is academic. Putting it very simply and positively, I feel that once a business has reached the stage where it qualifies for a *properly designed* public stock issue, no other form of financing can provide as much benefit.

The advantages of a public stock issue are as follows:

1. *Capitalization of earnings.* As you will see below, the evaluation of a corporation going public is based on its earnings. So long as a company remains privately held, any value based on what its earnings might impart is only a vague guess as to what a potential sellout would bring. The establishment of a public market for the stock firmly establishes the going business value of the company.

2. *Estate benefits.* As mentioned immediately above, the estate of a principal owner of a business is fairly and accurately evaluated. This can benefit the principal even while living. In the event of a buyout of other principals, a firm valuation is established which functions even better than the standard "buy and sell" agreements between principals which are invoked when there are irreconcilable differences, or when one principal wishes to retire and the remaining active principals do not wish to see a large block of stock get out of their hands. In case of death of a principal, there are benefits both to the surviving principals and to the heirs of the deceased. The heirs are not subject to an arbitrary evaluation of the going business made by Treasury Department agents to determine inheritance taxes. Valuable equities in going firms have had to be sold to meet such taxes.

On the other hand, the government agents can rarely argue the value of stock whose worth is set by the price at which it is traded over a wide public market. Further, the existence of an active public market makes possible the disposal without undue sacrifice of a portion of the stock in an estate to take care of the taxes needed to retain the balance. Not long ago I was consulted by the owners of a small chain of super-markets who, several years before, had had to dispose of their most successful single retail unit when a partner died and they had to raise money to buy his stock. Had this been a public company, the lucrative store could have been retained.

3. *Financial leverage.* Most public financing is either in the form of stock which becomes a *permanent* part of capital, or senior securities which have long amortiz-ations or conversions. They do not represent debt in the usual sense, as do other forms of financing. Therefore, in addition to the funds received from the public financing itself, a public issue also provides for far more capital leverage. For example, a private company with $1 million net worth might be able to borrow $600,000 on a reasonable basis. After a pub-lic issue which creates an additional $1 million in stock equity, a long-term debenture could be obtained for another $3 million plus another $1.5 million in unsecured bank borrowings. As compared to the original $600,000 availability, the $1 million stock issue actually creates a total availability of $5.5 million in financing.

4. *Acquisition potential.* The use of the stock of a public corporation is most helpful in making payments for acquisitions. Any corporation is allowed to use treasury stock — or to issue more stock — for value received. Acquisition of another company repre-sents such value. Moreover, purchase advantages can result from use of stock to acquire a privately owned company. The stock of public companies is usually priced by the market on a multiple higher than is accorded to private companies. For example, a private company earning $100,000 after taxes would do well to be evaluated at $700,000 in an acquisition. A public company can easily have a mul-tiple of ten to twenty times earnings placed on its stock by the public after it has been out on the mar-ket. Assuming a relatively low multiple of ten times

earnings for the public company, obviously the public company would be using "70-cent dollars" to purchase the private company.

5. *Personal gain for principals.* The capitalization of earnings mentioned previously accrues benefits to the principals of a company that goes public. Not only is stock sold to provide additional corporate capital, but it is also sold for the account of principals. The sale of principals' stock (see *secondary selling* below) produces capital gains income which can, at one fell swoop, put more cash dollars in the pocket of a principal than many years' ordinary salary drawings could produce. A correct basis of comparison would involve a principal whose corporate salary places him in a 50 percent tax bracket. Additional drawings — or dividends — will raise the tax bracket even higher. Such a principal who sells only sufficient stock to yield $450,000 would realize net cash of $300,000 after 33 percent capital gains taxes.[1] In the form of higher drawings or dividends, the same principal could take ten or more years to develop as much after-tax cash.

Against such an array of advantages most objections are easy to discount. Control is not lost, as some detractors claim; usually initial public offerings do not even involve a majority of a corporation's stock. Moreover, as corporations grow and issue more stock, 30 percent or less can constitute working control. This is because well-managed issues spread the stock widely and the individual public stockholders hold infinitesimal percentages (on which they invariably vote the proxies for existing management). As the pros say, if an outsider tries to buy up enough stock to seize control, the effort will drive the price of your own stock so high that you may be delighted to take your fortune and depart.

Types of Registrations

Public issues of stock require *registration* with government agencies. Although there are a number of different types of registration, commercial businesses seeking financing via this route generally use only the following three variations:

---

[1] The tax on capital gains has varied, at times falling as low as 20 percent.

- *Intrastate registrations.* Not all stock issues require registration with the Securities and Exchange Commission. The exceptions are those issues involving sales of stocks to bona fide residents of only one particular state. These are not found nearly as often as are the other two major forms of registration described below, and the services of investment bankers are not usually employed. Special purposes are served by these limited registrations, particularly when the funds are to be used entirely for corporate capital, where principals are not initially concerned about a national public market, and where the size of the issue varies from $50,000 to a few million dollars. With an effective registration of this type, local advertising and solicitation can be used to generate stock subscriptions. There is usually a time limit for solicitations and, until the expiration of this limit, all funds received are usually impounded. Filing, accounting, and other registration requirements vary depending on state regulations.

- *Regulation A Issues.* This is the *short form* type of registration with the S.E.C. It is suitable for modest-size public financings which still come under the scope of a national registration. Under Regulation A, stock may be sold to the public in an issue whose total amount may not exceed $1.5 million. Although, as is true for any kind of registration, the services of an investment banker are not required, they are usually employed in short-form issues. Regulation A requires the printing of a prospectus which can be much simpler than is required in a full registration. Also, the financial statements do not have to go back as far in the past, nor do they have to be fully audited. The general theory behind the short-form registration is, of course, to save cost in a small issue. But this saving can be less than anticipated. The usual cost will frequently be as much as 15 percent of the gross amount of the issue. Despite this factor, there is still much to be said in favor of the short form for a small issue.

- *Full Registration.* Beyond a gross offer to sell $1.5 million of stock publicly, a full registration, or "S-1," is required to be filed with the S.E.C. In addition to a detailed printed prospectus, the filing requires fully audited financial reports plus written documentation of the facts stated in the prospectus. Investment bankers are almost always used for underwriting the issue, and legal counsel both for the corporation and for the underwriters must be retained in preparing the prospectus. All major issues, and those handled by the better underwriters, require full registrations. The dollar cost of preparation of the issue may be higher but, depending on the total size of the offering, the percentage cost will probably be less than that of a Regulation A issue.

Types of Securities

We have covered in considerable detail, in Chapter 3, the many types of securities which can be sold by a corporation. All of these varieties can be offered in a public issue; however, the nature of the public market is such that the choice of securities to be sold is practically limited to just a few standard types. The older, well-established public companies may reflect wide varieties of securities on their statements, but a corporation that is going public for the first time would be ill advised to attempt to market all but a few types of securities. Preferred stock, for example, has experienced diminishing popularity during the past twenty years. Investors in young corporations are likewise not much interested in taking senior securities. If they seek lower-risk investments, they can find such opportunities in stable, established companies. Instead, the investor in a younger company which goes public for the first time prefers to have the growth and gain potential represented by common stock.

Therefore, if a new issue (IPO, or *initial public offering*) does not consist solely of common stock, it usually is designed to allow for ownership of at least some common stock, at the outset or in the future. One variation is the issuance of convertible debentures which provide a good interest income and senior position at the outset, but with the right to convert into common stock at a price 15 percent to 25 percent higher than the IPO share price. Debentures which may or may not be convertible are sometimes packaged in unitized combinations that give the investor the right to purchase common stock at a very reasonable price — but only in a certain ratio to the debentures the investor must also purchase.[2] Returning to our earlier statement, however, the most desirable new issue is the straight common stock offering. The corporation commissioners of many states are becoming increasingly unenthusiastic about nonvoting stock.

There is, however, one acceptable variation — the use of two classes of common stock for dividend purposes. Modest cash dividend features enhance some new stock issues; however, the payment of cash dividends on all the common shares of a corporation may remove needed growth capital. The corporate principals — who enjoy substantial salaries and who still own the majority of corporate stock — would prefer to see the value of their shares enhanced through retention of surplus rather than to receive dividends on their own stock. Therefore, if the stock issued to the public carries a dividend, the stock retained by the principals might not have a dividend feature. In subsequent years, management could be allowed to exchange, say, 20 percent each year for the dividend-bearing stock. In five years all outstanding stock becomes one-class dividend-paying common stock and will pose no problems in future distributions of principals' stock.

Choice of an Underwriter

Underwriters of public stock issues are found primarily in the security dealer field. Security dealers place this particular function into a group of activities which they perform and to which they refer as *investment banking.* Almost any brokerage firm holding valid security dealer licenses may handle an underwriting; however, there are some practical limitations. The great majority of securities firms are members of the National Association of Security Dealers (NASD). This organization, with offices in the principal financial communities, restricts its members from engaging in various types of transactions with nonmember firms. Since most public stock offerings involve a syndicate of more than one underwriting firm, it is almost essential that you choose a member firm of the NASD (see below).

Security brokerage firms tend to concentrate in certain specialties. Some handle only the investment accounts of

[2]For example, the investor who buys a $1,000 debenture bond is also allowed to buy 100 shares of common stock at $1.00 each.

institutions. Others concentrate in bonds, and another category forms the group of well-known national retailers of stock in the open market, utilizing many branch offices scattered throughout the country and staffed with *registered representatives*. While the head offices of such firms may have corporate departments equipped to handle underwritings, there is usually not an effective organizational link between these departments and the stock-retailing oriented representatives in the local branch offices. There is another group of very strong investment houses, primarily located in the Wall Street area in New York, which have few branch offices, but which have the power to sponsor substantial offerings. All along the scale are houses of various strength and scope, local or national, which can handle issues of varying magnitudes and qualitative levels.

A veritable hierarchy exists in the investment banking fraternity. At the theoretical top are a few firms handling only very substantial and important clients, and they are practically in the position of taking on no new clients. Other substantial houses are open to better quality new offerings — and so on down the line. The hierarchy extends to the underwriting syndicate where normally only firms of the same level are found in the management group. There is even an implied hierarchy in the placing of brokerage firm names on the prospectus. In a comanagement, the left-hand position is supposed to carry more prestige than the right-hand position on the same line.

Without going into further detail, there are certain things a business should look for in a prospective underwriter. The underwriter should be able to handle the *takedown requirement* (see below) readily, should be capable of forming a representative syndicate, and above all, should have demonstrated a certain moral responsibility. As you will presently see, public issues can involve much work and expense before an actual binding contract is executed. It is significant, therefore, that the business whose stock will be offered have as much assurance as possible that informal understandings will be faithfully implemented.

The Finder's Role

The role of a *finder* in an underwriting is a uniquely productive one, and its usage has been long established. For this reason the presence of a finder, particularly in first issues, is widespread. Generally a finder is an individual such as a financial consultant or a professional in the financial community whose other activities do not include a direct involvement in actual stock underwriting firms. Not only should the finder be well grounded in the entire field of business finance, but in this instance he or she should be well acquainted with the roles and positions of many investment banking firms. As described above, the hierarchy and varying functions of brokerage firms are both diverse and esoteric; therefore, someone who can authoritatively recommend the right firm is of definite value. Further, the experience and contacts of a well qualified finder gain easy audiences with investment banking decision makers who respect the finder's recommendations and know that he or she has used seasoned judgment in screening the application before presenting it. Also, as in many other types of presentations, an objective third party can frequently sound the praises of a business more effectively than its own principals can.

Acting as a consultant, the finder can advise when, and if, a company is ripe for an IPO. If it is, the finder can advise how to avoid certain future investment banker objections and problem areas, and how to initiate the preparatory stages, which can last a year or more. During the introduction to, and negotiation with, the underwriter the finder primarily serves as protagonist for the corporation.

Finders' fees range from ¾ percent to 1½ percent of the gross amount of the issue. They are frequently paid by the underwriters, or partially or wholly by the corporation. All investment bankers recognize the role of the finder and will join with the corporation in working out a satisfactory compensation package. Normally, on the basis of having made a good underwriting possible, and also of having provided criteria from experience against which the deal can be evaluated properly, the cost of the finder is more than offset.

Types of Commitments

There are three variations of underwriting commitments:

- *Best Efforts.* The underwriter will commit to use its best efforts to sell a certain amount of stock at a specified price. There is no guarantee that all of the contemplated issue will be sold — or that *any* of it will be sold. But an investment banking firm will not allow its name to appear on a prospectus, even on only a best-efforts basis, if it feels little chance of success. A certain time limit is established, during which the stock may continue to be sold. All proceeds from the sale are impounded until the selling period terminates. Though it is not the best possible solution, the best-efforts commitment may be the only route available to an aspiring company. It is also frequently used when a company underwrites its own intrastate issue.

- *All or Nothing.* In this type of commitment the proceeds from sale of stock are impounded as in the best efforts offerings; however, if the predetermined total issue is not sold, all sales are reversed and money is returned to the would-be purchasers. Some firm commitments (see below) are written on a contract which includes the phrase *all or none,* but the actual condition is quite different.

- *Firm Commitment.* By far the most desirable commitment is a *firm takedown.* In underwriter's parlance, a takedown is the amount of stock which the underwriter contractually agrees to buy, for resale to others. Under the conditions of a firm commitment, the underwriter agrees to purchase the entire stock issue at a fixed price on a specified date. Because of the work and expense involved in many full registrations, plus the inevitable publicity and possible repercussions, most substantial issues should not be undertaken except in anticipation of a firm commitment. As you will see below, however, this type of commitment is not contractually established until well along in the public stock offering process.

Pricing the Stock

As I have described in the earlier chapters on equity capital and acquisitions, evaluating a company for the purposes of a public stock issue is almost always based on an *earnings multiple.* The multiple, which is applied only to after-tax corporate earnings, is usually set on the most recent fiscal year-end profits. Since most companies that go public demonstrate a consistent growth curve, the use of the current earnings figure provides the most advantageous pricing base. S.E.C. requirements call for certified accounting figures as far back as five years, if available, and a company that hopes to sell stock publicly in the future should try to anticipate well in advance so that the CPA firm doing the audit will be able to provide the type of unqualified audit the S.E.C. insists on. It will be on the most recent unqualified audit after-tax profit that the multiple will be set. Although it is permissible to show subsequent quarter profits in the prospectus, the underwriters normally set the price only on a full year's figures (or occasionally on the most recent trailing four quarters).

Prior to May 1962, a new issue boom occurred in stock offerings, during which earnings multiples were set at ridiculously high levels. When the bubble burst, not only did the multiples settle down to more realistic levels, but also many high-priced issues sagged drastically from their issue price. Both underwriters and corporate executives learned a lesson from this sad history; as a result, the outlandish overpricing of a new issue may be a thing of the past.

It must be remembered that a first public stock issue for a previously private company comes into the market at a *negotiated price.* The price is set as the result of an agreement between the underwriters and the issuing corporation. Thereafter, once the stock is out on the market and is stabilized, it sets its own level, by the simple rule of supply and demand. It is true that certain stocks sell for as high as thirty times earnings or more; however, these are stocks which have been out on the public market and usually involve companies with outstanding growth potential. (There are also public companies whose stock trades on the market at four or five times earnings, sometimes at a price less than book value; these are companies whose profit potentials are downgrading.)

Generally speaking, IPOs are priced on a multiple of eight to twelve times per share earnings *before dilution.* Dilution results from the issuance of additional stock to the public. To understand how these figures are arrived at, let us follow the usual few steps taken in setting a stock offering price.

Assume that a corporation earns $150,000 net profit after taxes in its most recent fiscal year. If a ten times multiple were placed on company earnings, 100 percent of the corporation would be evaluated at $1.5 million. The corporation has 100,000 shares of common stock outstanding. Therefore, each share of stock has been priced at $15 ($1.5 million divided by 100,000 shares). Looking at it another way, each one of the 100,000 shares has earned $1.50 profit ($150,000 profit divided by 100,000 shares). Thus a

$15 price represents a ten times multiple on per share earnings of $1.50. So far, this computation has been on a before-dilution basis.

Now, let us assume that an additional 50,000 shares are authorized to be issued by the corporation, to be sold to the public in an underwriting. When these shares are added to the original 100,000 shares held by the principals of the company, the new total of outstanding shares is 150,000. The per share earnings (obtained by dividing $150,000 profit by the new total of 150,000 shares) are now $1 per share. Obviously there has been a one-third dilution as the result of the public issue. The *after dilution* multiple is therefore fifteen times earnings because the stock, as mentioned above, was sold at $15 per share.

While pre-dilution multiples may normally range from eight to twelve times earnings on first issues, after dilution multiples can vary widely. In the case cited above, where the after-dilution multiple came to fifteen times earnings, the underwriters might want to reduce the ten times pre-dilution multiple to avoid the higher multiples resulting from the dilution of such a large percentage of new stock being sold.

Of course, the range of multiples I have quoted are only guidelines and are subject to many qualitative adjustments. In some industries, particularly in the financial and banking fields, book value may have some influence on the multiple. More general with all industries, however, is the difference which can result from the presence of a long history of sustained earnings. High multiples are justified by the expectation of a future continuation of higher evaluation premium. For example, a fifty-year-old company may be evaluated at a 50 percent higher multiple than a company which, although it has the same earnings growth, has been in business less than five years.

Size of the Issue

There are two categories of selling which can be included in a public issue, as follows:

- *Primary selling*— the sale of stock which is issued by the corporation, in addition to its already existing stock, the proceeds of which go to the corporation.

- *Secondary selling* — the sale of stock already owned by principals and other shareholders of the corporation. No new stock is created by the corporation for

> this purpose; therefore, secondary selling *creates no dilution.* The proceeds of such sales go to the selling shareholders and not to the corporation.

Either one — or both — types of selling can be found in a common stock issue. The first category to be considered is primary selling for the corporation. Every responsible underwriter wants to be sure that, as a result of the public issue, the corporation seems to be adequately financed for the immediate future. Therefore, a careful analysis is made of corporate financial needs to determine, in a gross dollar amount, what would constitute an adequate addition to permanent equity capital. In the example we have previously used, $750,000 additional capital was raised for the corporation. At the same time, however, it is possible that some of the principal shareholders wished to obtain some capital gain and to put some cash in their own pockets. Therefore, another 25,000 shares — at $15 per share — were registered to be sold in the same issue for the benefit of the selling shareholders. This increment of secondary selling was acceptable to the underwriters. First, it caused no further dilution of the per share earnings. As explained above, the number of shares outstanding does not change as a result of secondary selling; only the names of the stockholders owning those shares change. In addition, the secondary selling added $375,000 to the issue to bring it to a total of $1,125,000, a respectable offering in the lower volume range. The additional 25,000 shares gave promise of providing a wider stockholder group, after the issue, than if only the shares for the corporation were sold.

Limitations

There are several limitations on secondary selling. If the underwriters will take down only a certain maximum dollar amount — and this maximum is wholly required to satisfy the financing needs of the corporation — the would-be selling shareholders will have to wait for another day. Actually, this is very seldom the case. A more serious limitation imposed by the underwriter is to avoid the appearance of a *bailout.* If principals sell too large a percentage of their stock holdings in a first issue, the public (and their stockbrokers) can become suspicious that these insiders of management are not optimistic about the future of the business and wish to unload. As a general rule, any offerings (in a single issue) in excess of 25 percent of the holdings of management, prior to the issue, risk appearing to be bailouts.

On the other side of the coin, principals must sometimes be induced to sell more of their shares than they originally intended, in order to secure a wide enough public stock holding. If, for example, only 20 percent of a company is held by the public, small possibility exists of an active market made in the stock after the issue, and the stock price can respond wildly and unnaturally to sell or buy orders for even small blocks of stock.

Principals must be willing to provide some of their shares to round out a first offering if the corporate financing requirements have been met and there would still be insufficient shares in the hands of the public to provide a decent *after market.*

There is one more consideration in determining the size of the issue. If the corporation desires listing on one of the recognized exchanges, it is important that sufficient shares are issued — and sold to a sufficient number of stockholders — to satisfy the minimum requirements of the stock exchanges on these points. The exchanges also have other requirements, including earnings levels, as a prerequisite to becoming listed.

Identity of Interests

Beyond the satisfaction of minimum requirements for listing, or for obtaining a sufficiently widespread public holding in the after market, it is wise to limit the size of the first public issue. Here we come to what I consider among the most important attitudes to be adopted in connection with going public.

First, a basic fact: *Whatever benefits the public stock-holders will also benefit the insiders.* The principals of a public corporation will inevitably find themselves in the same boat as their public stockholders. A reasonably priced first issue presents the possibility of a price rise in the after market. When the stock goes up, the public benefits — but so, also, do the insiders. In fact, the value of the unissued stock held by principals frequently appreciates far more significantly from after-market reaction than could have been achieved through attempts to negotiate a higher issue price with the underwriters.

Therefore, it is wise to limit the first issue in size, in recognition of the fact that subsequent issues will yield the higher values set by the public in the after market. Share-holders who, for example, sell 20 percent of their holdings for $1 million in a first issue may find they can obtain an additional $1 million from a second issue for the release of only 10 percent more of their stock.

The Cost of Going Public

The expenses of small public issues can be high, frequently 10 percent or more of the gross amount of the stock sale. But as the issue size increases, the cost becomes much more reasonable. The cost for a $1 million issue would include the following:

Special CPA audit for prospectus	$18,000
Corporate counsel	4,000
Underwriters' expenses and counsel	6,000
Prospectus and contract printing	7,000
Blue sky registration	2,000
	$47,000

The above expenses approach 5 percent of a $1 million issue. They would drop to 3 percent for a $2 million issue and 2 percent or less for issues over $3 million.

In addition the underwriter receives a commission, referred to in investment banking circles as the *spread,* or *concession.* Underwriting commissions vary from about 15 percent to 6 percent on common stock first issues. The higher range applies to small issues, such as those filed under Regulation A. Issues of a few million dollars generally do not require commission over 10 percent; thereafter, depending on size, the percentage drops lower.

Combining the preparation costs, shown above, with the underwriter's commission, a new issue for $3 million might be expected to have a total cost of about 10 percent, or $300,000.

The underwriter's commission is not nearly so high as it appears. This is because the fee is broken up — and passed down along the line in the underwriting syndicate — in a series of *reallowances.* The largest single portion of the fee will go to the individual registered representatives (stockbrokers) in the field who place the stock with their personal customers. Out of a 10 percent commission, the registered representative may get 4 percent, the selling group stock brokerage firms 3 percent, the underwriting group 1½ percent, and the managing underwriters 1½ percent.

Letter of Intent

When the corporation and underwriter have established at least a tentative interest in exploring the possibility of a public stock issue, arrangements are made to provide the underwriter with sufficient information and audit material to make a decision about going forward. Not only will the underwriter be concerned with the corporation, but also with the entire industry in which it functions, plus reviewing every possible economic area which can conceivably bear on the company under study. When the review is completed on a satisfactory basis, representatives of the underwriter and of the corporation will meet informally to discuss details of a possible deal. If there seems to be general agreement, the underwriter will forward a *letter of intent* to the prospective client.

The letter of intent is frequently misunderstood by those not actively engaged in the investment banking field. First of all, it is *not* a binding contract. Yet it is as close to a contract as either party can come, prior to a few days before the actual issue date for the public stock. As you will see, the actual underwriting contract is executed only at almost the very end of the underwriting process. There is no alternative. Until that time either party can walk away, with no further obligation. Yet a great deal of reliance can be placed on a letter of intent from an ethical brokerage firm. The letter contains various contingencies and *market outs*, but it is a fact that an ethical investment banking house begins to feel a moral obligation once the letter is submitted and accepted. Only a serious break in the market, or a drastic change in the company itself during preparation and registration of the S-1 (the form for full registration with the S.E.C.) will cause the letter of intent not to be fulfilled.

Here is an example of a theoretical letter of intent:

April 30, 1994

Mr. John Jones, President
Jones Distributing Company
Los Angeles, CA

Dear Mr. Jones:

At the time of our visit on April 14, we agreed to submit to you in writing our general recommendations with respect to a public offering of Jones Distributing Company, Common Stock for the account of the Company and certain shareholders. Accordingly, in this letter we have outlined for you the thoughts which Williams Investment Bankers has regarding such a contemplated offering.

First, let us compliment the management of Jones on its exceptional performance in developing the business so successfully over a very short period of time. We have been unusually impressed by our contacts with management and by the comments we have received from a variety of others whose views we have solicited in the normal course of investigating your fine organization. If we mutually agree on proceedings towards an eventual public offering, we will, of course, continue to investigate and analyze your business, but we have every expectation that this will result in a verification of what we have learned to date.

In order to provide you with as specific a financing plan as possible, we have used a number of assumptions which we would like to set forth at this point:

1. *The public offering would take place after the completion of fiscal 1994 which ends August 31. Based upon the present backlog of registrations being reviewed by the Securities and Exchange Commission, and the normal five to six week lag between the end of a fiscal year and the availability of audited figures, we would estimate that a Jones filing could be accomplished by mid-October. The actual public offering would, therefore, take place sometime around mid-November. A filing could be accomplished earlier this year based upon interim 1994 figures, but such timing would not be in the Company's or the selling shareholders' interest primarily because current earnings are in such a sharp uptrend that a significantly fuller realization in terms of market valuation can be achieved at year end as opposed to an earlier date.*

2. *Net sales according to your estimate for fiscal 1994 will approximate $40 million and net*

income after taxes will be in a range of $2.5 million

3. The Company requires new capital of approximately $6 million to $8 million and the selling shareholders will sell up to $3 million of their holdings.

4. Present shareholders and management of Jones have no strong views as to whether or not a reasonable quarterly dividend rate is established on the Common Stock. If a dividend is necessary for marketing purposes, or if shareholders require it, a dividend could be established consistent with the Company's financial position.

5. No material changes in the nature of Jones' business are contemplated by management, nor does it expect that the trend of growth as indicated by the record over the prior three years will be significantly different.

6. General stock market conditions will remain strong, and the improving investor attitudes towards merchandising type stocks, on which valuations were quite modest throughout 1993 and early 1994, will continue to improve.

We recommend a split of the shares presently outstanding to enable the establishment of the initial offering price which reflects prestige yet indicates the youth and vigor of a growing company. We suggest a split involving the issuance of one new share for each of the existing 1 million shares presently outstanding, resulting in a new share capitalization of 2 million shares outstanding. Estimated earnings per share for the fiscal year ending August 31, 1994, would be $1.25 on net income after taxes of $2.5 million.

Based upon this new captialization, we would suggest that the company sell 400,000 shares which would increase the number of shares outstanding after the completion of the offering to 2.4 million shares, or a dilution, by the addition of the new shares, of approximately 20 percent. Estimated earnings per share for fiscal year 1994 on the basis of 2.4 million shares outstanding would be $1.04. We recommend that the selling shareholders make available up to 200,000 shares for inclusion in the offering. Therefore, the total offering would consist of a maximum of

600,000 shares, which in our judgment would provide sufficient shares for good secondary market trading activity on the National Over-the-Counter Market (NASDAQ).

The pricing of initial stock offerings is always difficult and frankly still remains an art which is not subject to highly definitive statements until the proposed offering is only a matter of days off. In the case of Jones, pricing projections are even more hazardous because we are looking ahead to November in the stock markets; economic conditions and world affairs can all have changed markedly during the interim.

As we have attempted to indicate in the above paragraphs, if general market conditions, pricing of similar issues, and the overall business situation continue to improve, then we think an offering of Jones common stock could be accomplished late this fall in the 10 to 12 times earnings range. It is our opinion that the objectives of the company and its shareholders and the present financial condition of Jones are such that an offering which could only be accomplished at a lower price basis is neither necessary nor desirable. We would, therefore, advise that no offering take place until this kind of valuation could be achieved. Under different circumstances, however, our conclusions in this respect might well be different.

The offering price per share would be $12.50 to $15.00 related to estimated earnings per share of $1.25. An offering price in the 10 to 12 earnings multiple range related to estimated 1994 net income of $2.5 million would place a total valuation on Jones of $25 million to $30 million prior to the sale of shares for the account of the company. Using an average 11 times earning multiple, a total offering of 600,000 shares would amount to $8.25 million with $5.5 million being sold for the company and $2.75 million for the account of the selling shareholders. After the offering, the general public would own 25 percent and the present shareholders would account for 75 percent of the 2.4 million then outstanding shares.

We estimate that direct expenses of such an offering, other than underwriting commissions, such as legal, auditing, printing and other costs should not exceed $45,000 to $50,000. The greater portion of such costs can be paid by the Company although certain *expenses are customarily assumed by the selling share holders. Of course, auditing and certain other expenses would be incurred at fiscal year end regardless of the public offering and so are not really added expenses to the Company.*

If we were to proceed with a public offering as outlined above, it would be our intention to form an underwriting group of established investment banking and brokerage firms with offices in principal cities throughout the United States to distribute Jones Common Stock on a national basis. The gross commission charged by the underwriting syndicate would be approximately 8 percent of the public offering price, although the actual size of the offering would have a bearing on the final determination of this commission. Underwriters bear their own legal expenses, advertising costs and the other direct expenses involved in merchandising such an issue.

The following sets forth in abbreviated form an approximate time schedule for a Jones offering along the lines discussed in this letter:

October 5 — Audited Financial Statements for Fiscal Year Ending August 31, 1994, Available

October 9 — Registration Statement Filed with S.E.C.

October 30 — Receipt of Deficiency Letter from S.E.C.

November 10 — A Public Offering of Jones

November 18 — Closing with Company and Selling Shareholders

This timing is based upon the present backlog and processing schedule of the S.E.C. and, of course, can be subjected to a variety of changes.

The foregoing statements in this letter are preliminary recommendations and should not be construed as a binding contract of Jones Distributing Company, or yourself, or of Williams Investment Bankers, or any other proposed underwriter. We have stated to you our interest in this potential financing and our ideas as to how it might be successfully accomplished. All relevant terms, conditions and circumstances and legal matters relating to such proposed stock sale must be mutually satisfactory to us and to our counsel.

Very truly yours,

WILLIAMS INVESTMENT BANKERS, INC.
Henry Brown
Vice President

You can see from the above example that a great deal of thought and careful preparation goes into the letter of intent. Considering the costs of an abortive issue, both to the corporation and to the underwriter, the parties are careful not to go beyond this stage unless they feel they can deliver the performance stipulated in the letter. If the corporation figures and facts are borne out, only a serious break in the stock market will cause delay in the underwriting. Therefore, when an acceptable letter of intent is negotiated, the corporation is justified in committing for the expenses incurred prior to the actual stock issue.

Recapitalization

Almost all companies which go public for the first time face the necessity of taking special steps to provide the proper stock structure. If the company is a proprietorship or other form of noncorporate entity, it must first incorporate to create the stock which it will sell, as well as that increment which will be retained by the principals. Most companies which reach the public issue stage are, of course, already incorporated, yet they, too, usually require stock restructuring.

The usual problem is that there are too few shares to sell at a reasonable price. Most private corporations do not bother to issue additional stock, beyond the original authorized amount, as they grow. Therefore, you will find fairly large companies with only one thousand to several hundred thousand shares of authorized stock. When a public issue is undertaken, more shares must be created to provide a sufficiently broad holding in the hands of the public.

We have previously described the method of evaluating an aspiring public corporation as the result of negotiation between management and the underwriter. After the evaluation, the size and shape of the issue is determined. In other words, there is agreement on the percentage of the company stock to be sold—and how much of the proceeds of the issue will go to the corporation or to the selling shareholders.

The total amount to be sold is computed in dollars. If, for example, a corporation earns $600,000 after taxes and is evaluated at $6 million, an issue which contemplates sale of 40 percent of the company stock would involve a gross underwriting of $2.4 million. Now the underwriters must resolve the problem of determining the number of shares among which this gross amount will be divided. There are several definite guidelines which influence this decision, as follows:

- Will there be sufficient shares to assure a proper stockholding in the hands of the public?

- Will the individual share price be correlated to the quality of the stock being offered?

Small issues, such as those governed by Regulation A, have involved stock which sold as low as $3 per share. Many Regulation A issues in the past followed the pattern of offering 100,000 shares at $3 per share. Full registrations in the modest range can be designed to offer stock at $4 to $6 per share. But when an offering moves above the $1.5 million-dollar range, and is handled by more substantial underwriters, the per share price requirement is elevated. A "respectable" price for a larger issue is $10 or more (which gives the stockbroker a minimum $1,000 sale for a "round lot" of 100 shares); most new issues range from this minimum up to slightly over $20 per share. Only very large, long-established firms, such as the renowned first issue of the Ford Motor Company at well over $50, are exceptions to this practice.

Returning to our example where $2.4 million worth of stock is to be sold, it is quite likely that the underwriters will decide to offer 200,000 shares at $12 per share. With this number of shares to market, an underwriting syndicate which does its job well by restricting large purchases will obtain a fairly wide public distribution. But we find that our example has a total of only 100,000 shares authorized and outstanding stock, so a *recapitalization* is necessary.

Through the recapitalization process, additional stock is authorized, and new share values are set, usually by applying to the corporation commissioner of the state in which the corporation is domiciled. The total authorization might be increased to 1 million shares with a permit to issue 200,000 shares to the public in the first offering. But the shares retained by the principals must also be adjusted in the recapitalization.

Before the issue and the recapitalization, principals held 100,000 shares which represented 100 percent of the stock in a company evaluated at $6 million. After the issue, principals will retain 60 percent (40 percent being sold to the public) worth $3.8 million. Now, remember that the price per share for the public issue — the issue price — has been set at $12 per share. On this basis, the principals would have to be the holders of 300,000 shares of new stock ($3.6 million divided by $12). To accomplish this, the corporation approves a 3-for-1 stock split, and the principals receive 300,000 shares of new stock for their original 100,000 shares for which permission has been obtained from the state corporation commissioner. Therefore, after the public issue, there will be 500,000 shares of stock outstanding — 200,000 shares in the hands of the public, 300,000 shares retained by principals.

Timetable

The filing of a registration requires the teamwork of a group of qualified professionals. Probably the first category to go to work will be the accountants; in fact, since a well-advised corporation will anticipate far in advance the possibility of a public issue, the CPA firm may have been engaged — and told of the possibility — a year or more before the beginning of a filing. The choice of CPA for Regulation A and the smaller issues is fairly free on the part of the corporation. When tackling a larger issue, however, ($10 million up) the underwriter will have to be satisfied and this will probably limit the choice to one of the nationally known CPA firms. If one of such accounting firms has not previously been retained by the corporation, possibly an arrangement can be made for an affiliation of effort between the local CPA firm used and a national firm. It is important that the CPA firm engaged have experience in preparing the financial reports for a public issue.

The corporation must also have its own attorneys for the issue — *corporate counsel* — and, since this is one of the many specialties in the legal profession, a qualified law firm must be chosen. Upon this firm falls the major burden of prospectus writing, as well as working on the

recapitalization and preparation of the voluminous sup-
porting documents required by the S.E.C. In addition to
doing this specialized job correctly and efficiently, it is the
responsibility of corporate counsel to safeguard the corporation from any possibility of civil or criminal exposure
which could arise from improper filing procedures. The
underwriters have their own counsel — the *underwriter's
counsel* — who will exercise similar protective functions
on behalf of the investment bankers and will also handle
the *blue sky* requirements. Blue skying is the term
applied to the registration of a stock for sale in the individual states. This is simple in some states — merely the
mailing of a prospectus to the corporation commissioner
or secretary of state — more involved in other states where
special applications must be filed. Although the requirements for blue-skying may be complex in some states like
California, they can be complied with easily by most
sound offerings. A few states, among them Texas, have
such ridiculously unrealistic codes that most underwritings bypass them. Many issues blue-sky in the eight or ten
major financial states; others go for sales in twenty five or
more states. After the issue is out and the market has stabilized, the free trading of a stock throughout the country
will make its sale unrestricted; blue-skying applies only to
sales of the original issue.

When the letter of intent has been confirmed by both
sides, a meeting is usually held to coordinate the schedule. Most underwritings are timed to incorporate the
financial reports of the latest full year of operation, so the
fiscal year end date becomes significant. The schedule
can be expected to look something like this:

- Four months before the corporate fiscal year end, the
  letter of intent is confirmed, based on reliable year
  end operating figures.

- Applications for recapitalization of corporate stock
  are processed as quickly as possible after the decision to go ahead with the issue.

- Accountants begin working on past year's figures for
  conformity and, at least two months before fiscal
  year end, begin making tests of inventories and
  receivables so that the entire procedure does not
  have to be accomplished at the last minute.

- During the month prior to fiscal year end, corporate
  counsel begins to gather prospectus information

and, within thirty days after the year end, prepares first rough draft of prospectus and sends copies to underwriter's counsel. This is usually done before the financial information is received from the accountants.

- Approximately six weeks to two months after the fiscal year end, the accountants have their financial reports ready. Meanwhile, both of the counsels have been working on redrafting various parts of the filing, including the prospectus. The filing is then put together with the financial and the first S-1, including the prospectus, is actually printed. The prospectus printer does this within twenty four hours, then keeps the type set awaiting corrections. At this point all parties, their counsel and accountants, get together for a hectic two or three days to polish the prospectus which, inevitably, is reprinted sometime between midnight and dawn, then flown to Washington by one of the counsel for filing with the S.E.C.

- Three weeks after filing, a *deficiency letter* is received from the S.E.C., listing certain suggested corrections. About ten days to two weeks later the *effective date* — the actual issue date of the stock — is set. Firm underwriting contracts are finally signed.

- Seven to ten days after the effective date is the *settlement date*, on which the corporation and selling shareholders receive their money from the underwriting.

From the above, it is obvious that a minimum of three months after fiscal year end is required before reaching the effective date of the issue. Four months to settlement date is more normal. Considering the fact that certain things have to be accomplished prior to the fiscal year end, including the early contact and negotiations with the underwriter, it is also obvious that a lead time of nine months or more can be required to transform the idea of a first public financing into actuality.

The Underwriting Syndicate

When a filing, such as the S-1 registration, is made with the S.E.C., it includes a full printed copy of the prospectus. In connection with the underwriting, many more copies of the prospectus are printed and distributed under the control of the underwriter. But, these first prospectuses carry a unique designation, printed in bright red wording across the face of the front page, which states that they are *preliminary prospectuses*, or what are known among stockbrokers as *red herrings*. Although restricted from distribution to the public, red herrings are freely circulated in the investment banking fraternity for the purpose of forming a *syndicate.*

In all but the very small issues, the originating investment banker participates with other brokerage houses in making the offering. This joint effort is triggered by the circulation of red herrings to a great number of potential participants who are invited to join the underwriting syndicate. The investment banking firm which has negotiated with the corporation, and issued the letter of intent, is known as the *managing underwriter.* From the time the issue is first filed with the S.E.C., the managing and other underwriters will be checking with some of their regular customers for possible interest in buying shares of stock in the new issue. During the red herring stage, no purchase orders can be accepted, but stockbrokers are allowed to accept *indications of interest.* While these indications are not binding, over 90 percent usually stick, so the *feedback* which they provide to the managing underwriter gives real assurance relative to proper share pricing and general acceptability. Other underwriters, who begin to see feedback from their own customers, request invitations to join the underwriting syndicate.

The managing underwriter will take the largest share of the offering; however, this increment will rarely exceed 25 percent of the total issue. Not only is it prudent for the managing underwriter to spread its risk by laying off parts of the total commitment to others, but the managing underwriter also hopes for reciprocity from other brokerage firms which will invite it into syndicates of their own originations.

Setting the Price

When the red herring is first circulated, several items are left blank. Chief of these is the price per share and the space provided for the underwriting syndicate. Usually only the name of the managing underwriters appears. During the syndication, the other brokers are advised of the probable price range and the feedback information helps firm the issue price. Just before the effective date the syndicate is definitely formed and the precise price is set. The final prospectus shows this price, which is what the public will pay, and also lists the underwriting syndicate in detail. The managing underwriter receives about 1½ percent (or about 15 percent of the total brokerage commissions). The other members of the underwriting group may, along with the managing firm who is also in the group, receive another 15 percent of the gross commission.

This means that between 60 percent and 70 percent of the gross commission remains for the *selling group,* which normally passes on at least half of this to the individual registered representatives who are on the front line making the actual sales to the public.

Recognition of this division makes it obvious that the managing underwriter, which has done so much work in negotiating and bringing the issue to the market, receives no inordinately high compensation for its work.

Takedown Requirements

The members of the underwriting group assume responsibility for payment to the corporation of the full cash committed proceeds. This group comes under certain S.E.C. *takedown requirements* which vary depending on the type of issue (bonds vs. stocks, etc.). The requirement for the usual common stock financing issue, for example, is that the underwriter takes the takedown commitment into its books with a *haircut* of 30 percent and that the underwriter have, at the effective date and thereafter until settlement is made, sufficient liquid cash assets to meet all common creditor obligations (which include the obligation to pay the corporation being underwritten for its stock which is to be resold to the public).

Using an example, let us assume that one of the underwriters makes a takedown commitment for 25 percent of the 200,000 shares being sold, or 50,000 shares at $12. The gross value of these shares is $600,000 which, less an underwriting commission of $60,000, leaves $540,000 worth of public stock which can be counted as a liquid asset, less the 30 percent haircut, or $378,000.

Therefore this underwriter must be able to show that it has sufficient liquid assets to pay all its common creditors plus $162,000 for the takedown.

The takedown requirements are frequently academic, although they are always complied with. Normally the issue is *presold* on the basis of indications of interest received prior to the effective date. After the effective date, customer confirmations are sent out and, since payment is required four days after confirmation in new issues, funds flow in to provide the cash required seven to ten days later on the settlement date. On that day the under-writers hand their check to the corporation—and the long process has been completed.

The After Market

When the final settlement has been paid by the underwriters to the corporation, the financing role of a particular public stock issue has been completed. But management must then consider the behavior of the stock which has been sold to the public. The principals who still retain some of the corporate stock (although they might have sold a portion of their holdings in the public issue) realize that, as the market price of the publicly held stock rises or falls, the values of their own holdings do likewise. Also, growth companies, during their histories, will probably have many additional public issues subsequent to the first offering.

Stock sold in the first issue is evaluated as the result of a *negotiated price* with the underwriters. Subsequent issues will go out based on the market price of the issue at the effective date; therefore, a stock which does well in the market will yield more money to the issuing corporation in ratio to dilution.

The performance of the stock of a corporation after its first public issue is known as the *after market.* There are several categories of after market, as follows:

● Major stock exchanges

● Over the counter market (NASDAQ)

● Regional exchanges

The major exchanges, which are national in scope, are the New York Stock Exchange (NYSE) and the American Stock Exchange (AMEX). The activities of these exchanges are well recognized and the quotations of the stocks traded on them are reported daily in the newspapers. These daily newspaper transaction reports cover the stocks of every corporation listed by the exchanges and it is therefore common to refer to such stocks as *listed securities.*

A corporation which desires to be listed on one of the exchanges must meet with certain qualifications and must also agree to abide by the rules of the exchange including the issuance of stipulated financial statements. There are a number of qualitative admission requirements which any good company should be able to meet. Most significant, however, are certain size requirements as to the following:

- Profits
- Net worth
- Number of stockholders
- Number of shares held by the public

The requirements of the New York Stock Exchange in the above categories are higher than those of the American Stock Exchange, as shown in the following table:

	NYSE	AMEX
Pre-tax Profit	$2.5 million	$750,000
Net worth, tangible	18 million	4 million
Number of stockholders	2,200	800
Shares of public stock	1.1 million	500,000
Market value of public shares	$18 million	$3 million

There is a particular significance to the last three categories as the number of stockholders — and the number of shares which they hold — actually constitute the *trading market* of the stock. If too few shares are held by too few people, there will be very little activity in the stock.

Freetrading Stock

The shares held by the public are known as *freetrading stock*, the sales of which are reported in the newspapers. The last price at which these shares are bought and sold daily — the *closing price* — constitutes the quotation. If there are few transactions, the stock price may remain dormant even if a company is progressing. Conversely, where there is a very limited stockholding, the sale of even a small block of stock by someone who must liquidate holdings can cause an unnatural drop in the stock prices. Therefore, these minimums are sensibly set, and it is wise to consider them prior to completing the planning of a first public issue.

The major exchanges constitute what is known as an *auction market* because buy and sell orders are matched by price in open trading on the floors of the exchanges. Many excellent descriptions of the workings of a stock exchange have been written and we will forego this aspect as our concern is limited to the implications of the after market relative to corporate finance. There are many arguments pro and con about the relative validity of an auction market compared to the nature of the over the counter market, which is a *supply and demand* market. From a financing point of view, I think this difference is academic.

The *over the counter* market (NASDAQ) is made up of the trading activities of stock brokerage firms throughout the United States, each of which has an OTC trading department. When a new stock is first issued, the managing underwriter *makes the market* immediately thereafter. By so doing, the managing underwriter stands ready to buy or sell reasonable amounts of the stock being traded. This is handled through nationwide trading wires so that, even if the broker making the market is located in San Francisco, a buy or sell order can be placed with a stockbroker, for example, in Atlanta. The prices quoted in OTC trading consist of a *bid quotation* and an *ask quotation*. The bid quote is the price being offered on a particular day by prospective buyers; the ask quote is the price demanded by sellers. If you wish to sell some OTC stock you will be paid the bid price; if you wish to buy you will be charged the ask price. Normally the difference between the bid and ask prices — the *spread* — is about 5 percent (for example, bid 10, ask 10½). The spread comprises the broker-dealer's commission, including the share of other brokers in the transaction, and the broker-dealer's costs of maintaining an inventory of the stock.

'In the Sheets'

Once a stock has been on the over the counter market for a short while, several broker-dealer firms may trade actively in it to make the market. This is done by a listing *in the sheets*. These sheets are daily reports put out by general quotation bureaus reflecting the bid and ask prices and the names of the broker-dealers who have decided to join in making the market. Each broker so listed is announcing to all the security dealers in the country that it stands ready to buy or sell reasonable quantities of the stock.

There are no particular requirements for admission to the OTC market. The very fact of having a public issue places the stock of a company in the OTC market. Therefore most new issues find their aftermarket to be over the counter. But there are no specific waiting periods required for a listing on one of the two major exchanges. For this reason some companies which qualify for the NYSE or AMEX will be listed on one of these exchanges a few weeks after their first public issue becomes effective. During the short interim period, their stock will trade over the counter.

The regional exchanges present few significant differences with regard to financing considerations. Some small stock issues may apply for regional listing because they have a limited local market at best. Many other regionally listed companies are also listed on one of the national exchanges or are very actively traded over the counter. Some specific categories of stock are traded on specialized exchanges, such as the San Francisco Mining Exchange, to get more attention than they might otherwise command.

The big decision is between a major exchange listing and being traded over the counter. If a corporation can qualify for either, management must carefully weigh the choice, particularly for a growth company which looks for stock price enhancement to abet future public financings.

It is not quite correct to assume that prestige companies are all listed on one of the major exchanges. Stocks of many important banks and insurance companies are traded solely over the counter. Such well-known companies as Avon Products, Amgen and Apple Computer have been on the roster of the OTC market.

In the past, the OTC market did not impose some of the regulations and reporting requirements called for by the major exchanges. Also, proponents of the OTC market claim that through the activities of the broker-dealers who regularly trade in an OTC stock, it gets more play and can benefit more from this sponsorship. This may be true, particularly immediately after a first issue when the managing underwriter will over-allot sales of the stock to *stabilize* the price. But after the stock has been out and free trading a while, this aspect decreases in importance.

Reporting Requirements

Present S.E.C. tendencies indicate that OTC reporting requirements will be brought closer to those of the major exchanges. Even though NYSE listings are growing longer, they are small in comparison with NASDAQ, which probably includes the stocks of over 40,000 public companies. While the sponsorship of a broker-dealer can make a significant difference in the OTC market, the lack of sponsorship can create a very stagnant market. Even though there are advantages which can be recognized for either type of after market, it is my opinion that the major exchange listing, because of stricter regulations, provides more prestige and eligibility for institutional investors. The computerized *stock watch* functions of the major exchanges tend to assure investors of more legitimate auction market pricing and controlled spreads.

Subsequent Public Issues

After a company has gone public, a wide range of financing possibilities becomes available. As the company makes progress and its growth requires additional funding, management can choose among the following possibilities:

- Issuance of debentures or long term notes;
- Issuance of convertible debentures;
- Issuance of commercial paper;
- Issuance of additional common stock; the use of rights

The public issuance of debt usually takes the form of a *debenture bond* or long term notes. Debentures may be longer term (from fifteen to twenty years) and frequently have a sinking fund requirement that calls for annual principal reductions after the first two years. Notes, even in large amounts (for example $100 to $300 million) are usually issued for shorter terms, from three to seven years, and usually have no sinking fund requirement. One of the great advantages of publicly issued debt is that it involves far fewer restrictive covenants than debt privately placed with institutions.

There is also a major difference in the method of setting the interest rate. Interest rates on privately placed debt are negotiated on behalf of the corporation by its investment banker and frequently may be higher than public debt because it is not rated. Publicly issued debt, however, requires a credit rating to be established prior of the effective date of the issue.

There are three major rating agencies — Standard & Poors (S&P) Moody's, and Duff & Phelps. When a public debt issue is about to be underwritten, the managing underwriter visits the rating agencies and attempts to obtain at least two satisfactory ratings. The three rating agencies do not use exactly the same letter-number combinations but the financial community is well aware of their significance. While the highest S&P rating is AAA ("triple A") and a "single A" rating is still highly regarded, any bond rated BAA ("B double A") by S&P is considered *investment grade*. The equivalent minimum investment grade rating by Moody's is BBB ("triple B"). While some of the most conservative institutional managers invest only in "A" rating or above, many have a certain percentage of BAA's in their portfolios in order to obtain higher yield.

The ratings are based on dependability of earnings, low debt to equity ratios on the balance sheet, and length of time in business. Obviously a young company, even with conservative ratios and a recent strong earnings history, will not receive the top ratings until it is more mature.

Most significantly, the ratings determine the interest rate of the note or bond. A pivotal base rate is that of the 10 year U.S. Treasury bond, to which is applied a risk-reward approach. U.S. Treasury bonds — *Treasuries* — are considered to be the lowest risk investments; therefore other fixed income notes and bonds having a higher risk should provide a higher reward (pay a higher interest rate).

For example, common stocks of well regarded companies theoretically have 6 percent more risk than Treasuries. Therefore if the government bond presently yields 6 percent interest, the common stock should have a 12 percent *total yield* — that is, dividends plus stock price appreciation. The pricing of senior notes and debentures falls somewhere in between these two extremes.

Each bond or note rating level has a different interest rate, expressed as the *spread* above Treasuries. That spread is usually quoted in *basis points*. A basis point is 1/100th of a percent; therefore ½ percent equals 50 basis points. Depending on the market, "A" rated bonds might have a spread of 200 basis points (2 percent) above Treasuries and a "BAA" might be priced at a spread of 350 basis points (3½ percent). Therefore, if the Treasury bond has a current interest rate of 6 percent, the "A" bond would be priced at 8 percent and the "BAA" bond at 9½ percent interest. These rates are consistent during any single phase of the market.

All similarly rated bonds are usually priced the same. On rare occasions investors feel that the rating is too conservative because of a promising company outlook and pay slightly lower interest in order to lock in the loan to a company which in a few years may be more highly rated.

Convertible Debentures

The market usually has a strong appetite for *convertible debentures.* This is because the investor receives a steady income stream while possessing what could be a valuable option to purchase common stock at a bargain in the future. Convertible debentures have the following characteristics:

- They pay interest at a rate as much as 3 percent to 4 percent lower than straight public debt.

- They are usually subordinated to long term senior debt of the company.

- They may be converted at any time to common stock at a fixed price regardless of the market price of the stock at the time of conversion.

The conversion price usually ranges from 15 percent to 20 percent above the market price at the time the debenture is originally issued. If, for example, the underlying stock price is $30 per share when the convertible debenture is issued and the premium is 15 percent, the debenture could be converted at any time into shares costing $34.50 per share. Should the share go to $50 per share, the investor would profit by $15.50 per share when selling the stock. Prior to exercising conversion rights, the investor would still be receiving the debenture interest payments.

It is this extra kicker which makes the investor willing to receive lower interest and even to accept a subordinated position for the fund.

Obviously the relative lack of restrictive covenants and the low interest rates which characterize convertible debentures make them very attractive to corporate management. The occasionally offsetting negative is the fact that the principal invested in the debentures may ultimately be converted into common shares and that, of course, will create some dilution of per share earnings.

This can be quite acceptable because as a company grows it may need more common equity than retained profits provide. But it is always desirable to leverage the equity by a reasonable amount of straight debt, so the decision maker must balance the use of straight debt and convertibles in order to achieve an optimal outcome.

Commercial Paper

One of the fastest growing pools of domestic finance in recent years has resulted from the issuance of *commercial paper*. Commercial paper describes a group of relatively short term notes placed by corporations into an active trading market. As you will note below, this type of financing can only be used by established companies with *back-up banking* in place.

Corporations sell commercial paper because it is flexible, almost free of restrictive covenants, and low-cost. As an alternative to bank borrowing, commercial paper can bear interest rates 1 percent to 2 percent below bank prime rates. Commercial paper is sold by the corporation as a group of individual notes, say for $1 million each, of varying maturities. The maturities may be 30 days, 90 days, 180 days or even 270 days. They are bought by treasurers of large corporations, insurance companies, savings institutions and other organizations looking for ways to invest money on a short term basis in a highly liquid market. Some investors buy commercial paper just to keep their money working over a long weekend, as will be described below.

In order to issue commercial paper the corporation must:

- Create a group of notes with maturities from 30 days to 270 days.

- Arrange with a large investment banking house to become the market maker for the commercial paper notes.

- Obtain a rating from a rating agency. Commercial paper ratings are preceded by the letter "P" — for example, P-1, P-2, P-3, etc.

- Arrange for a backup line of unsecured credit from a commercial bank, or a syndicate of banks.

When the above steps are complete, the notes are given to the investment banker who sells them to clients and maintains an orderly market. When the paper matures (in

90 days, for example) the issuing corporation may either pay off the present noteholder or direct the investment banker to *roll over* the paper for another 90 days, which is accomplished either with the same investor or by selling into the market of commercial paper investors.

The market for commercial paper is like any other large security market, in that there are almost always enough buyers and sellers. If the corporation wishes to reduce its outstanding indebtedness, it can do so by paying off notes on any rollover date or by buying its own notes in the open market. Investors can always use the market to buy or sell the notes, so they are not constrained by stated maturity dates; they also receive stated interest for the time they hold the notes.

The interest cost is lower because of the liquidity, flexibility and security of the notes. If for some reason the demand dries up for notes about to be rolled over, payoff is made from the proceeds of the unsecured backup bank line. Corporations include coverage of this possibility in their regular unsecured bank line agreements so that, at any one time, they may borrow partially from the bank and partially from the commercial paper market. The bank line agreement has a maximum credit limit, which the total of a corporation's outstanding commercial paper and direct borrowings from the bank cannot exceed. Banks charge a standby fee of about ¼ to ½ percent for the backup line not used for direct bank borrowing. Since the commercial paper net interest cost will still be considerably less, it is not surprising that, in recent years, banks have lost about 50 percent of their direct corporate lending business to the commercial paper market.

Subsequent Issues of Common Stock

The decision to issue more stock depends on the balance desired between debt and equity. In order to increase per share earnings, it is always helpful to add a prudent amount of debt. But a growth company will require frequent additions of both equity and debt capital. There is one major difference between pricing the sale of common shares in an IPO and in subsequent offerings. The pricing of the stock in the IPO is negotiated with the investment banking syndicate which underwrites the issue and is, in a sense, arbitrary. The underwriters usually try to hold down the share price in order to make it more attractive to the market, thereby making their job easier.

But all subsequent stock issues are *priced at the market* completely free of underwriter negotiation. On the *effective date* set by the bankers and the S.E.C. for the sale of the securities, all the shares underwritten by the syndicate are sold. The price at which they are sold is the *closing price* in the market. That price represents the last trade of the day and, if the specialists or broker-dealers are doing their jobs correctly, the price should be very close to the level at which the stock has recently been trading. Let us say that the stock closed the previous day at 24½ and opened on the effective date at 24¼. One should expect that an orderly market will maintain close to these two prices and that the closing price might be between 24 and 24⅜. The corporate representative should let the specialists on the floor of the exchange or the OTC broker-dealers know that a large price change at the end of the day, on small volume, would not represent a conscientious effort to maintain an orderly market — which is the stated responsibility of the market maker. After all, in a 10 million share issue (not particularly large) a drop of ½ point on a relatively small 500 share sell order at the end of the day would amount to a loss of $5 million to the corporation. I actually experienced such a happening and complained so strongly that the underwriters gave up ¼ percent of their 4 percent underwriting fee to offset the loss (we later reported that improper trade to the stock exchange governors).

Evergreen Registration

When a corporation reaches the point that it frequently makes debt or equity offerings, there is a way to expedite the individual issues of securities. The procedure, known as an *evergreen registration,* makes it possible to keep a *shelf* registration on file with the S.E.C. Beginning with a full blown detailed prospectus, the corporation files quarterly updates which meet the required standard. In return, the S.E.C., upon request, makes a quick review and gives the corporation approval to print a brief *jacket* to be wrapped around the basic offering circular. Using such a procedure I have been involved with security offerings which culminated in an effective date seven to ten working days after the decision had been made to seek the financing. As a means of being able to hit the market at a most favorable time, use of the evergreen registration process can be very valuable.

Chapter 13
Evaluation of Potential
Acquisitions, LBOs, ESOPs

In the period from 1980 to 1989 we witnessed in the American economy the greatest splurge of acquisition activity in our history. Growth by acquisition became an important analytical consideration for investment fund managers. Frequently, during sessions with investment analysts, corporate officers would be asked about the possibility of the potential acquisition market drying up — in other words, would there be fewer and fewer candidates left in the field of activity of the acquirer, thereby reducing the present rate of corporate growth? When this issue was first raised, a group of opportunistic executives embraced the concept of the *conglomerate.* By using the word conglomerate, management could acquire any type of business and throw it into the corporate pot — a veritable salad of diverse activities.

Early Problems

Conglomerates were very exciting to the stock market for several years until a few facts of life began to surface and, at first, the conglomerate managers came up with some satisfactory answers. They began to use the word *synergistic* to imply that, somehow, each of the diverse entities being acquired reinforced the other business activities in the total corporate bag. This fiction persisted for a period of time until the public began to realize that widely diverse activities required different types of management expertise — and it was almost impossible to find all of those types in one corporate entity. Moreover, this condition was aggravated by the fact that, after acquisition, many top executives of the acquired corporations were either terminated or left of their own volition. As a result, companies were trying to run widely divergent activities from central committees comprised of generalists who could not completely provide the definitive expertise and individual attention needed in certain types of operations.

Finally, as a result of several swings of the pendulum, the picture clarified and acquisitions, properly considered and evaluated, became an integral increment of corporate growth. But the science of evaluating acquisitions remained indefinite. It has been only recently that certain value approaches have been recognized as being valid, based on actual experience gained during the post-acquisition period of successful acquirers.

'Purchase' and 'Pooling' Accounting

The acquisition era of the 1960s came upon the scene so suddenly, and to such a great extent, that professionals in the field of investment and finance found themselves groping for realistic benchmarks of evaluation. The New York Stock Exchange went through a period in which the number of listed companies remained fairly constant for several years. The addition of newly listed companies was being regularly offset by the disappearance of old listed companies which had been acquired or merged. The Accounting Principles Board and the Securities Exchange Commission went into a flap which lasted approximately four years, during which the relative valid-ity of *purchase accounting* and accounting by *pooling of interests* were contested. When an acquisition uses *pool-ing*, the balance sheets of the two companies involved are simply merged. All the assets are combined along with all liabilities and all capital. There is, however, no good will created in pooling.

In a *purchase* acquisition the acquiring company picks up the assets and liabilities of the seller and reflects the cost of the acquisition as an addition to capital. Assets such as cash and receivables are picked up as actually reflected. Other assets such as equipment and real property are appraised by an outside appraiser and picked up at their newly acquired value, which, because of depreciation taken in the past by the seller, may realistically appraise much higher. If, after reflecting all assets and liabilities at appraised and actual value, the net worth acquired is *less* than the purchase price, the difference must be reflected as good will and written off over a reasonable period of years against *after tax* profits.

At first, pooling was considered almost a dirty word, and it was thought that *purchase accounting* represented a more valid picture. During the long period over which this con-troversy stretched itself, an entirely different conclusion was reached by actual experience. It became obvious that many of the acquisition-oriented companies were obtaining *instant earnings* by using the purchase accounting method. Pooling was then retrieved from the doghouse and analysts began to talk about *dirty purchase accounting.*

Requirements

Pooling was redeemed by two sets of requirements. First, a strict set of pooling qualifications was formulated, calling for, among other things, the following:

- A continuity of the same type of business activity by the acquired corporation.

- A continuity of a substantial portion of the former management.

- Acquisition of at least 90 percent of the acquired corporation.

- Payment of the acquisition price initially; no *earnouts* on future earnings are permitted.

- Acquisition payment by the exclusive use of common stock of the buyer.

Another pooling requirement was a continuation of the practice of *restatement of prior years' earnings.* After a pooling acquisition it is necessary that all subsequent financial reports of the combined entities reflect *prior years' earnings as if the two corporations* — acquirer and acquired— *had been combined in the five years* prior to the acquisition. This, in part, eliminates the *instant earnings growth* of an accomplished acquisition. For example, Company A reflected $1.02 earnings per share for the year 1989 and, without an acquisition, would have shown $1.22 for the year 1990. But during 1990, Company A acquired Company B on a pooling basis, and Company B 1990 earnings will add 12 cents a share to Company A earnings for a total 1990 per share earning of $1.34 for the combined entity. On an *as stated* basis, therefore, Company A would show an earnings increase of 32 cents per share ($1.02 for 1989 and $1.34 for 1990). But Company B earned 10 cents a share in 1989, and pooling requires that this amount must also be added to the Company A 1989 earnings on a *restated basis* — as if the two companies were already combined in previous years. Company A 1989 earnings on a *restated pooling basis* would, therefore, be $1.12 per share (Company A's $1.02 plus Company B's 10 cents) as compared to $1.34 per share combined for 1990 — or a *restated* earnings increase of 22 cents instead of the 32 cents increase which would have been reflected on an *as-stated basis*. Analysts and accountants agree that the restated basis gives a more valid picture of true growth by comparing the earnings increase as if the two entities had already been combined — and they are correct.

No Restatement

In *purchase accounting* there is *no restatement for previous years;* therefore, the earnings of an acquired company contribute to total earnings from the day the acquisition is completed.[1] Using the same examples given above, Company A's 1990 earnings of $1.22 per share would be increased by Company B's earnings of 12 cents per share *proportional to the percentage of the 1990 year Company B is owned.* Thus if B is acquired at midyear, then 50 percent of its earnings are added — or 6 cents per share — to Company A's total of $1.22, yielding a combined 1990 total of $1.28 per year. But the combined total is *not restated* for the previous year; therefore, it would be compared to Company A's 1989 earnings ($1.02 per share), reflecting an earnings gain of 26 cents per share per year — a greater rate of earnings growth than can be shown on a pooling basis. Obviously, if Company B had greater earnings in comparison to the per share earnings of Company A, which we have given in our example, the *instant earnings growth* effect of the purchase accounting would be even more pronounced. It is also more pronounced if the acquisition is made in the earlier part of Company A's fiscal year (as a larger percentage of Company B's earnings would be added to the combined 1990 total of the A-B entity after the acquisition) and the inflation of the per share earnings growth rate would be more drastic. This artificially inflated effect may persist for two years, because purchases always compare to *non*-restated past years, but there is then a reverse effect; after a while the earnings growth begins to drag unless a steady stream of new purchase acquisitions is maintained. Since poolings require restatement from the very outset, they do not have this future problem. Recently, however, there have been some accounting rule changes which somewhat mitigate the purchase accounting instant earnings growth advantages. Chief among these has been the requirement that *good will be amortized* in purchase acquisitions.

---

[1]The capital gains tax has varied, sometimes going as low as 20 percent.

The good will depreciation factor can be quite serious. Many growth companies which are acquired for their earnings command prices far in excess of their book values. Such companies are acquired for their contribution to earnings growth and the purchase price is primarily based on an *earnings multiple.*

For example, *purchase-treated* Company K shows earnings of $150,000 after taxes which, based on a 15 times earnings multiple, gives a purchase price of $2.25 million. But the net worth book value of Company K is only $525,000 — therefore, the good will would be $1.7 million. The maximum depreciation period allowed is 40 years (less in certain cases) so the good will amortization is $42,500 per year which *must be deducted from after tax earnings.* For the acquirer, therefore, the reportable earnings of Company K drops to $107,500 — a serious hindrance, yet a sound accounting principle to protect investors from possibilities of false growth reporting in the absence of sufficient net worth.

There are, of course, cases where companies are purchased which have greatly depreciated assets on their books, primarily real property such as plants, warehouses, hotels, retail stores, etc. In such cases, accountants accept qualified outside appraisals of the true higher value and some of the good will can be allocated to such physical assets. Any future depreciation of such assets will, at least, be an expense *before taxes,* and the balance sheet, by reflecting less good will, will exhibit stronger tangible worth to an investor.

Until the 1972 rules were clarified, there were many cases in which an acquisition could be treated either as a pooling or a purchase, but this optional possibility has now been eliminated. Under the new regulations, those acquisitions which meet pooling criteria must be pooled — and the converse goes for purchases. Since the evaluation of any acquisition can be seriously affected by its accounting treatment, it is necessary that — almost from the first exposure to a potential acquisition — an early look at the balance sheet be taken to determine *a priori* whether a purchase or a pooling is involved.

Asset Value Evaluation

The most elementary form of evaluation of a going business takes into consideration only the true value of the assets, less the liabilities shown on the balance sheet. To this net worth is usually added a good will factor which will vary according to a set of criteria. In general, these criteria relate to the staying power of the business, the degree to which one can expect the business to continue at its present level of earnings — or better — because of some sort of franchise or exclusive location, established reputation, relative freedom from competition or from obsolescence through changing technology. Until some time after World War II, most evaluations took this simple approach. Transactions involving small businesses — particularly outside of the U.S. — may still use this evaluation.

In arriving at *true asset value,* the assets on the balance sheet are brought up to their present values, usually on the basis of an outside appraisal. If management has been understating its inventories for tax purposes, a new physical inventory is taken, costed and totalled. If reserves, such as for accounts receivable, are unnaturally high, the values are restated to conform to normal practice. Heavily depreciated real property (which may have actually appreciated far beyond its original cost) is appraised by outside professionals. From the total of all these restated values are subtracted the liabilities, to yield the present true value. Then, frequently, good will is added — which, historically, was the first step developed to recognize the difference between *asset liquidation value* and the potential of the same assets to create profits in a going business. Various industries developed their own differing good will factors to be added to true value. A service industry company might add a good will factor of three years after tax profits. Heavily entrenched manufacturing companies might add five years after tax profits. Employment or advertising agencies with little book value would add good will equivalent to one year's billings (or more).

Return on Investment

These factors evolved empirically and related generally to the return on investment which could be anticipated from those gross revenues. Some good will was even based solely on unrealized potential, particularly in the media field. It has been jokingly stated that, until fairly recently, FM stations were evaluated on the basis of three times losses — and this almost seemed proven by the increasing sale prices of FM stations, many of which had yet to show a profit. Of course, these stations represented valuable franchises in a field tightly controlled by government, and it was recognized that wider use and population growth could create future yield values.

In some countries which have not yet reached the degree of evaluation sophistication found in the U.S., some systematic approaches have developed. I encountered one such system during a negotiation in France. With the balance sheet before us, the seller presented a manual, apparently prepared by a national accounting or appraisal group, which contained a set of tables for determining appreciation to present value of certain categories of assets. These tables ran for ten years and were applicable to good, well built properties in solid areas of established and growing communities (which was the case of the company involved in this negotiation). The land had been purchased by the seller five years earlier, and, since land appreciation had been running 16 percent per annum, the table suggested the land be increased by 109 percent (16 percent compounded for five years). The building had been completed two years before and — based on the combined consideration of twenty five years' depreciation expense offset by increased current construction cost — was qualified for an increase factor of 18.6 percent. To these increased values were added all the other tangible assets — minus all the liabilities — on the balance sheet, to attain *current value.* Then, to the current value, the seller claimed we should add one year's gross revenues as good will. Incidentally, this was a high margin business (10 percent net after tax profit on gross revenues) and — by strange coincidence — the final price was not far off from the 14 times multiple of after tax earnings my board of directors had authorized. While there was indeed some professional basis for this coincidence, it only took place because of the high-margin aspect (to be explained later) and because certain other growth criteria were present. Using the same French approach, a business with lower margin and a slow growth prognosis might be valued fairly close to the same figure — which is the fallacy of such an approach. As we will see later in this chapter, only an earnings basis can provide true going-business evaluation.

Discounted Cash Flow

Up to this point we have described evaluations of potential acquisitions on the basis of *static* criteria, primarily the elements reflected on the balance sheet, adjusted to true, or present realistic value. It was a major evolutionary step when, early in the 1950s, emphasis shifted to the *dynamic* aspects of a business — namely, the return expected to be gained annually on the assets or good will being purchased. Attention moved from the balance sheet and began to focus on the operating statement. Acquirers would make profit and loss forecasts on a pro forma future basis for as much as ten years from the time of acquisition. On these forecasts cash flow figures would be developed (after tax profits plus non-cash expenses, such as depreciation). Then — to explain the matter simply — a computation would be made to determine what amount of purchase price could be repaid out of the forecast cash flow over a limited number of years. In other words, how much money could be recaptured by the acquirer in five, seven, or ten years?

The Payout

Of course the first step in such a process would be the somewhat arbitrary determination of the number of years the acquirer was willing to wait before recapturing the purchase in the cash flow generated by the acquisition. This would depend on the assumed staying power or stability of the business being purchased. I would say that almost the maximum time found to be acceptable was ten years. Even stable industries were expected to *pay out* in seven or eight years. And the payout had to include an added increment to replace the interest earnings on the money tied up in the acquisition. Since the buyer did not receive a payback from the cash flow soon after the acquisition (except in some cases of raids on cash-rich companies — see below), the buyer had to postulate a value of the *future* payout *discounted to present value.*

Elementary economics speaks of the *opportunity cost* of money — the cost attached to invested money which represents the amount of interest it might have earned if it were left on deposit in a bank, or invested in high-grade bonds. This cost varies, of course, with the money market, but because money markets go through complete cycles in a few years, from high interest to low interest, it is usually valid to assume an average 6 percent per annum opportunity cost on a ten year payout — equal payments each year over ten years. Using those assumptions, the present value of the payout must be discounted approximately 40 percent. In other words, $100,000 received in ten equal annual installments is really worth no more than $60,000 cash received immediately, today (and this makes no allowance for the additional loss from possible future currency inflation). Therefore, an acquisition must create at least 140 percent of its purchase price in cash flow, if the payout over ten years is deemed to be acceptable.

In the discounted cash flow approach, the purchase price is obviously determined by the total cash flow projected over an acceptable time. Assume that a potential acquisition earns $250,000 after taxes per year, after depreciation expense of $50,000. Beginning cash flow is $300,000 per year. It is a stable business and the buyer determines that a ten year payout is acceptable. During the ten years it is forecast that cash flow increases smoothly to $500,000 a year — or will average $400,000 during the payout. Therefore, total cash flow for the ten years will be $4 million, which — discounted 40 percent — will justify a purchase evaluation of $2.4 million cash to be paid now for the acquisition.

Tax Considerations

Although discounted cash flow has largely been supplanted by price-earnings ratio approaches, it still has a value when used in conjunction with newer price setting methods, particularly in adjusting the evaluation for acquisitions involving unusually high or low asset values — or unusually tight or liquid balance sheets — in relationship to the after tax earnings. Discounted cash flow is also found in acquisitions where the acquirer is a private company or — in particular — when a private or public company sets out to acquire a company with a large tax loss carryforward, or a cash rich company. In the case of the tax loss company, it is obvious that these loss carryforwards will, for a few years, shelter the earnings from taxes, and the cash flow will recapture the purchase price more quickly in the first few years.

In the case of the cash-rich company, you can have the same effect. The corporate raider looks for cash-rich companies, public or private. If the company is private, it has usually developed excess cash because its owners were in high personal income tax brackets and did not wish to pay out corporate earnings in the form of high taxable dividends. Public companies which have accumulated excessively large cash reserves may have an unprogressive self-perpetuating management without sufficient shareholdings to assure practical control in the face of a tender offer.

A corporate raider can offer a price higher than the prevailing market based on the ability to utilize the excess cash, declaring a massive dividend to the acquiring corporation immediately after taking control, thereby reducing the payback discount, to justify the original acquisition price.

Evaluation by Earnings Multiple

The evaluation of a going business by an earnings multiple has become much more recognized and, in fact, prevalent in the U.S. The money used to acquire a business is undeniably capital; therefore, where such capital is invested should be determined by the return which can be generated on that capital, compared to other *equal-risk* investment opportunities. The return is a function of the profit level of a business being bought. A multiple of that per annum return is the converse of yield on investment.

For example, if a business is acquired on the basis of five times annual earnings, it means the acquirer would earn a yield equal to the total investment in five years — or 20 percent per year, a typical return on a high risk investment. In a 10 times multiple, the return is equivalent to a 10 percent per annum return on an investment — a lower risk rate of return, but obviously higher than even more conservative investments such as bank deposits or holdings in high grade bonds, both of which yield considerably lower returns.

The risk level and staying power of the acquired business have much to do with the multiple, as is illustrated by Dewing's table which has been reproduced in Chapter 10. This table describes gradations of earnings multiples from 10 times for *businesses with long existence and established good will among many customers* to 1 times for *businesses of a personal service character or businesses dependent on the skill of a single person such as an author's agency or an animal hospital.*

But there is one important element missing in using a static table for evaluations, at least in the more substantial situations. I am referring to the element of *potential future growth of earnings.* The earnings multiple is applied to the *current* earnings level (remember, this level is always after tax earnings); therefore, if earnings increase, the effective earnings multiple over the period until payback is lowered.

The importance of this factor—and means of quantifying it — are described in the last section of this chapter. It is the predictable growth element that sometimes justifies earnings multiples above 10 and as high as 20 times or more.

Earnouts

There are some cases when a company being acquired is very obviously headed into a period of increasing profits. For example, the company may have been operating at full capacity and it is doubling its facilities with some assurance that revenues and profits will increase substantially as the additional facilities are constructed and come on line as more staff is trained. Perhaps this expansion program will take several years to complete, but the groundwork has been done. An earnings multiple of 10 times *current* earnings is offered but the seller feels he is getting nothing for having set the scene and prepared the plans for the higher rate of earnings which seems inevitable. If no accommodation is made, the seller may say, "Come back in several years when I am earning much more, and then I will accept your 10 times multiple offer on the higher profits." But the buyer wants to make the deal now since it may reinforce other sectors of the buyer's operations, and sees good continuing growth. The buyer *cannot pay today* for future profit levels which are still several years off; otherwise the return on investment for the first two years will be too low (for a public company this can be a real interim depressant on the market price of its stock). This problem can sometimes be solved by using an *earnout* formula.

The earnout formula has two parts — an original purchase based on current profits and a second incremental payment based on additional earnings gained in the future. Good earnout formulas also provide a special earnout base to take into consideration the normal anticipated growth, beyond which the substantial profit growth is compensated for by the earnout formula. Let us say that Company K is presently earning $100,000 per year after taxes. But its goods or services are very much in demand and an expansion program is planned which is anticipated to jump the profits to $300,000 in four years. Buyer and seller agree on 10 times the current profits, or $1 million as the price for acquisition. It is further agreed that the seller will be compensated for the additional profits after four years. Usually, in a case such as this, the earnings for years three and four will be averaged. Therefore, the earnout period begins at the start of year three. Assuming *normal* profit growth to be 10 percent per annum (the earnout formula is devised to accommodate *unusually substantial* growth) the current earnings might be increased 20 percent to 30 percent to establish the *earnout base*, beyond which the earnout profits are to be computed. Since Company K currently earns $100,000 per annum, the earnout base might be $130,000. Then, the amount by which the average earnings of years three and four exceed the earnout base of $130,000, represents the figure used in making the final payment.

If Company K earns $200,000 in year three and $300,000 in year four, the average earning is $250,000. That average exceeds the $130,000 earnout base by $120,000, which is the earnout overage. Buyer and seller have previously agreed that the second payment will be 6 times the *earnout average*; therefore, the seller receives an additional $720,000 at the end of the fourth year. The earnings multiple paid on the earnout is usually less than that paid in the original purchase because it is recognized that the *buyer* contributes time, effort and capital during the earnout period to help make it successful. Sometimes, if substantial capital contribution is required of the buyer to complete planned expansions during the earnout period, an agreed money cost is deducted from the earnout average.

Stock as Consideration

If stock of a public company is used as consideration paid for the acquisition, there are two important factors to consider:

- The value of the stock to be paid at the end of the earnout must be based on the *then*-market price of the shares, not the share price at the time of the original purchase; otherwise, if the stock price has risen considerably during the four year (as in the example given above) earnout period, the buyer would have to book a far higher acquisition cost than would be indicated by total dollar value of the earnout (since the share price must be computed at market value at the time those shares are issued).

- There should be an upper limit to the number of shares to be issued for the earnout, to protect against temporary downside market risk. Usually the limit is set at a number of shares equal to the number issued at the time of original purchase. In the example used, if the acquirer's shares had a market price of $20, then the original purchase for $1 million would have involved 50,000 shares; therefore, an additional 50,000 shares would be reserved for the earnout. If the earnout of $720,000 takes place when the acquirer's stock is selling at $40, only 18,000 shares would be used. But if the acquirer's stock dropped to $10 in four years, 72,000 shares would theoretically be required, but only the maximum of 50,000 would be issued, thus illustrating the protection against excessive dilution, particularly were there a temporary market low at the time of the earnout settlement. There is a good argument to present to the seller in favor of a maximum: The buyer can spoil a tax-free exchange if he or she receives more than 50 percent from an earnout.

Recently, the use of earnouts has been diminishing, particularly by listed public corporations. Pooling is no longer allowed where there are earnouts. If there is no good will problem, and the acquisition is not qualified for a pooling, the earnout arrangement might be used for purchase-treated acquisitions. Also, for purchases, the buyer can purchase a portion of a business, say 75 percent, at the outset. Then, several years later, there can be put and call options between buyer and seller to purchase the remaining 25 percent on an earnout overage formula, in proportion to that part of the selling company retained by the seller.

Pricing Influence of the Acquirer's Business

The evaluation criteria presented in this chapter relate to the value determination of the business to be acquired — and, since this is the element which is being sold, its value is the primary determinant of its price. There are, however, certain mitigating factors which arise from the position of the buyer. When the buyer has made an evaluation — and is going to pay the entire purchase price in cash — then the cash paid should coincide with the buyer's evaluation. If part of the purchase price is paid with notes, and the notes bear at least 6 percent interest, there may be no premium demanded by the seller if he or she has confidence in the buyer's ability to pay off the notes as agreed.

The use of stock presents the possibility — in some cases only (see below) — that the seller may demand, and receive, a higher price than if the consideration were to be paid in cash. It should be first realized that there are many sellers *who prefer to receive stock rather than cash, because only through the use of common stock can a seller receive a tax free exchange.* Therefore, do not minimize the value of stock used as consideration for an acquisition. On the other hand, there are some elements which can tend to diminish the value of stock in the seller's mind.

If stock is offered by a private corporation, the seller must have faith in the package and in the fact that he or she will ultimately be able to liquidate the stock. For that reason, the buyer may demand more than the for-cash valuation of the business, and this premium may run up as high as 20 percent or more. But if the stock received gives the seller a tax free exchange and a dominant position in an attractive after-acquisition entity, the seller may ask little or no premium.

Restricted Stock

If restricted stock is offered by a public corporation, the seller realizes that the ability to liquidate is limited and subject to delay. Stock received in an acquisition is called *restricted stock* or *lettered stock* because the certificates bear a legend describing the restriction. This legend is removed when the shares are ultimately sold, but, in order to be sold, they must either be *registered* or must qualify for *exemption from registration.* To register a stock, the acquiring corporation must file a registration with the S.E.C. (and if it is a listed corporation, a *listing* application with the stock exchange). Therefore, if the seller plans on registering stock sometime in the next year or two, for total sale of all shares (at which time the seller will be liable for taxes on all capital gains, thus ending the tax free exchange period) the seller will ask for registration guarantees. One such guarantee is a *mandatory registration* which commits the buyer's corporation to register at least once, within a stipulated period of time (usually two or three years) all of the stock received by the seller. Another approach is the *piggyback* registration which commits the buyer to include the seller's shares in any (or the first) future registration which the corporation makes after the acquisition. If, for example, the acquiring corporation registers a public common stock issue for additional financing, the seller's shares must also be included in that registration and be sold by the underwriters, along with the company shares which are being offered.

If nonregistered stock is exchanged by a public company to the shareholders of a private company, there are two possibilities. Where there are a number of private shareholders, not active in the business being sold, those shareholders come under S.E.C. Rule 144 which provides for exemption from registration with the passage of two or three years — at which time the stock can be freely sold by any stockbroker.

In the case of a *control* selling shareholder, or one who continues in an executive or directorial position after the acquisition, the exemptions come under S.E.C. Rule 145, according to which the shareholder can sell stock on a periodic basis, through regular stockbrokers, under certain restrictions, the most important of which is that the shareholder may sell only 1 percent of the total outstanding shares every six months.

This may not be as much of a restriction as it initially appears. If a seller receives 50,000 shares from a company which has three million shares outstanding, the 1 percent limitations would still allow the shareholder to sell 30,000 shares (1 percent of 3 million) every six months. Therefore, if the sellers receive stock in a company in which they have confidence — and if there is sufficient normal daily trading in that company stock so that, when the sellers wish to dispose of their shares from time to time they will not depress the market price they will receive — then there should be little or no difference in the acquisition price, cash versus stock, particularly since there will be the advantages of tax free exchange.

Finally, there is the case where *registered stock is offered by a public company.* Many public companies today have *shelf-registered* shares of stock for use in future acquisitions. Therefore, they can issue fully registered shares to all of the sellers who can immediately sell, if they wish, through their stockbrokers (subject to Rule 145 in the case of *control* persons). Here the potential of tax free exchange gives the seller the best of two worlds: a) immediate liquidation or partial liquidation and b) holding some or all shares on a tax free exchange basis for future appreciation. *Naturally there is no premium over the cash sales price given to the sellers when free trading registered shares are exchanged as consideration in an acquisition.*

Acquirer's Multiple

I have many times been involved in negotiations on behalf of acquiring corporations fortunate enough to enjoy market prices on their shares which reflected high multiples on their earnings. The shares of one such company, listed on the New York Stock Exchange, regularly sold at a price-earnings ratio of 30 to 40 times earnings — a price well deserved because of consistent high per share earnings growth over a period of years. Frequently the sellers in acquisitions would have the fallacious idea that, because the acquirer had a high earnings multiple, a higher multiple should be paid to the sellers in an acquisition. It is true that the P/E multiple of the buyer does somewhat influence one of the limitations on the acquisition valuation — namely, the cost of capital (see below) but that factor is secondary.

Let us make one unequivocal statement: *The earnings multiple of the buyer has no influence on — or relationship to — determination of the proper multiple of earnings set as the evaluation of a business being acquired.* Would the seller accept a very low price from a buyer with a low price earnings ratio on stock? Of course not. *The earnings multiple valuation is intrinsic to the company being acquired —* its staying power, its future potential, its profit margin and profit growth.

Many executives of acquisition-active corporations make the mistake of thinking that their high-multiple companies can make successful acquisitions merely by buying companies at lower earnings multiples than their own company enjoys. That is true — but only for the first year *unless* the acquired company also enjoys a high rate of earnings growth. If not, the acquirer will have an earnings growth millstone around its neck in the future. If you enjoy a 20 times multiple — and buy a company for a 6 times multiple — you will receive a one-shot benefit in per-share earnings the first year.

But if your 20 times multiple is based on your corporation's 20 percent consistent per annum profit growth — and the company you acquire for 6 times earnings has only 5 percent per annum profit growth — you will have a future drag on earnings *ad infinitum* after the first year following acquisition.

I repeat: *The price-earnings ratio of the acquirer's stock has no bearing on the valid evaluation of the prospective acquisition.*

Cost of Capital

The determination of *cost of capital* is important in many aspects of financial planning. It is used in determining feasibility of expansion programs and financial planning. The topic can be quite complex at times and an interested student can find much reference material on the subject. Within the purposes of this book, however, we will touch only on an elementary explanation and then go directly to application of cost of capital principles to acquisition evaluation.

Cost of capital studies are determinations of the cost of all elements of capital structure found on the liability side of the balance sheet of a particular corporation. Normally, the capital shown thereon will consist, at least, of the following:

- Bank borrowings;
- Long term institutional or mortgage debt; and
- Equity, in the form of common stock and earned surplus.

Cost of capital is the weighted average cost of the above. If all capital were debt, the cost of capital computation would be rather simple, since debt costs are simply the interest rate plus concessions, if any, such as warrants, compensating balances, etc. Although it was previously held that bank debt, being relatively short term, should not be included in the cost of capital, I feel otherwise, particularly when considering acquisitions in the presence of bank credit agreements for two or more years (and they sometimes run up to five or seven years). Under such conditions the bank borrowing cost is as easy to determine as the interest cost on long term institutional loans.

When we come to the cost of equity, the determination is not so simple. Basically, the cost of equity varies according to what the company will have to pay to attract such capital, and, of course, this is the same principle which applies to the debt market. Obviously the market price of the common shares at the time of any funding by a stock issue bears a direct relationship to the cost of equity. The higher the price/earnings ratio — and therefore the higher the market price per share — the lower the cost of equity. This is because the dilution of earnings, resulting from the sale of such equity, is less. But when you are dealing with a high P/E ratio stock, it is shortsighted — in fact, fallacious — to base your calculations solely on present conditions.

Debt vs. Equity

The stock exchanges list many good stocks with moderate earnings multiples, among which most of the companies on the Dow Jones index are included. These are solid companies with long histories of stability and payment of good dividends. Normally, such companies average 3 to 6 percent growth per annum and therefore their shares sell at 9 to 18 times earnings, with some notable exceptions. At times of market peaks the Dow Jones Industrial average multiple may be $17\times$; during bear markets the DJI multiple has averaged as low as $8\times$. For such companies the cost of debt will usually be lower than the cost of equity, and many economists have concluded that the equity cost of such corporations is 10 to 16 percent per annum. Since they can borrow at lower rates — and since the interest on borrowings is tax deductible — debt is, for them, cheaper than equity (provided they do not borrow too heavily and drive up their own cost of borrowings by lowering the quality of the balance sheet with too high a debt/equity ratio).

The fast-growth, high-earnings multiple corporation finds the opposite situation. At first glance it appears the cost of equity is almost ridiculously low. To find *immediate* cost of equity in *today's market,* the following formula is used:

$$100\% \div \frac{\text{Market Price}}{\text{Earnings}} = \text{Cost of Equity}$$

Therefore, a fast-growth stock which earns $2 per share, and which has a market price of $40, would compute as follows:

$$100\% \div \frac{\$40.00}{\$2.00}$$

$$100\% \div 20 = 5\% \text{ Cost of Equity}$$

To this cost of 5 percent must be added approximately 15 percent for cost of underwriting, prospectus printing, attorneys, accountants, underwriters commissions, etc. But this is not the *true equity cost.*

Attraction to Investors

One factor that bears on the future of the company in the marketplace has been overlooked — namely, the attraction to investors.

Obviously, the investor who buys this stock at 20 times current earnings of $2 per share does not believe the earnings will increase 5 or 6 percent next year. This investor is buying a fast-growth stock — hence the investor's willingness to pay such a high multiple now — and expects the stock to earn $3 next year and $4.25 the following year.

The analysis of the investor's rationale is consistent with the principle that people buy growth stocks in *anticipation* of near-future earnings appreciation. From the company point of view, recognizing that it must continue to seek financing in the future, the *anticipated multiple* must be taken into consideration, particularly since equity shares stay with you forever — diluting future earnings growth — and common shares are normally not retired as is the case with debt amortization or payoff.

It is therefore important that the growth company use its anticipated price/earnings ratios two or three years down the line. Let us take the case of a company which has a track record of 20 percent compounded per share earnings growth per year. This year it earns $1.33 per share and its shares sell in the market for $26 (approximately 20 times earnings). The investor expects $1.60 per share earnings next year — and nearly $2 per share the following year. This assumes that the historical 20 percent compounded growth rate will continue.

The investor is "buying" the earnings level two years down the line (a fairly common procedure in American investing) and the price paid relates to that $2 per share earning the investor looks for in the future. But at $2 per share, the $26 price would represent a much more conventional 13 times earnings. Since that is the *price* the investor pays, it is also the *cost* to the growth company which recognizes it probably cannot forever sustain its high rate of growth. It is proper and conservative for the company to assume a 10 or 15 times multiple two years down the line (still quite handsome a P/E ratio compared to the Dow Jones average of 8 to 12 P/E), and should the multiple move downward to that level two or three years hence, the company, by having postulated the lower future multiple, will not have overpaid for an acquisition and will therefore still be able to have additional stock issue financing in the future.

Taking our second example, immediately above, the formula based on the earnings anticipated two years down the line would be:

$$100\% \div \frac{\$26.00}{\$2.00}$$

$$100\% \div 13.00 = 7.6\% \text{ Cost of Equity}$$

To the above cost is added 15 percent for underwriting expense, so the cost of equity would be approximately 9 percent.

Now let us compute a complete cost of capital. Assume that long term debt is 8 percent and constitutes 25 percent of total capital. There are some medium term bank lines at prime plus ½ percent plus 20 percent compensating balances, consisting of 25 percent of capital (assume 6 percent plus ½ percent times 20 percent equals 7.8 percent). Equity, computed at 9 percent above, constitutes the remaining 50 percent of capital. Since the interest on debt is tax deductible (assume 50 percent corporate bracket) the debt cost is reduced by the tax; however, the dilution caused by equity shares is after tax, so its full cost must stand. The weighted average will be computed as follows:

Medium Term Debt 7.8%	After tax 3.9%	× 25%	1.0% rounded
Long Term Debt 8%	After tax 4.0%	× 25%	1.0%
Equity Cost 9%		× 50%	4.5% rounded
	Weighted Cost of Capital		6.5%

Theoretically any acquisition which does not yield at least 20 percent more per annum than the above cost of 6.5 percent (about 8 percent) would be too costly. Translating 8 percent into earnings multiple (100 percent ÷ 8 percent) would indicate that a maximum of approximately 12 times earnings should represent the limit to be used in an acquisition; but this approach has its drawbacks (see below).

A single broadbrush approach to find corporate cost of capital is as follows:

$$\frac{\text{After Tax Profits + Interest Paid on Long-Term Debt}}{\text{Total Capitalization}}$$

From the investor's point of view, the above fraction computes the return which is presently being made on all capital. Theoretically, if the same return or better can be achieved from an acquisition, it is feasible to proceed. But the same flaw exists even with this method.

Most old established companies have high ratios of equity to debt — 85 percent equity to 15 percent debt, up to 70 percent equity to 30 percent debt. Since their earnings growth is not rapid, the equity capital costs more than the debt, and therefore total cost of capital would appear to be 10 to 14 percent, and payment of more than 10 times earnings for an acquisition would seem improper if viewed strictly on a cost of capital basis. On the other hand, fast growth companies may have lower or higher profits in relationship to total capital, but their low costs of equity can imply feasibility for an acquisition which, in the future, will turn out to be too costly. Whereas cost of capital can be helpful as a guideline — as a partial limit — and as a tool for calculating the cost of an entity's need for additional capital after acquisition, one variable is not properly weighted. *I am here referring to the predictable earnings growth rate of the proposed acquisition.* The *static aspect of yield* is analyzed properly, but the *dynamic aspect of profit growth* is not.

Evaluation by Risk Return Ratio

We have come now to the value which is intrinsic to the acquisition itself — the predictable compounded profit growth rate. It is this factor which primarily influences the value of the company under consideration for acquistion. If an established acquiring company has a cost of capital of 11 percent — and turns down an acquisition potential with an annual earnings growth trend of 20 percent because it is priced at 14 times earning multiple and the first year yield is only about 7 percent (admittedly less than the acquirer's 11 percent cost of capital) — then the executives should be faulted for failing to recognize a good buy. The 20 percent compound earning growth rate will in subsequent years increasingly exceed the acquirer's cost of capital and enhance its per share earning.

By the same token, a fast-growth company with a low 7 percent cost of capital has no justification for making an acquisition which, on the basis of the price demanded to acquire, will initially yield 12 percent (8½ times earnings is the purchase price) but which has indicated *future* profit growth of only 4 percent a year. The 14 times multiple in the first case is actually cheaper than the 8 times multiple in the second case because of the much higher profit growth rate of the first potential acquisition. In both instances cited above, the intrinsic growth of the company being acquired has not been properly evaluated — and this error has negated a fine acquisition in the first case, and encouraged a poor acquisition in the second case.

What establishes a price/earnings multiple of a public company? A number of considerations, but by far the most important is the *rate of profit growth*. And the same principle applies to a potential acquisition candidate. By its own rate of growth it can contribute to — or cause to lag — the acquiring corporation's per-share earnings growth rate.

The setting of a P/E multiple is actually done by the investor who, based on expectancy of future earnings, assigns this value. The basis of all intelligent investment decisions between situations of equal risk is the determination of which company offers the best *future yield* possibilities. If, between two companies of equal risk quality, the first company's profits grow 7 percent per annum and the second company increases at the rate of 9 percent per annum, obviously the investor will opt for company number two. The more difficult part of the problem is the actual gauging of the yield.

The benchmarks for yield are the blue chip corporations — old, established, stable, usually with long dividend paying records. Historically, these companies have produced an average annual yield of about 9 to 11 percent to the investor. The total yield has normally been comprised of 3 to 4 percent dividends and 5 to 7 percent appreciation due to profit growth. Such companies will carry P/E multiples from 5 to 8 in bear markets and from 12 to 17 in bull markets. Let us use an 11 times P/E ratio as a hypothetical base. In order to attract an investor to pay a higher multiple for a stock, it is obvious that there must be an anticipation of a return higher than 9 percent per annum. Therefore, a 15 percent compounded growth rate of earnings per share would command a higher P/E multiple, but how much higher?

The precise relationship between various rates of earnings growth and the applicable P/E ratios has been set forth in what are known as *risk-return tables*. These tables give the proper value to growth, expressed in P/E ratios.

The table will show, for example, that a stock growing 20 percent a year in profits is a better investment at a cost of 30 times earnings than a 10 percent profit growth stock costing 14 times earnings. It is simply a matter of higher yield — or a quicker return of the investment. Consider the following:

- 20 percent compound earnings growth will increase the investment 100 percent in four years.

- 10 percent compound earnings growth will increase the investment 50 percent in four years.

- 6 percent compound earnings growth will increase the investment 25 percent in four years.

The relationships are quite obvious. A stock with 20 percent annual profit growth should carry four times the multiple of a stock with 6 percent growth. If the 6 percent growth stock carries a 5 times multiple, the 20 percent growth stock should carry a 20 times multiple. Variations in rate of annual per-share profit increase will change the price of a company's shares in relation to its current earnings.

Although P/E ratios will change between good times and bad — in bull and bear markets — following is a general average of multiples by category of profit growth:

Rate of Annual Profit Growth Per Share	Average Price/Earnings Ratio For Share Market Price
3% to 5%	4× to 6×
6% to 8%	5× to 8×
9% to 11%	6× to 12×
12% to 15%	8× to 15×
16% to 19%	10× to 20×
20%	12× to 24×

These ratios would apply primarily to established public corporations.[2] They would have respectable balance

---

[2]From 1928 to 1993 the S&P 500 stocks sold at an average P/E ration of 13.7×. In May 1994 that ratio had risen nearly 40 percent, to 18.7× because of consumer investments in mutual funds (as an alternative to low-interest bank CDs). As interest rates increase, the P/E ratios will move lower toward historic averages. Further, the 1994 high growth of corporate profits during 1994 increased per share earnings, which began to catch up with the high multiples, so that by the end of the year the average earnings multiple of the S&P 500 stocks had settled down to about 15×.

sheets; if lacking in liquidity or growth capital, it would be assumed that such companies might have to do more equity financing — diluting their earnings — so the multiple would be lower. In the lower growth ranges on the table above, there will usually be a 3 percent to 5 percent dividend paid. At the upper ranges the dividend might drop to 1 percent or even zero (high growth stocks are not expected to pay much in the way of dividends, in order to conserve capital for growth). It would also be expected that there are a large number of traded shares outstanding, creating a valid market, plus reasonable institutional holdings. Smaller public companies, without all these factors present, should be evaluated somewhat lower, although, if it is determined there is an honest market being made on the stock of a small growth company, premiums of 20 percent to 50 percent above market price can be paid in an acquisition, provided evaluation of the multiple stays below the above table.

When evaluating a *private company* for acquisition, the values in the above table should be *reduced 30 percent to 50 percent*, the higher discount being applied to the higher ranges of multiples. Of course, the financial position of the acquired company will have an influence, which can go either way:

- If the acquisition candidate is cash-rich, the acquirer can figure on utilizing the excess cash as a reduction of the price being paid. Let us say a private company has 8 percent profit growth and is evaluated at 7 times earnings. The earnings are $100,000 after tax and the seller wants $1 million for the business. The buyer feels $700,000 is the proper price but notes that — beyond all needs of the business, and beyond that which is required for a good balance sheet — the seller has $300,000 excess cash. The seller can mentally subtract this amount from the $1 million price tag (since the cash is not needed for the continued profit growth of the business) to arrive at the $700,000 purchase price. The transaction will actually pay the seller $1 million, of which $300,000 is the seller's own money.

- More frequently the acquired company is short of the desired capital; lack of growth capital can be one reason for selling a business. In this case the buyer must postulate the effect of supplying the needed capital. Sometimes the figure needed is based on that required for expansion of facilities, or to finance the expected future growth. In other cases, theoretical supplementation of capital is made to meet the acquiring corporation's own financial profile discipline. For example, a company which has good financing capability might insist that each new acquisition create no more debt than equity. The capital structure would be 50 percent debt-50 percent equity. Let us imagine an acquisition which earns $200,000 after tax-evaluated at $2.4 million. Its capital consists of $500,000 equity and $800,000 debt. The buyer feels the need to reduce the debt by $300,000, and, since the combined cost of capital is 7 percent, the buyer mentally reduces the $200,000 earnings by $21,000 (7 percent of $300,000) to arrive at a pro forma earnings of $179,000. On the basis of the same 12 times multiple, the evaluation would now be $2,148,000.

The above examples illustrate that there definitely can be differing evaluations placed on similar growth companies, to compensate for stronger or weaker balance sheets. With that weighting taken care of—and the lack of ability to make financial strength adjustments removed as an obstacle—there can be no further objection made to the heavy reliance placed on *earnings growth* as the prime criterion for evaluation.

We have initially taken the position of the investment fund manager, who uses risk-return tables for evaluations. We have then used this same process to establish the value of the indicated profit growth of acquisition candidates. I have seen acquisition-prone companies boom — and then go flat. But companies which adhered to the risk-return ratio process, along with the other disciplines described in this chapter, in the evaluation of their successful acquisitions, have usually been able to maintain their established growth company track records.

LBO Evaluations

As mentioned in Chapter 10, companies can be acquired with relatively little equity capital by borrowing against the acquired company's assets. In such cases the cash equity provided by the borrower is *leveraged* by the use of debt or other securities. Where the amount of cash equity provided by the buyer is quite low relative to the total purchase price, the acquisition becomes a *leveraged buyout (LBO)*.

LBOs take place under the following circumstances:

- A family-owned business is sold to employees because the family has no heirs available or willing to continue in management.

- The top-management group of a large public company *takes the company private* by buying back all the public shares.

- An outside group of investors makes an unfriendly offer to buy all, or a controlling amount, of the outstanding common shares of a company.

In each of the above cases, an LBO is usually involved. The first case of the family buyout is a friendly transaction which in many deals involves not only debt but also the retention by the selling family of a security (notes or preferred stock) which is junior to senior bank or institutional debt.

Management buyouts represent a different situation and are based on several motivations. By purchasing all publicly held shares, management perpetuates its control. The company can be downsized by personnel reduction and spinoffs of certain activities to make it more profitable. A few years later it can be taken public again, usually at a nice premium, with all the capital gain going to the small management group.

A good example of this case was Hospital Corporation of America, a $5 billion corporation, which took itself private, made some spinoffs to reduce LBO debt, then went public again several years later. (It has since merged to become Columbia/HCA.)

The third case is the one that makes headlines in business journals. It involves the takeover of a large public company by a group of outside investors — for example, the takeover of R.J. Reynolds by the KKR Investing Group for more than $10 billion. But the same methods can also be employed in much smaller situations.

Opportunities for LBO takeovers arise when a corporation is perceived as not producing the results it should for the benefit of the stockholders. A self-perpetuating management may be sitting on a pile of cash and liquid assets that are producing little or no profit growth, more personnel may be employed than necessary — in general the company is viewed as fat and slow-growth.

When a takeover group identifies such an opportunity, it buys a relatively modest amount of stock in the open market and then starts to talk publicly about *enhancing shareholder value.* Soon the group makes a tender offer for all, or for a controlling amount, of the stock at a price as high as 40 percent to 80 percent above the present market price of the shares. *Voila,* shareholder value is enhanced, and the existing shareholders tender their stock for a windfall profit.

The takeover group has already lined up the LBO financing. Usually LBOs are financed by a combination of short to medium term bank loans, senior debt, and junior debt (frequently called *junk bonds).* All the assets — and stock of subsidiaries which can be sold (divestitures) — are pledged to the lenders. The banks receive good commitment fees, the senior debt holders get warrants to buy stock at a good price in the future, and the junk bonds get high interest rates, more warrants, and higher commitment fees.

Usually a major investment banking firm acts as advisor and offers short-term *bridge financing* to provide interim funding while it is placing the senior and junior debt securities.

Obviously the takeover target has sufficient assets to finance the deal, but the buyers and lenders must be able to see how they can handle the tremendous debt burden involved. The questions to be answered:

- How to reduce or repay debt.
- How to service the remaining debt (how to pay interest and meet amortization requirements).

The first strategic priority after takeover is to reduce debt — and to do it quickly. This is usually done by stripping the company of all short-term investments and cash not needed for operations, and by selling off previously identified subsidiaries and physical assets, such as office buildings, to raise cash. The buildings may be greatly depreciated on the books — and the subsidiaries may be worth far more than their historic cost value — so the transaction may generate profits as well as increased liquidity.

The ability to service the remaining debt will then be determined by cash flow analysis. It is this same analysis which leads directly to the evaluation of the takeover target and the determination of the price paid for the outstanding shares by means of the tender offer.

Members of the financial community involved with LBOs use a special set of shorthand terms. They are:

- EBIT (pronounced "eee-bit") — an acronym for *earnings before interest and taxes.*

- EBDIT (pronounced "eb-dit") — an acronym for *earnings before depreciation, interest, and taxes.*

- EBITDA (pronounced "eee-bit-dah") — an acronym for *earnings before interest, taxes, depreciation, and amortization.*

The prime concern is to assure enough cash availability to get through the early takeover stage. At that point there are few if any taxes to pay because of the huge interest costs and transaction fees. Therefore, EBIT will reflect pretax corporate profit and indicate what income will be available for interest payments.

EBDIT is the most significant measurement as it adds back *non-cash depreciation expense* to obtain cash flow available to pay interest and service the debt. Obviously EBITDA cranks in that part of cash flow which would be available for *principal reduction of debt* — amortization.

The pricing multiples applied to cash flow are lower than the usual P/E multiples because the latter are computed after all expenses, including taxes, interest, and depreciation. Most LBOs have been priced at 5 to 8 times cash flow (EBDIT) although there have been some cases of $10 \times$ and $11 \times$ pricing based on unusual circumstances. In my view, $5 \times$ to $7 \times$ would be appropriate in most cases.

The multiple used may be based on assumptions that the buyer can cut expenses by restructuring, thus postulating higher than current cash flow, but timing is a factor in accomplishing such changes. Also, as with other forms of acquisitions, there will be some weight given to a target company which reflects large cash and short-term investment positions on the balance sheet.

Employee Stock Ownership Plans

ESOPs were created by an act of Congress for the purpose of encouraging stock ownership in a company by employees. In some cases this is initiated by a stock grant from the corporation followed by dividend reinvestment programs. Such plans do not usually wind up establishing a large or controlling block of stock ownership. A quite different case is where financing is arranged for employees to be able to take over substantial ownership of the company by purchase of its common stock.

ESOPs generally develop either because the present owners wish to sell out to their employees on a friendly basis or — on a totally different basis — where a corporation decides to spin off a portion of its business to a group of employees who will own and operate the spinoff as a separate business. It is the latter case which more closely resembles LBO financing.

There is one important attribute to ESOP financing. The federal legislation which created ESOPs provided a special incentive to banks and financial institutions significantly reducing the tax on the interest and fee income earned by making loans to facilitate employee stock purchases under the plan. Not only does that tax saving encourage financial institution participation, but it also makes it possible for them to charge lower interest than would usually be the case.

In an ESOP corporate spinoff to a group of employees, it is quite normal for the corporation to take back a lower ranking security, thereby providing substantial comfort to the other lenders, and increasing the possibility of being able to accomplish the deal.

When I was CEO of American Medical International (AMI), a large multinational corporation, our board of directors approved the spinoff of a group of domestic facilities which did not fit our long-term strategy. The *all-in* price — purchase price plus financing and professional fees — was just under $1 billion ($980 million). A group of AMI executives were the primary buyers and formed the new management. We were sorry to lose their services but recognized that this deal could provide them with significant personal gain after a few years.

To facilitate the transaction, AMI, the parent company, agreed to take back $400 million in preferred stock along with some common stock warrants. An initial bank line commitment of $110 million was obtained from a Swiss bank, and a major investment banking firm underwrote the balance of the financing, meanwhile advancing a bridge loan until that financing was fully subscribed and funded. The resulting capital structure, which was fairly typical for an ESOP of this size, looked like this:

Senior Bank Line - 6% 5 Yr. Term + Fees	$110,000,000
Senior Notes - 10-1/2% 7 Yr. Term + Warrants	250,000,000
Junior Notes - 13% 10 Yr. Term + Warrants	220,000,000
Preferred Stock - Noncumulative + Warrants	400,000,000
Employees' Common Stock	500,000
TOTAL	$980,500,000

Management of the spinoff did a good job, and after less than six years, the entity was acquired by a major public company at an excellent price. All loans were retired, the preferred stock was paid off, the warrants were cashed in for a good profit (AMI made $63 million on the transaction), and the employees, now happy capitalists, made the biggest gain of all. The ESOP financing, although initially a highly leveraged buyout, provided the basis for what was essentially a sound and highly rewarding transaction.

CHAPTER 14
EURODOLLAR FINANCING

What is a Eurodollar? How did Eurodollars originate?

When I think of Eurodollars, I am sometimes reminded of Einstein's theory involving the interchangeability of matter and energy. Most of us have heard of the theory and are aware that it has been proved. A few of us may know how to make use of the theory, yet none of us really knows why it works. We find the same sort of limited knowledge in the financial community regarding Eurodollars. To a majority of laymen as well as bankers, Eurodollar financing is somewhat mysterious. Its origin is not clearly understood. But the pool of Eurodollars is now unmistakably with us, estimated to be more than $1 trillion.

What is a Eurodollar? Even the definition is a subject of argument among financiers. There is no such piece of currency, no Eurodollar bill in any denomination. But it is rather freely exchangeable into Euro*sterling*, Euro*francs*, Euro*guilders*, etc. To illustrate the exchange flexibility of these funds, it might be more academically correct to refer to the entire subject as *Eurocurrency* financing. Even the prefix "Euro" is no longer correct, because we now see the strong entry of Japanese yen into the picture. An *Australian* corporation recently had a debenture issue underwritten by a syndicate headed by some *German* banks, the total issue being denominated in *yen*. What would one call that particular issue? Euroyen? Asiadollar? The tag we put on it is unimportant. We are talking about a new, fast-growing pool of available growth capital, and regardless of source or denomination, the present tendency is to leave all of the varieties under the same heading used when the pool first became recognized in its present form and usage — Eurodollars.

An oversimplified definition of Eurodollars is *dollars deposited with banks outside the United States, usually owned by non-U.S.A. persons or entities and available for investment*. Eurocurrencies are currencies deposited in banks outside the countries which originally issued such currency. Probably some of the earliest cases involved official reserves of foreign central banks and government treasuries which, possessing dollar reserves, kept them in banks outside the United States. Certain large international insurance companies which did business in the United States made a practice of keeping part of their policy reserves in dollars, but on deposit in European or London banks. Other European and Asian multinational companies, engaged in such global businesses as oil and shipping, did the same. One of the more amazing aspects of the Eurodollar pool development was the practice of Communist-controlled banks which attempted to camouflage their ownership of dollars by placing these funds on deposit with European banks. (How quickly political differences fade when money is involved!)

A Sign of Stability

All of the foregoing may represent the early beginnings of the Eurodollar pool, but these practices could not alone have created the picture as we see it today. Something else happened. A number of European countries developed economic stability in the decade of the 1960s, and the demand for capital in these growing economies offered foreign holders of dollars more advantages than could be obtained by keeping the same funds on deposit in the United States. With safety and liquidity equal to that found in U.S. banks, the foreign holder felt more secure about seeking a higher return in London or European financial centers. In this way the holder still kept funds in dollars, but enjoyed multinational diversification and yields. In the 1970s, holders began shifting into various Eurocurrencies, depending on the strengths of those currencies. Many foreigners remember that during World War II the U.S. froze Swiss assets in the U.S. (on the assumption that many were the camouflaged property of Axis governments and corporations) and were concerned that any assets or deposits belonging to a country that might experience a Communist takeover could possibly suffer a similar blocking by the U.S.

Against the background briefly outlined above, many independent holders of dollar credits began to swell the ranks which formerly consisted only of central banks, official government reserves and holdings of the largest multinational companies in the world. The amount of dollars grew as foreign firms increased their sales to the U.S. — and retained their dollar profits. Profits from tourism, from costs of American occupation troops abroad and from the development of world trade in general, increased the Eurodollar fund. Swiss bankers say that the Eurodollar pool grew because of the fiscal irresponsibility of the U.S. government in deficit spending and, later, in balance of payments deficits. They are partially correct — but that is not the whole picture. Even if the U.S. does balance its budget and does again achieve a positive trade balance, I believe this new private world currency pool will persist and it will continue to grow. Having started, the trend will attract more and more capital to the view of global investment.

Interest Rates

The Eurodollar market has an interest rate situation which is unique. It is one of the most classic examples of cost (rate of interest) being determined by supply and demand. This is because interest rates of these external funds are virtually independent of any single government controls, such as those exercised by the Federal Reserve activities in the U.S. or by control of bank discount rate or money supply by the Bank of England. Normally, Eurodollar interest rates are slightly higher than those in the U.S., both for long-term issues and for short-term bank lines, but the differences are not unrealistic for the borrower. When the world is in a tight money period, the spread between Eurodollar rates and U.S. domestic rates is greater, because the law of supply and demand is exerting more influence. When money is loose, the rate differentials are less.

During the peak of the tight money period of 1969-70 when U.S. prime bank rates reached 8½ percent, Eurodollar rates ranged from 12 percent to more than 15 percent per annum — for shorter term loans. In the crunch of 1979-80, domestic prime rates passed 15 percent, but the Euro rates stayed closer this time, probably because today the Eurodollar market is so large. (It must be realized that the comparison should be adjusted to the fact that U.S. banks look for an average of 20 percent compensating balances, whereas Eurodollar bank lending normally involves no balance requirements; therefore the differential is less marked than it would initially appear.) In tight money times, the big U.S. bank branches in London begin to seek Eurodollar deposits — which they re-lend to customers in the U.S. This illustrates another point — that the acceptance of such deposits actually constitutes *borrowings* by such banks. Thus we find ourselves in an era during which, if the customer is willing to pay the cost, banks can usually find, through the Eurodollar market, more funds to lend, even in tight money times.

The reader should not jump to the conclusion that the Eurodollar market is a high-cost source of money. It is simply realistic, and realism creates broader differentials in times of stress. During 1972 there was only about 1 percent difference between the Eurodollar deposit rates and the negotiated certificate of deposit rates in the U.S., and the short-term borrowing rates were very close together. Also during 1972 the Eurodollar medium-term rates were slightly higher, but the long-term rates were almost identical, or even lower, depending on currency denomination. To illustrate the sensitive realism of the market, during the summer of 1972, Eurodollar deposit interest for 6-month deposits was approximately 6 percent. At the same time, however, when dollar speculators scrambled to cover short sales at the end of June, the rates for 3-day loans zoomed to more than 20 percent per annum, while the 3-month and 6-month rates remained unchanged. The same thing happened in 1979.

Special Purposes

The example mentioned above highlights one of the major attributes of the Eurodollar market — that money is usually available for special purposes, perhaps at a high cost in some instances, if the end justifies the borrowing. During the tight money period of 1970 the American entrepreneur Kirk Krekorian borrowed more than 50 million Eurodollars to purchase a dominant block of Metro-Goldwyn-Mayer stock. It was publicly reported that part of this loan carried interest in excess of 13 percent per annum and another increment, in excess of 15 percent. The borrower obviously reckoned that the returns he sought justified the cost; also, his interest expense was tax deductible. It must not be assumed, however, that the rate of interest reflected a high risk to the lenders. The loan, arranged primarily with German banks by a London merchant bank, was amply secured by free-trading MGM stock and other securities.

I have given some extreme examples of Eurodollar interest rates; however, they are not representative of the broad picture. Normally, Eurodollar financing costs are attractive and realistic for the special purposes which are served so well. These purposes will be described below; however, as a summary to the general background, several points should be made.

The professional academicians in the field state that dollar assets do not become Eurodollars until they are deposited in banks outside the U.S. — and until those banks relend the funds. For the purposes of this book, I think that qualification is too academic. We are interested in potential sources of capital, and the fact that such capital is *potentially* available represents the reason attention should be paid to this new funding pool. The Eurodollar market functions between banks — but, of course, finally provides financing to the business borrower. By "banks" we mean to include more than the usual commercial banks we know in the U.S. The term also embraces private banks, merchant banks, foreign savings, investment banks, etc. The corporate borrower will still receive the funds, as described below, but the solicitation or syndication for Eurodollar financing will not include any direct approaches to individuals, as is the usual case in public stock issues in the U.S.

The Eurodollar market looks as if it is here to stay. It seems to have grown beyond a phenomenon to fill a temporary gap on the world financial front. It has accomplished international cooperation among financing sources yet, at the same time, has remained free from national controls and inflexibilities. The Eurodollar market is truly competitive and is capable of unusual speed, both of which are benefits to the seeker of capital.

Purposes and Types of Eurodollar Financing

Eurodollar financing is usually obtained for one or more of the following reasons:

- To obtain offshore funds, free from U.S. government restraints, for investment in foreign operations.

- To borrow growth capital offshore, to use in foreign subsidiaries.

- To obtain competitively priced junior convertible securities, with relatively few restrictions by the investors, for *use in the U.S.* or offshore.

- To obtain special situation spot financing, for use in the U.S. or abroad.

- To obtain major financings much more quickly than the same amounts could be obtained by the route of filing a prospectus with the Securities and Exchange Commission for an underwritten security issue.

- To obtain medium-term financing for a period not generally available in the U.S.

Before commenting in detail on the above purposes, it should be recognized that Eurodollar financings are generally accomplished in the following formats:

- Short-term bank loans, secured or unsecured, for one year or less.

- Medium-term bank loans, secured or unsecured, for terms from three to ten years.

- Long-term unsecured senior debt, generally in the form of 20-year debentures, with only interest required to be paid for the first ten years, principal and interest thereafter.

- Long-term unsecured junior debt, broadly subordinated, generally in the form of convertible debentures, usually for 20-year terms, interest only payable for the first ten years, principal and interest thereafter.

From the above we can see that financings involving a wide range of types and terms are available in the Eurodollar market. Let us now take an in-depth look at these variations.

Investment in Foreign Operations

For many years the U.S. imposed few if any restrictions on investments by persons or corporations in foreign operations. Among the major financial powers, few other countries with the exception of Switzerland took such a *laissez faire* attitude. In fact, after World War II few countries could afford to have their national capital resources dissipated, and strong currency controls were in effect in Great Britain, France, and many other world financial centers. Japan sustained the strictest policy for the longest period of time but, in so doing, rebuilt a strong producing economy, ultimately with enormous positive payments balances and foreign currency reserves. Only in 1972, when the Japanese balances continued to strengthen at the expense of other world financial powers, were these controls relaxed. By the end of 1972, Japanese merchant banks began aggressively to seek financing opportunities throughout the world, under their newly gained freedom to act as international lenders and investors.

In 1968, the United States government, recognizing increasing problems arising from uncontrolled external investments, imposed foreign investment controls. These were made the responsibility of the Office of Foreign Direct Investment (OFDI) in Washington. The controls consisted of two basic segments: a) limitations on future foreign investments made by major multinational corporations, establishing a control related to a base of existing foreign investments at the time the controls were initiated; and b) an annual dollar limitation on new foreign investments, subject to change. Since this book is addressed to those interested in learning about the subject from scratch, we will consider only the second of these as it relates to future Eurodollar financings for those persons in corporations who have not yet gone into the Eurodollar pool for financing.

The maximum foreign investment allowed by an American citizen or corporation was initially only $100,000 per annum, but increased gradually to $2 million per annum. This "allowable" is noncumulative, so any year of zero investment is a lost allowance. President Nixon increased the per annum allowable to $4 million and, based on the theory that returns on such investments should ultimately accrue to the payments benefit of the United States, indicated he might like to go further, and finally the controls were lifted altogether. There have been strong objections by some members of Congress, with complaints of the exportation of U.S. jobs and reduction of needed capital at home, the validity of which is questionable. But it is not within the purpose of this book to debate those questions; rather it should be pointed out that the controls are subject to congressional and presidential whim, and the situation provides little confidence to a financial planner who wants to expand abroad. On the other hand, all Eurodollar financings are, under the controls, permitted to be *added* to the allowables; therefore, you can count on any foreign investment aspirations being limited only by the amount you can raise in the Eurodollar or foreign national currency markets. To summarize, the reasons for seeking Eurodollar financings for *interests in foreign operations* are as follows:

- Freedom from possible future OFDI limitations set by the U.S. government.

- Assurance of being able to expand internationally to the extent of the Eurodollar financing you can obtain.

- The ability to *add* to your domestic U.S. financing arrangements. Usually, U.S. bank line and long-term debt agreements will permit foreign borrowings for foreign operations.

- The readiness of Eurodollar sources to finance operations in their own countries and in foreign areas — as compared with the reluctance by many U.S. banks and insurance companies to lend out of their own areas (surprisingly!).

After making initial investments in a foreign operation, such operations, if successful, should grow and require more capital. The reasons for using Eurodollar capital for these purposes are generally the same as those stated in the immediately foregoing paragraphs. It might be added that, once you have been able to consummate a Eurodollar financing successfully (as described later in this chapter), many of the participating banks will ask for the opportunity to bid on future growth financings in their local areas. Once you become a "member of the club," the welcome mat is out, provided your operation suffers no materially adverse changes.

Eurodollars in the U.S.

Here we come to the aspect that is surprising to many corporate executives and bankers — that *the proceeds of this type of Eurodollar financing can largely be brought back to the U.S. for domestic financing needs.* The money need not be used exclusively for foreign investments, although where such foreign investments are contemplated, it is indeed the ideal funding to use offshore as well.

The practice of underwriting Eurodollar convertible debentures for U.S. corporations developed quickly in the late 1960s, reaching almost hectic proportions by 1968-1969. Then, with the recession and tight money period of 1969-1970 in the U.S., this activity diminished. There were several notable cases of issues for companies which went sour, such as the Four Seasons Nursing Home chain. Not all of the European merchant or investment banks participated in these debacles, but they had the effect of refining analysis and diligence, and today the marketability of convertible issues is usually strong, except for occasional pauses during money crunches or times of international economic uncertainty.

Convertible Debentures

Convertible debentures are very appealing to the Eurodollar investing community, and the reasons are quite understandable. Europeans are traditionally long-term investors, usually committed to the idea of making a first review of the investment after five years. Unlike American or Japanese investors, who switch a great deal over shorter periods, Eurodollar investors look at the bond coupon (the debenture interest rate) as downside risk protection for a number of years. The expectation of capital gain as a sweetener, arising from conversion of the debenture to underlying common stock which has appreciated, is anticipated much later. For this reason the earlier Eurodollar debentures contained prohibitions against *calling for conversion* (see Chapter 11) for the first five years. In 1979, while negotiating a convertible issue, I suggested that we might introduce a sliding scale of conversion provisions for the first five years, as follows:

- During the first year the debentures could be called if the underlying common share price rose to 200 percent of the conversion price.

- During the second year the debentures could be called if the underlying common share price rose to 175 percent of the conversion price.

- During the third year the debentures could be called if the underlying common share price rose to 150 percent of the conversion price.

- During the fourth year the debentures could be called if the underlying common share price rose to 125 percent of the conversion price.

Initially there was resistance, but after the underwriting bankers polled their syndicate, they came back with a flat requirement that the common share price must be 175 percent of the conversion price (see below) any time during the first five years, in order to qualify the corporation to make a call of the debentures for conversion into common stock. This provision is now widely available.

Following are the normal terms of Eurodollar convertible debentures:

- Term — 20 years.

- Interest payable semiannually or annually.

- Only interest is payable the first 10 years.

- Principal is repayable in 10 equal installments during the last 10 years, although in many cases this repayment may be eliminated by conversion to common stock.

- Principal amounts of issues have usually ranged from $10 million to $70 million, with a few large exceptions.

- Interest rates will depend on the international money market. But smaller convertible issues ($10 million or so) for less well known companies coming to the market for the first time have ranged between 6 and 8 percent. Larger issues for better-known companies or for those coming to the Eurodollar market for a second time have ranged from 4½ percent to 6 percent, depending on the world money market.

- Conversion premium — The debentures are usually convertible into common stock at a price 10 percent to 20 percent above the market price of the common stock at the time of the debenture issue.

- The debentures constitute junior debt and are very much subordinated to other types of financings; therefore, they represent an excellent building block for a large financial structure.

The appeal of the classically structured Eurodollar convertible includes the fact that there is no withholding tax required by the U.S. on the debenture interest payments and — depending on the status of the ultimate investor — may be relatively tax-free to him or her. This facet of the convertible is accomplished through compliance with certain international tax conventions. One of those most popularly used involves the tax conventions between the U.S. and the Netherlands, under which non-U.S. persons may invest in obligations of a Netherlands company which lends money to a U.S. corporation, the interest payments on which are not subject to U.S. withholding tax. The Netherlands government and economy has long had a reputation for stability, which instills confidence in the investor. But since the Netherlands Antilles, possessions of the Netherlands in the Caribbean, have lower local taxes, the corporate vehicle required is usually incorporated in the Antilles, for example in Curacao. Following are the steps which are usually taken:

- The borrowing corporation (let us call it American Widget Corp.) forms a Netherlands Antilles *financing subsidiary* which we will call Widget International N.V. The capital of Widget N.V. must be an amount equal to 20 percent of the intended Eurodollar financing total.

- A Eurodollar prospectus is prepared by the European managing banker or underwriter. This prospectus will state, among other things, that 1) the debts of Widget N.V. to the Eurodollar investors are guaranteed by the parent U.S. corporation, and 2) the convertible debentures will be sold only to *non*-U.S. persons.

- Based on the above facts — particularly the exclusion of U.S. persons from the investor group — a ruling will be obtained from the U.S. Internal Revenue Service that interest payments are not subject to U.S. withholding taxes.

- The parent corporation guarantees the Eurodollar investors against U.S. withholding tax liability.

- The managing bankers complete a trust indenture for the bonds — a *fiscal agency agreement* — and alert their possible syndicate to the offering.

- Corporate executives travel with the managing bankers to visit the leading prospective bank members of the syndicate to answer any questions regarding the prospectus.

- Within eight to ten days, all investment commitments are received and totaled, allocations are made if the issue is oversubscribed (it normally is), and a settlement date is set, usually fifteen days later.

- On the settlement date, money for the entire issue is received in collected funds.

- If desired, *all* of these funds can be lent to the parent company immediately by the Netherlands Antilles subsidiary. The 20 percent original capital of the N.V. subsidiary can be invested in a foreign operation or placed in an interest-bearing deposit with London banks. The funds are free to travel anywhere in the world, or to be repaid and reborrowed at any time by the parent U.S. corporation.

The above procedure can take place very quickly (see below). It is interesting to note that the entire placement is among foreign banks, who make these investments for their customers' accounts. The debentures are denominated in $1,000 bonds, and these are *bearer* bonds with detachable interest coupons. The issuing corporation has no contact with the ultimate investor as the debentures are not registered. Interest payments are made by the corporation in a lump sum to the trustee, or fiscal agent, in London, who in turn remits payments to the bankers who send in the coupons which their customers clip and remit.

Spot Financing

As mentioned earlier, the Eurodollar market is a true supply-demand type of money source. Money is usually available for any credit purpose, provided the cost demands can be met. Commercial banks in the U.S. normally attach to their lending arrangements the requirement that the borrower be, or show a possibility of becoming in the future, a regular bank customer with demand deposit accounts, payroll or trust accounts, etc. Balances maintained are part of the compensation sought. Therefore a large *spot* borrowing for a special or nonrecurring purpose is not warmly greeted by U.S. commercial bankers. Not so with Eurodollar bankers, who represent funds frankly seeking straight revenue returns with safety. For this reason the Eurodollar market is a good source for special borrowings for terms of less than one year, or for two to three years. These loans can be arranged by London merchant bankers or branches of U.S. or other banks foreign to the United Kingdom, located in "the city" (the E.C.2. district of old London, around the Bank of England). The rate is based on the *interbank* rate — the interest charged by one bank to another — plus an amount known as the *spread*. The spread can be less than 1 percent for highly regarded loans, or up to more than 2 to 3 percent. As mentioned earlier in this chapter, the Krekorian loans to buy MGM stock bore 12 to 15 percent interest, but that was when the world money market was tight, the interbank rate was high, and the spread was high. In the fall of 1992, the interbank rate had fallen to approximately 5 percent.

One of the most definitive characteristics of the Eurodollar market is its speed. Private placements with banks can be made in a matter of weeks after the first application, provided credit information is complete. But there is an even more dramatic time differential between domestic U.S. and Eurodollar convertible debenture issues. Eurodollar issues are *completely outside the scope* of the S.E.C. or any other national securities regulatory body, as the Eurodollar managers have done a fine job of self-regulation. For this reason I have seen Eurodollar debenture issues take only five or six weeks from the date of decision to proceed with the issue to receipt of funds. Moreover, the timing of Eurodollar issues is less subject to artificial cutoff dates relative to accounting or to other technical requirements encountered in the U.S.

Medium-Term Financing

It has long been a complaint in U.S. financial circles that we have one big gap in our financial spectrum — the medium-term loan. Banks prefer short-term loans, rested once a year, but they usually also extend two- and three-year revolving lines, or amortizing lines up to five years. Our institutional lenders, like insurance companies, feel their preparation and monitoring make it mandatory that their loans be a minimum of 12 years — preferably 15 years and sometimes 20 years. The gap between these two extremes remained unfilled until fairly recently, when the Eurodollar banks stepped in. Probably these sources realized that, lending being their prime activity, they could capitalize on the medium-term void in the U.S.

There is now available in the Eurodollar market secured and unsecured financing with terms of from four to eight years, or up to ten years in special cases. This medium-term financing is being pushed by *consortium banks*. The consortium banks function in many ways along the classic merchant banking lines; however, they have been formed by groups of U.S. commercial banks in combination with private or London merchant banks, plus many of the largest French, Belgian, Dutch and West German banks. Almost all of the consortiums have head or major offices in London. Their interest charges will be negotiated on a spread over the interbank interest rate. The rate may be fixed for the full term of the loan, or it may fluctuate with the interbank rate.

Choice of Currency Denominations

As mentioned earlier in the chapter, the bulk of Eurocurrency financing was for many years denominated in dollars. Following the dollar devaluation at the end of 1971, and again during the time of uncertainty created by the float of the pound sterling during June, 1972, investors began to consider issues which were denominated in other currencies such as Deutschemarks, guilders, yen, etc. In other words, in the case of notes or convertible debentures, the corporate borrower can commit to repay the debt when it is finally due in a currency other than dollars. During 1979 when the Deutschemark and the yen were viewed as having relatively stronger value than the dollar or the pound sterling, the investor showed willingness to accept a lower interest rate if repayment were guaranteed in those currencies. Therefore, the corporate borrower who wished to enjoy a lower interest rate could arrange for a Deutschemark or yen denominated obligation. At the same time it should be recognized that the corporate borrower is risking the possibility of a further upward revaluation of those currencies against the dollar. It is a two-way gamble because, over the maturity of a long-term obligation it is quite possible that the dollar will again gain strength against other currencies. Relative currency values are established on the basis of today's foreign exchange markets. For this reason, in late 1972, French franc, guilder, Swiss franc and Deutschemark denominated debt or convertible debt issues all carried lower interest rates than did the same types of obligations issued by similarly rated U.S. companies in domestic U.S. underwritings. By 1988 the situation had reversed as the dollar strengthened.

Regardless of the currency denomination, the proceeds can immediately be switched into another currency, such as dollars, at the going rate of exchange. Such switches would always be the case when the proceeds are to be used largely in the U.S. On the other hand, if you are borrowing for the expansion of a foreign subsidiary in a country in whose currency the obligation is denominated, the switch may not be necessary—and the cost may be less. To avoid *currency translation,* or *exchange* losses, you should always try to borrow in the same denomination as you have cash flow. For example, if you have Swiss franc assets and cash flow you should borrow in Swiss francs to create a perfect hedge.

Qualifying for Eurodollar Financing

Generally the qualifications for Eurodollar financing are the same as those in the U.S. Obviously, the minimum size of the financing will depend on the type of funding selected. Local Eurocurrency loans for local growth of a foreign subsidiary can be quite modest. Short- and medium-term loans can go from several million dollars to over $50 million; debenture issues from $10 to $70 million. If you qualify creditwise for these ranges in the U.S., you should also qualify in Europe.

Obviously, convertible debentures require the existence of underlying common stock whose price is readily determined. Therefore, the issuing company preferably should be listed on the American or New York Stock Exchange.

The worldwide Eurocurrency pool functions in some ways like a private club and the avenues of approach are not widely known. If you can make contact with anyone who has been active in this market, this individual can probably assess your chances and assist you if you qualify.

There are also a number of institutional avenues to which you can turn for assistance. These consist of certain commercial banks in the U.S., domestic investment banking firms, and specialized financial consultants. But among these categories, you will probably find Eurodollar expertise only in the largest financial centers, such as New York and Los Angeles, and even there it is necessary to be selective about the individual whom you approach, and be persistent about your objective. In the case of investment banking firms and commercial banks in the U.S., it only makes sense to approach those having international connections. A number of our leading investment banking firms maintain offices in the city of London and in such other world financial capitals as Paris, Amsterdam, Geneva, and Zurich. A few of the largest commercial banks in the U.S. are members of consortiums with offices in the same world financial capitals. However, only a few individuals in those qualified investment banking firms and commercial banks have had actual exposure to the Eurodollar market, so an inquiry must be directed to such individuals and should not be diverted to alternative plans of domestic financing if — based on the reasons given earlier in this chapter — a Eurodollar financing is the preferred method of funding.

Finally, Eurocurrency financing represents an expanding development in international cooperation. Chauvinistic attitudes are being broken down; a single standard of financing for all nations appears to be developing. In a rapidly shrinking world, this viable pool of capital may be the financial community's major contribution to global unity and equal economic opportunity for all people on the planet earth.

INDEX

Index

Index

Index